An American Family
on the African Frontier

Major Frederick Russell Burnham, from a photograph taken after the death of Queen Victoria and shortly before he was invested by King Edward with the cross of the Distinguished Service Order. From *Scouting on Two Continents* (Doubleday, Page & Company, 1926).

An
American
Family
on the
African
Frontier

The Burnham
Family Letters, 1893-1896

Edited by Mary and Richard Bradford

ROBERTS RINEHART PUBLISHERS

To our Parents

Published in the United Kingdom, Ireland, and
Europe by Roberts Rinehart Publishers
Main Street, Schull, West Cork
Republic of Ireland

International Standard Book Number 1-879373-66-1
Library of Congress Catalog Card Number 93-85472
Printed in the United States of America

Contents

THE PRINCIPAL CHARACTERS

Americans in Africa

FREDERICK RUSSELL BURNHAM: American prospector and scout from Pasadena, California
BLANCHE BLICK BURNHAM: his wife
RODERICK (Roy) DEAN BURNHAM: their son
NADA BURNHAM: their daughter
JOHN BLICK: brother of Blanche Burnham, Fred Burnham's companion in Rhodesia
GRACE BLICK: sister of Blanche Burnham, nicknamed Chum or Chub, accompanies her brother John Blick to Rhodesia
JAMES BLICK: father of the Blick family, Pasadena contractor
HOWARD BURNHAM: brother of Fred Burnham
HOMER BLICK: brother of Blanche Burnham
JUDD BLICK: brother of Blanche Burnham
PETE INGRAM: Burnham's partner in prospecting and scouting, later marries Grace Blick
BOB BAIN: Canadian scout, friend of Burnham and Ingram
A. KINGSLEY MACOMBER: Pasadena prospector and adventurer, joins Burnham in Matabeleland

In Pasadena

REBECCA RUSSELL BURNHAM: Fred Burnham's mother
PHEBE BLICK: wife of James Blick and mother of Blick family
JOSIAH RUSSELL: Rebecca's brother, who attends to Fred Burnham's business interests in California
MADGE BLICK FORD: Blanche Burnham's sister
JACK FORD: Madge's English husband
LINNIE BLICK: Homer Blick's wife

KATE AND JOE BLICK: youngest children of James and Phebe Blick

Matabeleland Personalities

ART CUMMING AND FAMILY: friends of the Burnhams
JAMES F. DORÉ: South African capitalist who finances several of Burnham's enterprises
THE HONORABLE MAURICE GIFFORD: Burnham's friend and partner, younger brother of British South Africa Company Director Lord Gifford
DR. LEANDER STARR JAMESON: chief administrator for the British South Africa Company in Rhodesia
LOBENGULA: king of the Matabele nation
CECIL RHODES: founder and managing director of the British South Africa Company and prime minister of Cape Colony

PROLOGUE

I

The American frontier was at an end. As of 1890, according to the U.S. Census Bureau, the frontier's continuous line of settlement no longer existed.

Americans reacted in different ways. A young history professor, Frederick Jackson Turner, transformed the frontier's passing into a noted theory of American history. The frontier, said Turner, distinguished Americans from their European forebears by providing economic prosperity and political democracy. Now that the frontier was gone, Americans must find something to replace it. Some spent the remainder of their lives searching for new frontiers, hoping to find the opportunities that Turner claimed were the frontier's particular gift.

In April 1893 an American prospector, Frederick Russell Burnham, a former cowboy and Indian scout, hitched four mules to a Studebaker buckboard in Durban, Natal, and headed north toward a new frontier in Africa. On July 4 Burnham, his wife, Blanche, and six-year-old son, Roderick, celebrated Independence Day with American friends on the banks of the Crocodile River. Recognizing that the North American frontier was gone, he and his family sought new frontier opportunities in Cecil Rhodes's British South Africa Company colony in Mashonaland.

Burnham was a true son of the border. His family had settled in Connecticut in 1637 and produced lawyers, soldiers, and preachers who moved west with the nation. By 1860 his father, Edwin Otway Burnham, a Congregationalist minister, was a member of a colony in Minnesota settled by former New Yorkers. Frederick Burnham's English-born mother, Rebecca Russell, came to America in 1842 with her dissenting, reform-minded parents. The Russells eventually migrated to Blue Earth County, Minnesota, where

Fred Burnham at twenty. From *Scouting on Two Continents*.

Rebecca married Edwin Burnham and where Frederick was born May 11, 1861.

The Burnham family survived an uprising by Sioux Indians in 1862. For the next three years, their area was subject to raids by Sioux who had fled west to the Dakota Territory. The threat of raids and the harsh conditions of a Minnesota farming community toughened young Fred. In 1871 the family moved to Los Angeles. Following his father's death two years later, Fred became a mounted messenger for Western Union, then a boy hunter supplying game to mining camps of the Panamint Range east of Death Valley.

Later, Fred moved briefly to Iowa to live with puritanical relatives, Uncle Josiah Russell and his family. Unhappy with the life there, he fled west, where he worked as a cowboy in Texas and Kansas and prospected in Arizona. During the Apache uprisings of the early 1880s Burnham served as a civilian scout for isolated mining towns like Globe and for mining camps that needed intelligence of raiding Apaches. On Christmas Day, 1883, he struck gold, sold his claim to an eastern syndicate, and returned to Iowa to marry his boyhood sweetheart, Blanche Blick.

After his marriage Burnham continued to roam the West as a prospector and mining promoter. Although frontiersmen are often portrayed as loners, many were family men, and Burnham lived in the Daniel Boone manner, combining adventure with business in association with relatives. Both acquisitiveness and romanticism motivated him. His letters reveal a man hungry for personal success but ready to help his relatives get ahead as well. Like a Richard Harding Davis hero, making money was not enough—he must find King Solomon's mines.

Burnham identified with the mining community, seeing himself as an engineer scout, a prospector moving up in the world. During the 1890s American mining engineers such as John Hays Hammond and Gardner Williams pioneered the development of South Africa's gold mines.[1] The lure of gold later served as the catalyst for the Burnham family migration to what their contemporaries called the "Dark Continent."

II

During the 1880s Britain, France, Germany, and Portugal sought territory in what historians describe as the "Scramble for

Africa." Caught in the middle were the Boer Republics, the Transvaal and Orange Free State, which were peopled by the descendants of seventeenth-century Dutch Protestants. Discovery of gold in the Transvaal in the 1880s led to an influx of non-Boer prospectors. In Britain's Cape Colony, gold stimulated interest in moving north.

Above the Transvaal's northern boundary of the Crocodile River lay the native kingdoms of Mashonaland and Matabeleland, which were ruled by the Matabele king, Lobengula. For twenty years rumors had drifted south of gold in Mashonaland. These stories attracted the interest of the most powerful figure in South Africa, Cecil Rhodes. In 1888 Rhodes sent a small party of adventurers north to meet King Lobengula, from whom they gained a royal concession. Lobengula believed he was giving the English mining rights only in neighboring Mashonaland, but Rhodes claimed it was a concession to all of the king's domains. The following year Rhodes's British South Africa Company (BSA) received a Royal Charter to colonize the area. When Transvaal Boers appeared ready to trek into Mashonaland, Rhodes moved first, sending a column of four hundred men to occupy the kingdom. For the next three years the company sold mining concessions and farms, exaggerating tales of Mashonaland mineral wealth to attract settlers and to raise the price of company shares on the "Kaffir Circus," London's South African gold market. Mashonaland was celebrated as possessing the "Gold of Ophir," King Solomon's mines, and became the talk of the mining world.

Africa had fascinated Fred Burnham since childhood, and he decided to join the American prospectors scrambling for African gold. He was embroiled in lawsuits with California's Alvord Mining Company, and his letters contain frequent references to what must have been difficult times. The decade of the 1880s was one of labor strikes, depression, and the notorious Haymarket riot in Chicago. Burnham grew disenchanted with industrial America, foreseeing growing class strife as equality and prosperity declined. He believed this decline was caused by the disappearance of the frontier, which nothing could replace in providing opportunity. After reading Edward Bellamy's 1888 utopian novel, *Looking Backward*, he was committed to the socialism of Bellamy's Nationalism movement, whose key concept was equality among citizens.

Burnham became convinced that Africa held limitless possibilities. On January 1, 1893, he and his family left for Africa in search of a new frontier. Burnham hoped to establish his own "little empire," a just society where no man could deny another his bread.

They reached Durban, Natal, in April. Blanche rejected her husband's suggestion that he continue alone while she and Roderick waited in safety in Durban. They would go on as a family or not at all. Fred bought an American-built Studebaker buckboard for the long trek and chose burros for draft animals.

On April 23 they set out, their destination the British South Africa Company outpost of Fort Salisbury in Mashonaland. Historians of the American overland trail will find similarities between the Burnham's African trek and the crossing of the American plains in the 1840s and 1850s.[2] Fred mended harness, cared for the donkeys, and hunted to supplement their diet. Blanche cooked meals over a reflector and in a Dutch oven, washed clothes in streams, and shared her husband's longing for American pie and baked beans. Roderick caught the donkeys, gathered ox chips for campfires on the timberless veldt, and under his mother's instruction learned his letters from the California primary reader.

The family witnessed problems unique to Africa. Burnham, a free trader, fumed over the Boer Republic's high tariffs, and he and Blanche noted the tension between Boer and Briton. Apartheid laws permitted blacks into Durban only if they worked for whites, and the Burnhams drove past migrant black laborers traveling south to work in the mines. In Africa, unlike the American West, whites were a minority.

The Burnhams' views of Africans may shock readers. Social Darwinism was at its height in the 1890s, furnishing so-called scientific proof of Caucasian superiority. The Burnhams absorbed Darwin's tenets, and, like many of their contemporaries, they regarded the African as virtually a lower species. Burnham admired the Africans as pure savages capable of feats of strength and bravery, but that view did not change his opinion that blacks should be governed by the more civilized white race. As he criticized the African for not working, he could also believe that cheap native labor was spoiling the white man in Africa.[3]

At first the Burnhams traveled alone. North of Johannesburg they joined a wagon train for the dangerous last leg through lion country. In the train they met two Americans, cowboys turned prospectors, Pearl (Pete) Ingram and Bob Bain. Both men would become part of the Burnhams' circle in the north.

III

King Lobengula's mining concessions to the Chartered Company in Mashonaland threatened his own power. Matabele military society survived on raiding Mashona and other tribes to capture women for marriage, young boys to raise as warriors for the king's regiments (*impis*), and cattle for wealth. The king did not expect changes simply because whites hired Mashona laborers to work in their mines and on their farms. The Mashona, however, appealed to the British for protection.

An uneasy truce existed for three years as the king struggled to restrain young warriors who wanted to drive out the whites. Confident that Lobengula would eventually force the issue, officials of the BSA intended ultimately to extend their power over Matabeleland. Meanwhile, Dr. Leander Starr Jameson, the Companys' chief administrator, played down difficulties with the king to stockholders and potential settlers.

A July 1893 incident provoked war. Lobengula sent 2,500 warriors to raid Fort Victoria to punish the Mashona for stealing. Warriors obeyed orders that no whites be harmed but killed the despised Mashona in front of their horrified employers. Settlers threatened to leave the country unless the BSA furnished protection.

Jameson realized the colony could not stand disruptions of its black labor force. Confronting Matabele *indunas* (generals) outside the brick walls of Fort Victoria on July 17, he ordered them to retire immediately or face retaliation. Although one *impi* retreated, a mounted patrol caught another raiding a nearby Mashona *kraal* (village) and opened fire, killing several Matabele. Convinced that war was inevitable, Jameson used the native trader Johann Colenbrander, a company agent, to spread propaganda against the Matabele among the white settlers. Colenbrander portrayed the Matabele as bloodthirsty savages bent on revenge. Nearing Victoria, the Burnhams heard these tales, possibly from Colenbrander himself.

The Burnhams' wagon train encountered fleeing whites shouting that war had broken out between the English and the Matabele.

The announcement was premature, but the trekkers believed it and debated whether to continue north or to turn back. Burnham voted with the majority to go forward.

The threat of war and their own exhaustion changed the family plans. Salisbury was the Butnhams' original destination, but when they reached Fort Victoria they decided to remain and await the outcome of the fighting. Historians believe that Lobengula did not see war as inevitable until October of that year, but in August the Burnhams and their associates already spoke of it as an accepted fact.[4]

Burnham intended to stay out of the conflict until a letter arrived from the United States. Only a fragment remains in his papers, but apparently it announced the failure of a bank that held some of his money. Fearing financial ruin, Burnham enlisted in the company forces. The Victoria Agreement of August 14, 1893, enticed Burnham and others into the company's service by offering each enlistee 6,000 acres in Matabeleland, 15 reef gold claims, and 5 alluvial claims. The company promised "plunder" to those fighting in its service, and Burnham hoped to recoup his financial losses by winning mineral rights in Matabeleland.

Three columns invaded Matabeleland in October 1893. Major Patrick W. Forbes, an ex–regular officer, held overall command and led the Salisbury contingent. Burnham was a member of the Victoria column headed by Major Allan Wilson. His experience in Arizona's Apache wars and his natural ability made him the expedition's foremost scout. The two columns joined at Iron Mine Hill. A third under Lieutenant Colonel Hamilton Goold-Adams entered Matabeleland from the south.

Lobengula wisely ordered his generals to evade pitched battle and to resort to ambush. Thanks to Burnham and the other scouts, and bad luck, the Matabele could never surprise the British. Instead, at the battles of the Shangani Forest and the Imbembesi, the Matabele hurled themselves at riflemen concealed behind wagons. British Maxim guns, which proved decisive throughout the campaign, inflicted devastating losses on Lobengula's forces. Had the British not been armed with the machine guns, the Matabele might have overrun the columns with sheer numbers.

Burnham and two companions were the first whites to enter Buluwayo, the Matabele capital. Burnham was entrusted with dispatches and made a long ride to Tati, the nearest telegraph station, to wire the first news of Lobengula's fall to the outside world.

The British imperial government did not want the BSA acting independently. Government officials hoped Matabeleland would become a crown colony controlled by the British government, not by a private company. The company's rapid conquest of the Matabele spoiled that plan. Lobengula and his followers fled north toward the Zambezi River. Jameson needed to capture Lobengula to leave the British government in no doubt that the BSA controlled the king.

Jameson sent Major Forbes, with a patrol that included Burnham, to seize the king. Trouble dogged the mission from the beginning. In spite of its two Maxims, the patrol was underequipped. Forbes had performed capably when directing the invasion, but it was another matter to lead volunteers who believed the war was over. His regular-army mentality grated on frontier types like Burnham.

On the night of December 2, the troopers believed they had overtaken Lobengula. Natives reported the king to be a few miles ahead, across the Shangani River. Forbes sent Major Allan Wilson and twelve men to locate the king's wagons, with instructions to return before dark. Knowing that Burnham "was very quick at following a spoor" (trail), Forbes sent him with Wilson.[5]

Wilson and his men rode through camps that sheltered thousands of Matabele. When they reached a stockade in which they could see the king's wagons, an interpreter called out for Lobengula to surrender. There was no answer. Matabele warriors began encircling Wilson's group. Instead of retreating, Wilson sent a message requesting Forbes to send him the Maxim guns. Late that night Captain Robert Borrow and twenty men rode up, but without the Maxims. It was a fatal error. In the morning the Matabele attacked. Wilson asked Burnham if he could get through to tell Forbes to hurry with the Maxims or the smaller patrol was finished. Wilson also sent George Gooding, a young Englishman with the best horse in the patrol, and Burnham asked that Pete Ingram, his American friend, accompany them. The three evaded pursuers, but when they reached Forbes they found him under attack and unable to send help. The Matabele killed Wilson and all of his remaining men.

Nearly two weeks passed before the Forbes patrol reached

safety. It was a tragic end to what had been a triumphant war for the whites. Fred Burnham returned to his wife and son and was the messenger who confirmed the rumors of Wilson's disaster to a stunned crowd at a New Year's day picnic in Fort Victoria.

After Lobengul's defeat the British South Africa Company, not the Colonial Office, ruled what colonists began calling Rhodesia—its official name as of 1895. The BSA treated the Matabele as a conquered people, and in early 1894 word came that Lobengula had died north of the Zambezi. The Colonial Office blocked some company policies, but Rhodes and Jameson usually operated without government interference.[6]

IV

As a reward for his services, Jameson gave Burnham preference in selecting mining and land claims. During the campaign the scout had watched for mining sites nearly as carefully as for Matabeles. The Burnham Syndicate filed twenty-seven claims at Scout's Reef on the Gwelo River. In January the family, accompanied by Pete Ingram and Bob Bain, began mining operations.

Rhodesian mining changed Fred Burnham. Ever since his arrival in Africa he had criticized Europeans for their dependence on cheap black labor, but within two months after beginning work at Gwelo he adapted his views. His conscience troubled him, but the high turnover in black laborers at his mines led him to reluctantly support Rhodesia's contract labor laws, which forced natives to work a specified time before leaving an employer.[7]

Burnham worked in a whirlwind of activity, pegging land for speculators, prospecting, and forming syndicates to sell mining claims to London investors. From legends of ancient diggings and through observation and deduction he tracked down gold, copper, and coal. He speculated on land and dreamed of becoming a leader in Rhodes's proposed United States of South Africa.

Family interests extended beyond mining. In September 1894 Blanche's brother and sister, John and Grace Blick, arrived in Bulawayo. Grace intended to take a job with a fledgling frontier newspaper but instead became a companion to Blanche, who in May bore a daughter named Nada (the Zulu word for lily). John Blick worked for Fred and supervised other men's mining camps.

His experience demonstrates how a man could make money on the African frontier if, as on the American frontier, he was early on the scene and had a patron.

Problems began to appear in the land of Ophir. Rhodesia's gold was widespread, but not in thick profitable veins. Prospectors located the bulk of the ore in ancient diggings scattered throughout the country, mines that had been worked at some much earlier time. In September 1894, to quiet rumors that the gold fields were a bust, Rhodes brought in John Hays Hammond, an eminent American mining engineer, to conduct a mineral survey. In carefully phrased terms, Hammond reported that gold was sufficient for prospectors to make a living, but Rhodesia would not be another Rand.[8] In December Burnham abandoned Scout's Reef as worthless.

Meanwhile the frontier edged north. Rhodes hoped to occupy Barotseland, charter territory north of the Zambezi River, next, and he granted land in that area to Burnham, Ingram, and Maurice Gifford, brother of BSA Director Lord Gifford. The grants included the right to peg mineral claims in a region as unknown to Europeans as Rhodesia had been twenty years earlier.[9]

Burnham led prospectors across the Zambezi on behalf of the Northern Territories Syndicate. The expedition lasted from May to August 1895. Its members found coal and copper deposits, but the Gold of Ophir eluded them. Nevertheless, Burnham's favorable reports led to an expedition two years later that pegged five hundred square miles of copper-bearing land.[10] On the journey back south Burnham, who had separated from the others, and his native bearers nearly died of thirst as they struggled through thornbush deserts before locating water.

Meanwhile, Blanche Burnham was joined by additional family members. Her brother Judd Blick had arrived earlier and accompanied the northern expedition. In late summer her father, James Blick, and brother Homer Blick arrived only to witness the frontier boom's final stage. Rhodesia experienced an economic downturn; latecomers found the best jobs gone, and the demand for laborers fell off.

However, the Burnham family prospered. In December 1895, Fred and Blanche traveled to London accompanied by James Blick, who was returning home after only four months in Africa, and

newlyweds Grace and Pete Ingram. During their absence Rhodesia
came apart.

V

While the Burnhams enjoyed London, Dr. Jameson made his
famous raid in an attempt to overthrow the Transvaal's Boer government. Foreigners had flooded the Boer state following the discovery
of Rand gold, but President Paul Kruger's government refused to
grant voting and political rights to non-Boers. The foreign community resented discriminatory legislation to the extent that some
settlers considered revolution. Anticipating an uprising by Johannesburg's *uitlanders* (foreigners) and urged on by Rhodes, Jameson led a
band of four hundred men across the border. However, no rebellion
took place, and the raid ended in a fiasco when sharpshooting Boer
riflemen surrounded Jameson and forced his surrender. Jameson's
capture had fatal consequences for Rhodesia; his party consisted of
Rhodesian white police whose imprisonment left settlers defenseless.

In March the Matabele rebelled. The BSA believed the uprising to be the work of native witch doctors, or the priest class
(whom whites incorrectly labeled the M'Limo), but the Matabele
had ample reason for rebelling without looking to religious causes.
They had endured the BSA's hut tax and forced labor policies, but
other company actions were even more oppressive. Strangely, although whites recognized that the blacks' inexperience with
firearms was to the settlers' advantage, the company organized native police and gave them rifle training. The Matabele police soon
earned the hatred of their own people by enforcing company laws
requiring natives to work in mines and on farms. Then police
rounded up native cattle, the loot promised by the company to
those who had served in the 1893 campaign. While Lobengula
lived, few Matabele owned cattle, but after the conquest natives
began to appropriate the royal cattle, which to the Matabele had
both an economic and a spiritual significance. Thus the company
roundup united all Matabele classes against the whites.

Cattle inspired the rebellion in another way. In 1896 rinderpest,
a cattle sickness, struck Rhodesia. To halt the epidemic, the company
began destroying diseased cattle. The Matabele misunderstood the
motive, believing that the whites intended to starve them.

The uprising was planned for the new moon of March 28, 1896, but it began prematurely on March 20 when one *kraal* turned on native police killing three. The rebellion spread. Matabele tactics had improved since the 1893 war. Operating in small guerrilla bands, warriors avoided frontal assaults; thanks to the white-trained police, many of whom joined the insurrection, they were more skilled with firearms. But they failed to coordinate their attacks. Rather than a united assault on Bulawayo, the rebellion's early stages took the form of murdering isolated prospectors and settlers. Indeed, for a time whites refused to believe it was a general uprising. By early April, when rebels did surround Bulawayo, the settlers' situation was desperate.

The Burnhams arrived in Cape Town in late March and were met there by Pete and Grace Ingram. Leaving their wives in Mafeking, Burnham and Ingram dashed north by stage, throwing off mail bags to make room for ammunition. In Bulawayo Burnham returned to scouting. Throughout April the sisters awaited permission to travel into the war zone. Authorization came in May, and they set out on a northbound stage. Meanwhile, Rhodesian officials had sent Pete Ingram south to buy horses, and he met the stage en route and took Grace with him. Blanche traveled on alone until she was met by Fred, who rode guard into Bulawayo.

A new ordeal faced the Burnhams in the sickness of their two-year-old daughter. Blanche had left Nada in Rhodesia, thinking the trip to London would be too hard on the little girl. Nada had become ill during the siege of Bulawayo, and Blanche found her near death. After more than a week of semiconsciousness, Nada died, and her mother broke down with grief. Fred was on patrol at the time, and Nada's burial took place before he learned of her death.

Burnham became convinced that the siege's hardships had killed his daughter, and his role in the war against the Matabele took a personal turn.[11] On the night of June 5, he encountered a large army of Matabele within six miles of Bulawayo and gave the alarm. The next morning white forces and native auxiliaries routed the *impi*. Afterward, reports spread that the Matabele had watched the approaching white troops with indifference because their priests had assured them their magic would strike the whites blind. This reinforced settlers' belief that the M'Limos had instigated the rebellion.

The whites' victory was short-lived. In mid-June came the devastating news that the Mashona had joined the uprising. With rebellion spreading and costs mounting, the BSA searched for any means of ending the war.

VI

Officials continued to blame the uprising on the M'Limo, a term used by whites to mean a priest of the native cults. In fact, M'Limo was the Makalaka god of abundant harvest. The priest of the M'Limo cult relayed the various questions of supplicants to the god, who dwelt in a cave. Natives believed the priest's voice echoing in the cavern was M'Limo answering his followers. The whites' misuse of the term reveals the settlers' ignorance of native religions. Blaming the M'Limo priests for the rebellion was a convenient means of denying that exploitative company policies might be responsible.[12]

Assistant Native Commissioner Bonar W. Armstrong discovered a M'Limo cave south of Bulawayo in the Matopos Hills at Njelele. The shrine's priest was named Jobani. Armstrong asked General Sir Frederick Carrington's permission to attempt to reach the cave to kill Jobani. Carrington consented on condition that Burnham accompany Armstrong, and Burnham agreed. Carrington's last words to Burnham were, "Capture the M'Limo if you can. Kill him if you must. Do not let him escape."[13]

They rode to Fort Mangwe, two hours from the shrine. Burnham needed three days of preliminary scouting to select a route of approach and escape. On June 23 he led the way up the mountain and into the cave by a back entrance. They waited. At the foot of the mountain a native ritual was taking place. One man left the gathering and came up the path. Burnham later wrote:

> Now I gazed fully upon the M'Limo as he was about to enter the cave. He was a strong, active man, perhaps sixty years old, with short cropped hair. . . . His face was forceful, hard, cruel, and very wide between the eyes. . . . Here was the author of all our woes. Because of him, my little daughter was dead and the bones of hundreds of brave men and good women were scattered on the veldt by hyenas. Carrington's command, "Capture him if you can; kill him if you must," rang in my ears.

Capture was impossible. Burnham offered Armstrong the honor of killing the M'Limo. Armstrong replied, "No. You do it."

> So, as the M'Limo came in I made a slight sound and gave him his last chance to turn the white man's bullet to water. I put the bullet under his heart.[14]

They raced from the cave; Armstrong brought the horses while Burnham fired huts to distract pursuers. Two hours later they galloped into Fort Mangwe.

The company spread the story of the M'Limo's death in the hope that it would end the rebellion.[15] However, the affair became controversial among Rhodesian whites. One faction disliked Burnham because he was favored by Jameson and Rhodes. Enemies claimed the shooting had never occurred, and these accusations have damaged the scout's reputation ever since.[16]

The attacks on Burnham are exemplified in the writings of Hugh Marshall Hole, a company official in Salisbury who is not known to have ever met Burnham. In *The Making of Rhodesia*, although he never mentions their names, Hole writes that Burnham and Armstrong

> persuaded Carrington that they knew the actual hiding-place of the priest of the Mlimo and obtained permission to go and kill him. On their return they were greatly applauded for having achieved their dangerous errand, but some time later, when it was found that the Mlimo was still at work, an official inquiry was held, with the result that the whole affair was exposed as an elaborate hoax.[17]

In private correspondence Hole called the affair a fraud because Armstrong and Burnham said the M'Limo's cave was located "near Banko's kraal, close to the Shashi River, and within about 30 miles of the Matopos Hills." If Burnham had made such a claim, it would indeed have been a hoax, for the Shashi is fifty miles west of Fort Mangwe, in the opposite direction from Njelele. But Burnham said no such thing. Hole was quoting a report written in 1899 by Chief Native Commissioner H. H. Taylor, who attacked Armstrong for reasons unrelated to the M'Limo affair. Taylor wrote, "Armstrong had heard there was a certain cave near Banko's kraal, close to the Shashi River, and within about 30 miles of the Matopos, where the Makalangas used to offer up their sacrifices to the M'Limo." Hole copied an obvious error by Taylor. Burnham, in an interview less than a week after the expedition, spoke of "crossing the Shashani River," which is located about three miles from the cave.[18]

A company inquiry was made into the M'Limo affair. Hole asserts that the commission under Justice Watermeyer found that the shooting was fraudulent. Unfortunately the commission's findings have disappeared, probably destroyed when company records in London burned during the blitz of 1940. Even so, reasons exist for believing that Hole's version of the official findings is incorrect. First, General Carrington later recommended Burnham to Field Marshal Roberts for the position of chief of scouts during the Boer War. If Carrington had been a victim of a proven fraud in the M'Limo affair, it is improbable that he would have made such a recommendation. Second, Burnham continued to have good relations with many Rhodesians of good reputation. As a former archivist of the Zimbabwe National Archives has noted, "In fact the conclusion that Watermeyer reached was not nearly as positively opposed to Armstrong [and Burnham] as . . . Hole would have us believe."[19]

More significant is the recent claim that Burnham and Armstrong directed their attack against the wrong man. British scholar Terence O. Ranger, in his study of the 1896 revolt, argues that Jobani was a "friendly" native who was responsible for maintaining neutrality in his section of the country and for keeping open the southern wagon road over which supplies came into Rhodesia. The Makalangas, the tribe to which Jobani belonged, did not join the Matabele in rebelling.[20]

Burnham recognized that Jobani's territory was regarded as friendly. However, he thought some members of the Makalanga tribe supported the rebels. Whites were puzzled that the wagon road remained open, but it seems unlikely Jobani was responsible. The Matabele would have paid little attention to the wishes of a former subject tribe if they wanted the road closed. More likely the rebels simply lacked the power to close it effectively, for they did attack travelers in the war's early stages. At the time, whites believed the Matabele encouraged keeping the road open so that whites would use it to flee the country.

Burnham may have shot an innocent man, but if so, there was no premeditated plan. He was acting under orders. If Jobani was innocent, he was a victim not of Burnham but of white misconceptions of the M'Limo cult and of the difficulty in distinguishing friend from foe that marks irregular warfare.

The M'Limo affair was Burnham's last exploit in the rebellion. Afterward, regular forces took over the conduct of the war. Many of Burnham's friends had already left the country to await the return of peace. With Blanche still suffering from Nada's death and business at a standstill, there was no point in the Burnhams remaining.

On July 11, 1896, the Burnhams and the Blicks left Rhodesia to return to America. Though Fred and Blanche would return for a short time the following year, their first pioneering days in Africa were at an end.

In editing the Burnham letters we allow the family to tell its own story, but we supply sufficient information to clarify events for readers who don't have a background in African history. When the letter writer makes an obvious mistake, we correct it without making the reader suffer through a multitude of *sic*'s.

In some instances we modernize incorrect or archaic spellings. For the Matabele capital of Buluwayo, which in 1894 became the white town Bulawayo, we use the spelling Buluwayo and then switch, as do the letter writers, to Bulawayo. For Zambesi, we use the modern Zambezi. For African tribes, we use the Burnhams' spellings, for example, Matabele and Mashona, rather than the now-current forms Ndebele and Nshona. We allow to stand as written words which the letter writer admits to uncertainty in spelling. We have left variations in the spellings of names of people and places as they appeared in the original letters.

The Burnham letters describe the African frontier and offer comparisons with the American frontier. Exotic surroundings sometimes fascinated and sometimes repelled them. Like soldiers away from home, they remember and speak of once-trivial things in the past that now seem dear. John Blick worries over his former girlfriend's affections; Blanche and Roderick miss California fruit; James Blick pines for his wife of nearly forty years and vows to roam no more. Only Fred Burnham is content with Africa, dreaming of empires in which "no man shall take another's bread." That he, like his contemporaries, applied this idealism only to white men does not mean he was insincere.

The Burnhams, with their virtues, faults, building of castles in the air, and memories of their homeland, were a remarkable family. They were privileged to take part in one of the last pioneering efforts of modern history.

All letters, unless otherwise noted, are in the papers of Frederick Russell Burnham in the Sterling Library, Yale University.

The editors would like to thank Marta Burnham Burleigh and Frederick Burnham, grandchildren of Blanche and Frederick R. Burnham, for their help. We are indebted to the late Gayle Burnham, widow of Roderick Burnham, who provided information and encouragement. It was she who first gave permission for the Burnhams' letters at Yale University to be opened for our use. We wish to also acknowledge the assistance of Peter Craigmoe in the early stages of our research.

A special thanks to Frederick Rinehart, our publisher, who carries forward a certain frontier spirit that would have been familiar to Fred Burnham; to Connie Oehring for her copyediting; and to Judith Schiff, head of Yale University Sterling Library's Manuscripts Collection, who first made us aware that a hunch that Fred Burnham had left extensive papers was correct. The editors would like to thank the American Philosophical Society for a grant that helped us to begin this project, and we are grateful to the West Virginia Institute of Technology Research Committee for grants that facilitated our work.

NOTES

1. The definitive account of mining engineers is Clark C. Spence, *Mining Engineers and the American West: The Lace-Boot Brigade, 1849–1933* (New Haven: Yale University Press, 1970), pp. 279–280.

2. Compare the Burnham experience with these American travelers in John Mack Faragher, *Women and Men on the Overland Trail* (New Haven: Yale University Press, 1980).

3. The same views can be found in the American West. Army officers charged with conquering the Indians were often the native Americans' greatest admirers. American frontiersmen were considered agents of civilization for removing the "savage Indian." For a comparison of American and African attitudes, see George M. Frederickson, *White Supremacy: A Comparative Study in American and South African History* (New York: Oxford University Press, 1981).

4. The best account is Stafford Glass, *The Matabele War* (London: Longmans, Green & Co., 1968).

5. In W. A. Wills and L. T. Collingridge, *The Downfall of Lobengula* (New York: Negro Universities Press, 1969 [originally published in 1894]), p. 158, Forbes is quoted as saying that he sent for Burnham, who was burning huts at the king's last camp.

6. John S. Galbraith, *Crown and Charter: The Early Years of the British South Africa Company* (Berkeley: University of California Press, 1974), pp. 336–338.

7. The company labor policies cost Rhodes support in England. See A. Holmberg, *African Tribes and European Agencies: Colonialism and Humanitarianism in British South and East Africa, 1870–1895* (Göteborg, Sweden: Akademiforlaget, 1966), p. 220.

8. For an analysis of the Rhodesian mining and farming frontier, see Dane Kennedy, *Islands of White: Settler Society and Culture in Kenya and Southern Rhodesia, 1890–1939* (Durham, NC: Duke University Press, 1987).

9. Galbraith, *Crown and Charter,* p. 208.

10. L. H. Gann, *A History of Northern Rhodesia: Early Days to 1953* (London: Chatto and Windus, 1964), p. 77.

11. In his autobiography, *Scouting on Two Continents* (Garden City, N.Y.: Doubleday, Page and Company, 1926), Burnham blames Nada's death on "hardships of the siege" and writes, "constantly before my enraged vision rose the picture of my wife vainly holding to her breast our dying Nada."

12. For a modern study of these cults, see M. L. Daneel, *The God of the Matopo Hills: An Essay on the Mwari Cult in Rhodesia* (The Hague: Mouton, 1970). The Mwari cult of the Mashona was known to the Matabele as the M'Limo.

13. Burnham, *Scouting on Two Continents,* p. 251.

14. Ibid., pp. 256–257.

15. Whites were not alone in attacking spirit mediums. In later conflicts, natives killed mediums when they believed the mediums were supporting white rule. See Peter Fry, *Spirits of Protest: Spirit Mediums and the Articulation of Consensus Among the Zezuru of Southern Rhodesia* (Cambridge: Cambridge University Press, 1976), pp. 186–192.

16. Terrence O. Ranger, *Revolt in Southern Rhodesia* (Evanston, Ill.: Northwestern University Press, 1967), p. 187; Arthur Keppel-

Jones, *Rhodes and Rhodesia: The White Conquest of Zimbabwe, 1884–1902* (Montreal: McGill-Queens University Press, 1983), p. 489.

17. Hugh Marshall Hole, *The Making of Rhodesia* (London: Frank Cass & Co. Ltd., 1967 [originally published in 1926]), p. 367, note 1.

18. "Death of the M'Limo, Interview with Mr. Burnham," *The African Review*, August 8, 1896, p. 334. The interview is dated Bulawayo, June 29, 1896.

19. Peter Emerson, in the foreword of the reprint edition of *Scouting on Two Continents* (Bulawayo: Books of Rhodesia, 1975).

20. Terence O. Ranger, *Revolt in Southern Rhodesia*, pp. 185–190.

Part I
1893
Trekking and War

Frederick Russell Burnham (FRB)
to Rebeccaa Russell Burnham

100 miles from Sandy Hook
Jan 15, 1893
Steamer *Servia*

Dear Mother,

    A staunch ship and smooth water, nobody sick. Episcopal service in the saloon rather impressive and fine. I will mention several points of interest since our departure. First, the Sound and great N.W., tis a grand country, and we hit a clear spell in which to see it. Waters indigo blue and such timber on the hills and cliffs as grow in no other clime and all fringed by those monuments of nature that I love so well, the high mountains glittering white and seamed by glaciers. In their vast solitudes one draws deep the breath of life. For 500 miles we wind and twist and climb then out onto the boundless prairie of Assinibona and Manitoba. Buffalo horns polished and offered for sale by the remnants of the Cree tribe, $2.00 to $5.00 per pair. We did not have time to call on Uncle W nor at St. Paul. Winipeg 35° below zero. Think of it and then thank God you are alive and in a country fit to live in. St. Paul 24° below. Chicago 10°. The World's Fair we took in as thoroughly as possible. It really was just about as I had figured it up. The size of it is the most impressive part and it strikes me as a giant advertisement scheme in which the world is to buck at Chicago's game and 10 years after tis passed it will be forgotten or remembered as the Great Chicago Circus and Hippodrome. But I may be wrong. It is bound to enlarge the ideas of very many people. It will spread discomfort and that means change and that rightly directed means improvement or wrongly directed means decay. But Washington: I like Washington and the building is grand and harmonious. Its decorating suits me very well. I listened to the grave senators and eager congressmen. Great forces are gathered here strong enough to work wonders and miracles. But do they? Hardly, for so many are not in touch with the mass of the people. *Abas* [down with] senators who buy their seats. *Abas* judges who are owned by R.R.s. What a pity that its corridors are smirched by their footsteps. But there is a better time coming or a much worse one. Things are in change and these closing years of the 19th century will yet be a historical period. If the institutions of this civilization are not elastic enough, if the classes have served their purpose and will not bend, then we will make history in a sea of blood. Tis well. I can swim in that element for the animal in me is so strong that I am not troubled by that ghost of the many, *fear.* If the changes come in peace, that is well, for it answers to the secret desire of one's better nature. Only cast the die. I am anxious for it, if by force, then pity dies and mercy, mercy flees to the wilds. The location of great cities will be known only by the presence of a slag made up of iron, glass and brick well fluxed with human blood. That great strength and bulwark of the 19th century civilization, vested rights and inheritance, will be a prime factor in its complete undoing. But after all has been accomplished, when the old order of things have passed away as a dream of the night, will we rebuild on a better and truer basis? Being an optimist, I think *yes.*

We arrived in New York at midnight, witnessed a fierce fight between a lot of cab men and baggage men, an old man shamefully beaten and 3 policemen on opposite corner. But I suppose the attacking hoodlums had a pull with the ward boss. It greatly excited B.[1] and she did not sleep till 5 A.M., but had I interfered I would have got 50 days at Blackwells and been accused of causing the trouble by one and all. Still I did want to take a hand very much. R. Deane B.[2] was greatly impressed with the Goddess of L. and great bridge.[3] Bye the bye, when you cross the Pacific take the *Empress of India*, she is the most beautiful boat that leaves a post of the U.S. The Cunarders[4] are not as fine by 30%. Everything snow white and clean as wax. We crossed the Mississippi at LaCrosse, very cold. These English are such queer people, dogmatic, argumentative in the sense of constant repetition with liberal offers to back their assertions on all subjects which cannot be decided before the ship lands in any possible way. Two old duffers fought for 2½ hours on the merits and demerits of two steamships neither man had seen and two others all last eve and part of today, whether clothes were as cheap in London as New York. A decorative artist has in-

1. Blanche Blick Burnham (1862–1939), Fred Burnham's wife.
2. Roderick Deane Burnham (1886–1976), son of FRB.
3. Statue of Liberty and Brooklyn Bridge.
4. Cunard Shipping Line.

formed everyone on board at least 3 times each that he is the man that painted the ball on top of St. Paul's [London]—36 ft. high you know. Another duffer played checkers last eve but today refused on account of being Sunday. That was all right, but in a few minutes glibly said he was crossing for a pleasant time in London and the Continent but could not take his wife and children. It was so very expensive. Then I thought what a d—n hog you are. His equally religious companion frankly acknowledged he foresaw those very expenses so remained single, hog No. 2. The Lord is welcome to them and the sooner he calls for them the better. I am struck with the minister (Episcopal) on board. He is the broadest gauged man I have met for a long time.

In discussing the possibility of the U.S. becoming a competitor, on the sea or in boat building, of Great Britain it was unanimously decided that she could not because there were no Hamericans (sic) that could officer them, they not being competent as either engineers or sailing masters. Not being nautical, I dare not say a word, though I thought that Perry, Paul Jones, Foote, Farragut, Porter and some others got along passably well. Still taking the nation at large, I felt with shame twas partly true and by our own absurd laws, for England rules the wave is no idle boast, and by so doing holds the purse strings of the world, and even the greatest precious metal producing nation on earth has to humbly beg for a silver conference. The frogs wanted a real king and then got it and Harrison did the begging for us, the dear people, and Lombard and Wall St. have answered as could be expected.

Well this is the last letter you will get from me for a long time for as soon as this enforced leisure is over I will be so busy that no time will come to write or even talk on light themes and happy vein. But B. will give you all the items of interest, and this letter you must give to all the folks to read as tis impossible to write to each one, and I must write to Howard.

One thing I will surely gain by my wandering, a knowledge whether the country over the Mt. is ever to be reached and see with my own eyes if any of my dreams can be worked out even in part. If they cannot, then I will return and put them behind me forever. If they can, then I will work them till I die.

Friday—Warm as spring. B. still seasick. Roderick Deane O.K. and racing round deck. B. declares she will walk across the

Sahara desert rather than take boat, so as camelback makes one seasick we will load one camel with toast and one with cold Jap tea (all English on board and perfectly awful in taste), and she will ride a burro and meet Rod and I on the Zambezi River.

Concert tonight. There is one character on board that makes a great deal of such amusement. She is an English woman who has lived 25 years in France (mostly). She will declare the English are a nation of hypocrites singing psalms on Sunday and taking the channel boat Monday come over to Paris and go on a regular jag; that the bawdy houses are kept up by them in Paris and that 6 lords were arrested at one time in a recent raid on one of them by police; that English servants fawn on you and then steal everything loose including the floor rugs; that the English are so dishonest and won't pay their bills, their greatest papers tell lies knowingly, &c. Next A.M., feeling rocky and not liking the steamer menu, she will abuse the American supply co. and sigh for dear old England with all its home comforts and quiet family life where everything you want can be ordered within a block of your door. There seems to be but one unanimous sentiment and that is hatred of the Yankees. (In their best moods after dinner this degenerates into a mild form of toleration.) I am really quite glad I am not a Yankee. The idea of brotherly love and the solidarity of the English speaking races has received a rude shock. I am anxious to see the Briton in his own little island before he has been soured by a trip to America. There is a Russian Jewess on board, very smart and well posted on political affairs of Europe but foolish enough to try and reason or argue with an Englishman, so she was attacked yesterday by 4 men and I must acknowledge she defended the Jews in a masterly manner and rather got the best of it, and besides she did not lose her temper as the men did two or three times. I wanted to join in the wrangle but I have sworn off arguing or debating on any subject. I shall lead low and play 3rd hand high. Everybody drinks, men, women, and children and at 9 to 10 P.M. take crackers, cheese and ale or beer.

Am expecting this letter to be put off at Queenstown and go to America by return boat. I think this is about enough for this time. Probably I can write you another letter while on the African steamer and give you a few points on what we have seen.

Adios

Fred

—————

FRB to Uncle Josiah Russell

January, 1893

Dear Uncle,

You can pass the above letter around among all our friends and family. I think Mrs. Tallmadge would be interested and say to her that as usual we do not know just where we will go next but that we borrow no trouble on that account. I would dearly love to have you over here for a while. You remember what a pleasant trip we had down New Port[1] way caring nothing where night overtook us. It would be doubly interesting in old England. The soft sweet music and chants of its old cathedrals, quiet easy country life, its winding country roads, every foot historic ground where was refought and is still being fought the battles of liberty and popular rule since the dark ages. There is no denying this being a mighty nation. Give 35 million Americans a little island like this, put them along side a host of jealous peoples like the continent, and would they have built better than these? By comparison of countries, boasting for the time being at least dies within me and I think for *shame America* that any man within it should beg for work or seek it and not find it. We should have no poor, and the scales of justice should rest on an evener beam than anywhere in the wide world. Our political system needs some amendment and of a radical nature. I picked up a pamphlet addressed to all Englishmen calling for the annual expenditure of £100,000 per annum, the line of argument being so outside of money considerations that in America it would have fallen flat but here it has roused the whole country. The Englishman, arrogant and selfish as he is, loves country enough to put up $ on things that he will never see and can only be of value to maybe his grandchildren. If you chance to meet Mr. Foster and he enquires if I am coming home, tell him not for some time unless I should be compelled to attend to the mining suit and other mining business.[2] I shall call at Post Office, London for a line from you. I have no further news from my attorney Millard

———

1. New Port Beach, California.
2. At this time Burnham was engaged in a suit with the Alvord Mining Company of Pasadena.

save that the company was about to settle my claims against them, I too surrendered all interest &c., which suits me.

I will write you more from London.

Yours as ever,

Fred

———

FRB to Josiah Russell

Hereford, England
January 25, 1893

Dear Uncle,

Our English friends, the Fords, met us at the station and for the last few days we have been enjoying that peculiar English hospitality that puts one entirely at ease.[1] No excitement and in a few hours you feel as if you had in a measure always been expected and provided for. The first thing an American generally does is to describe English scenery not forgetting the oaks and parklike culture of the country, its hedgerows &c. and then branch off on cathedral lore and go into ecstasy over old Roman roads and ivy clad castles. So to be in good form I will give you a few impressions made by the cathedral and the solid old country town of Hereford. The local history of the cathedral runs about as follows. Supposed to be founded by St. Ethelbert about 825. Its present walls deceive the eye. The usual amount of saints' bones, armor, &c. is to be seen but what seemed to bring back the world as it appeared to the people of the 11th century most was a queer old map showing the greatest body of water to be the Mediterranean Sea, Jerusalem the center of the earth, the exact location of Eden, the tower of Babel and other equally absurd things. Should H.R.H. commission the commander of the fleet to make a hostile demonstration off the coast of China and place in his hands this map as guide he would soon be food for fishes. I will send you a copy of it. Notice in the lower right hand where Nebuchadnezzar, King of Babylon, is turned out to grass and is wandering around on all fours a la Wilson Peak burro, probably sighing for a tomato can.

1. The Fords were relatives of Jack Ford, Blanche Burnham's brother-in-law, who was married to Madge Blick.

The temperance question was a strong local issue here in the 13th century, for a pious priest spent 40 years in copying the bible and in his version, which was accepted, prohibited wine and cider. But alas in this degenerate 19th century we see, in spite of even the bible being sworn over to sign the pledge, that plenty of good Hereford cider can be bought at any public house for 1s a gallon.

At 4 P.M. we returned to the cathedral to hear the great organ and a fine choir. It was grand. We have nothing like it in America. It beats the opera and I do not wonder so much now why the nation will stand the taxes of the established church. Many of the marbles were systematically defaced during Cromwell's time by the Puritans as they hated images, but they did not destroy its wonderful architecture, and had I been shown the bones of the architect who planned and builded this from such materials as could be obtained in the 11th century, I should have been easily persuaded that they still had miraculous powers.

The weekly market is well worth a few hours time. Here are driven in from the farms each market day the finest of Hereford beefs, now such a popular breed in America. A 1600# beef auctions for about $100 here at present. But the stock is so gentle, the fence to hold a hundred head is no heavier than would hold a bunch of jack rabbits. The buyers walk around among them, take hold of their horns, feel of their ribs, lean up against them, and argue about their value and in fact treat them exactly as if they were pet dogs. Finally after the buying, the English cowboy is called in to drive them off to their destination. No lasso, no pistols and broad brim hat, no big Jacksonville whip whose crack is like a pistol shot, no bronco to ride, no spurs and fancy saddle. Just a plain red-faced stub and twist kid with nothing but a switch, two or three feet long. I would have given a good deal to have just turned loose one good lively longhorned steer from the Brazos just to see how they would have handled him. Nothing but the fire department could have saved the town. The fat sheep were in pens no higher than my knee and even that notorious animal the pig made no effort to bolt or be contrary and really it is not so disparaging to the Irish race to say they invite the pig into the parlor. The only improvement that I could possibly suggest in his breeding would be to lower the high soprano voice which is his habitual key and a slight nasal twang to what lower tones he indulges in. He may get the latter though from the visiting Americans for the native is never guilty of it.

The political fray is soon to open and I am anxious to watch it and will have a chance to hear the "Grand Old Man."[2] The railroad question is already on taps here and strong. It is in everybody's mouth, the government must control through parliament the terrible monopoly. Handbills are out for a great meeting and memorial to parliament at this place. It seems fares and freights are to be raised again and they are very high now . . . [letter incomplete].

———

FRB to Rebecca Russell Burnham
(letter is a copy in Rebecca Burnham's hand)

Paris,
February 7, 1893

Dear Mother,

As affairs in Africa are moving so rapidly, we have decided to sail on the 15th from Naples and down the east coast via Suez and Madagascar. . . .

We were told it was very fine weather for London. If so, what must the bad be? You *never* get a breath of pure air. At first my eyes and throat smarted but in a day or two that passed away.

In spite of the streets being paved with solid blocks and constantly cleaned, they are covered with a slimy dark mud that sticks tight. Its sidewalks are narrow and to walk is to fight your way along and to ride is to jolt along the same as in San Francisco. Miles and miles of narrow foggy streets and unadorned plain brick houses. No desert is so dreary and its poor are so wretched and dirty and cold.

I attended a meeting of the unemployed near London Tower. In a drizzling rain were gathered several hundred poor wretches, well guarded by a cordon of police and were being harangued by a poorly dressed man in such Cockney lingo I could not understand him. He was referring to the times of Henry VIII.

The crowd were silent, sullen. No cheers, no complaint. But it takes a mighty cause to hold a crowd in a cold rainstorm. There

---

2. William Gladstone, Liberal prime minister of Great Britain.

is in this mass a leaven that will yet reach Piccadilly and the West End, jeered though they may be at the present, and a man from the slums will yet make the blue-veined House of Lords listen to him. So much of outdoor London. Indoors it is another world.

The middle classes have plenty of books, magazines, warm fires, cozily furnished rooms, and every comfort. They do not work and rush as the Americans do, are in no haste to change the present order of things, and are as solid and steady-going set of people as can be found. Caste, they believe in and secretly have a lingering suspicion that the ruling sovereign can do no harm except ask Parliament for money. They still worship the Lords though denying that they are divine. It is by the sufferance of this middle class that the upper class live, for if they joined issue with the lower or even made up their minds themselves to change things it would be done.

The Tower with its blocks and its prisons, where in the good old days England put its smartest men and buried its dolts in the Abby, is of course one of the sights. The Abby is a marvel oft described yet always interesting. The clay of England's heroes are here and Chaucer's grave is covered with roses and wreaths, voluntary tributes of the people every day, while marble busts and slabs of men who looked down on such as he have crumbled and are forgotten. Surely to live in the hearts of the people is the longest life possible on earth and *that* is limited.

The dome of St. Paul's is tremendous and its whispering gallery brought back to my mind grandfather's description of it, also Primrose Hill to which he likened the little hill back of Sterling Center[1] and with grandma took me up on top and pretended to point out the interesting points of London. But my young eyes could only see the green prairie grass and scattered shanties of those early times. But his great-grandchild at exactly the same age has stood on the true Primrose Hill and been pointed out the modern London with its 5,000,000 souls. Grandfather would not know the modern Thames so thoroughly is it bridged and tunneled.

The zoo took a day of our time and it was well spent. In fact every moment spent in London was interesting and profitable. It

1. Minnesota settlement where FRB's grandparents lived in the 1860s.

was interesting to observe and study the stock and people that have in so large a measure builded America. Already the idea that we are a great nation or cut a figure at all is getting dim to me. One hears of Spain, Holland, Germany, Russia, Turkey, France, India, and Egypt but not of the U.S. unless to comment on a lynching in Virginia or a joke on Chicago copied from N.Y. papers.

There is no hiding the fact the English don't like us. I did not think so but it is true. It is only the radical who admires us at all, but they hate the Russians worse so we should not be offended. All eyes now are centered on Gladstone in England. He is without doubt the greatest man of the 19th century. He is far ahead of the mass of the people in ideas of reform but I fear his age will tell on him and he will go to his grave defeated. He is too grand for the average Tory vote or even a good part of the Liberals. Vested rights and custom are here as solid as the rocks and nothing but the persistence of a Gladstone backed by the fiery . . . [letter incomplete].

━━━━━━━

FRB to Josiah Russell

Off the island of Candia
In the Mediterranean
Feb 23rd 1893

Dear Uncle,

We have just had a severe blow and even now the sea is so rough tis very hard to write. It made one remember Paul's account of his little sea voyage, Jonah and others. But the waves were grand. Tis worth a storm at *sea* just to *see* it. I think my last letter to you was from Paris but mostly about England. Paris and the French were a great surprise to me. I found less squalor and filth in Paris than any spot in Europe I have seen. They are the most industrious, saving and clean people I ever saw and I only saw two drunken men while there. I spent one day in the region of the Bastille, but San Fran, Chicago or N.Y. can discount this for poverty and wretchedness. There is a tough foreign colony on the outskirts of the city made up mostly of Italians that comes nearer London and our own cities. But Paris is the city of earth. Its boulevards are really long parks. The Seine, a swift stream spanned by scores of the finest bridges, adds to its natural beauty. The build-

ings are artistic and of harmonious color. Its shops and stores a
continual panorama. And even the poor people make their clothes
fit them and they keep them clean. The idle class is very small.
The land is divided into very small holdings consequently France
is wealthy and excites the hatred and jealousy of all the surrounding nations. And as Blucher,[1] when shown over the city of London
by Wellington, exclaimed, "What a city to sack," so the modern
nations with their hands on sword say let's carve her up as we did
Poland, and some day they will. How can a republic live in such a
place? On her northern frontier is a victorious and brutal enemy.
On the east a poverty stricken horde of huns little better than was
led by the terrible Atila. To the south that treacherous and thieving
nation which has already joined the alliance against her. And on
the west lays England her old hereditary enemy and willing now to
pick her bones if there is a six pence worth of fat on them. All that
keeps their hands stayed a day is the growl of the Russian bear who
protected by vast steppes and hard winters is always the unknown
power that makes all Europe tremble. But she is so semi-barbarous
that it seems a strange alliance—the most highly civilized nation in
Europe to form a lasting alliance with—that it seems it must break
and when it does good bye France. Although it will be like the
badger in the barrel, quite a job to take it out. And the nation as
against a foreign foe is as united as Napoleon's guard, and they
love France better than gold. But she can never do again what she
once did, whip them all. It seems strange to see so many soldiers
marching to and fro, bands playing and colors flying. I asked an
Italian officer why they need keep 1,000,000 men under arms,
France can never attack you. No, he says, "but we want to be in at
the division of the spoils."

Well enough of politics, for probably none of these things
may happen. It looks at present as if cholera would give all of them
something else to think of than plundering each other. . . .

There is absolutely no use trying in a letter to write up the
standard sights of the different points of interest in Europe. A
good guide book can beat you all hollow in description. But the
sights are not disappointing. They excel *expectation*. To wander

---

1. Field Marshall Prince Gebhard von Blucher (1742–1819), Prussian commander at
Waterloo.

through the four miles of the Louvre is worth a year of one's life. Here is the product of thousands of the most brilliant minds of every nation for hundreds of years. In Westminster Abbey lays the sacred dust and a fitting place it is and very peaceful, only the footfall of the pilgrim and the music of the great organ to break the silence. But in the Louvre stand out the works in marble and bronze and gold, or worked in tapestries, or painted on canvas, is portrayed every human thought from the creation down. The tomb of Napoleon, massive, peculiar and in harmony with that wonderful man. His last wish gratified, "That his ashes should rest on the banks of the Seine among the people he loved so well." The tower of steel 1000 ft high,[2] and that more wonderful tower of the Bastile which showed to the world what an outraged people *can do*. So on and on until one's mind is staggered and becomes misty. One should drink in these visions of the past slowly. Tis strong food. Very loth I was to leave Paris, the only city I ever saw that I liked, and all in all they are a cheerful honest and happy people, never hypocritical or servile.

Through the Alps which of course draws sightseers from everywhere but fell very flat with me, for we could carve a Switzerland out of California and have scenery to spare. The quaint old town of Genoa known to the world chiefly through Columbus. Pisa made a reputation also by having a smart *architect in the family* who constructed a leaning tower that failed to lean clear over and to fulfill a wish of schoolboy days. I sat in its shade for it was a very prominent Italian scene in one of the old geography pictures and a very interesting tower it is.

From there to the Eternal City and round its seven hills and over I walked. Here is enough to inspire a Gibbon to write its fall. How *could* such a mighty empire *fall*? And what hope can a modern country have of continual national existence. Yet this is not a city of ruins by any means, for in spite of its thousand wars and its dearth of commerce there is still to be seen the most wonderful palaces on earth. The solid old castles of England, the artistic and beautiful of France are here both excelled. St. Paul's is like a huge barn compared to St. Peter's, and all modern palaces sink into insignificance compared to the Vatican. Thousands of rooms and

2. The Eiffel Tower.

miles and miles of galleries (11,000 all together). Under St. Peter's could be built every church in Pasadena and even their spires would not stick out the roof. . . . Here is poured out the wealth of Christendom. Art, sciences and religion blend to create these wonders and all modern Europe seems cheap beside them, as America seems cheap and new and temporary compared to Europe. Our modern skyscrapers and big cities seem as houses of cardboard and cities of paint and cloth. Here all is marble and stone and bronze. The Roman solidity has been preserved.

Yet vast as is St. Peter's, the palm of great buildings must be given to that monument of Jewish captivity, the Colosseum, the Roman Emperor believing if the Jews could build a Solomon's temple they could build him a lasting monument, a playhouse. But nowadays the Jew can always force the Christian to build for him by the proper use of money with interest. But thousands of ardent pilgrims have gone into print on the Colosseum, so how hopeless seems the possibility of saying one word new or discover one fact unknown before. My own feelings sitting on a marble cap looking into the arena can never be written. The flowers, so bright and plentiful in spite of the efforts of guards to hoe them up, seem an effort of nature to hide this bloody spot. But tis this very blood that has made its soil trebly rich and well suited for plant life. At the dedication of this edifice were slain 9,000 animals and 3,000 men in combat, lasting over three months. Here countless of the martyrs drenched the soil with tears and blood. Here ascended a stream of the most sincere prayers ever offered to a God. A crucible of human passion not for a day or a decade but for hundreds of years. One mile around its massive walls and seating capacity to hold ½ the people in Los Angeles County and then leave a large space for the combatants. Under the arena were kept the beasts which greatly interested Roy, for in the Louvre he saw a painting of the lions and tigers just emerging from the dens to eat a band of Christians kneeling in the center of the arena and here were the dens and arena and after a hearty meal of sirloin of Christian they were driven back to their dens with fire brands to await a fresh conscription of Jew or captive. But of modern Rome the less said the better, outside its palaces and churches, for Italy is so poor and its people so despicable. They care nothing for the halo of past grandeur and only look upon its modern magnificence as valuable from the amount of rich pilgrims and suckers it brings to their doors that they may fleece him of a few francs. There is no gold in the country and even its largest banks will not redeem the paper money of the country, even in silver, beyond 50 francs. The porter of the Hotel Suisse had to go 4 times to get even that for 3 times there was no silver in bank.

It is like America in war times. £350,000,000 per year interest she has to pay on national debt mostly to France. Portugal is worse off and Spain nearly so. How can the world run on a gold basis alone. Industry is hampered for lack of exchange and right glad are these people to see a silver piece.

Naples. Pictures in every geography and described in every European novel. Tis here or at Sorrento that the injured wife comes to die, and surely Naples without the Neapolitans would be a romantic and lovely spot wherein to die. Imagine Mt. Wilson to be a live volcano, always rolling up a volume of dense smoke and trailing it away for miles over the valley and San Pedro harbor to sweep in a graceful curve through Baldwin's ranch and by the Raymond with the Peunta hills an island (Capri and blue grottos). And the water is so clear and of a night gives out that peculiar light when touched by an oar. It's a poem to spend an evening on the bay of Naples, to watch old Vesuvius catching the last glow of the evening and see the wonderful shadows cast by the Castlelamar. Shadow and reality are here very close, too beautiful to last, slips away so fast hours are as moments. Tis dark and old Vesuvius looks the stern and black pile full of misery and destruction that it looked to those old Romans in the long ago, and as tomorrow we are to walk the streets of this old city we must end the vision and seek the dining room of the Hotel Geneva.

Pompeii. Surely I should not complain. Another day dream I have realized and unlike so many it fills every niche of fancy. Here we see the Roman not through somebody's pen nor through some old relic or twenty times restored buildings but as he lived 2000 years ago. Here are his utensils, his ovens, even the bread and fruit, dogs, horses and the Roman himself, pretty well preserved by the ashes that caused his death, his temples and churches for he was liberal and worshiped several gods as we do now. Theatres for comedy and one for heavy tragedy and adjoining a hollow square for the genuine play of life by the gladiators. They built and lived better than the modern Italians and were surely cleaner for the public baths are fine and they had a fountain in every house. The water brought in aqueducts and lead pipes still well preserved. Here we can see the house of the merchant, the banker, the artisan, the official, and slave. Forum, market place, and exchange. Its houses of ill fame, its temples and statues to the god. No restoring. Here it is as on the day when the play was interrupted by the mountain. I think these people must have been industrious and about as a modern city of 25,000 inhabitants usually is in morals and religion. Their streets were nicely paved. The streets named and houses designated. The purest of water and fine natural location must have made it the Pasadena of the Empire. I jingled an American dollar on the mosaic counter of the *banker* thinking perhaps its magical sound would call him back to life, for if it were possible to raise the dead that would surely have brought him to the front. Still it would have puzzled him to make the change, although as to its being the God we trust he would have soon understood. Whether he could grasp the far reaching influence of compound interest or not is an open question, quite likely he could, for these Romans were a strong people as can be seen in the features of its dead. The firm jaw, thin nose, broad head that showed a ruling race.

The land of antiquity and mecca of the relic hunter, Egypt, will soon be on our lee and I will close this. In my next will be able to tell you more of modern war in Africa as we take on 240 Soudanese to accompany us and help fight the Wahi[3] who number over 100,000. Yours as ever F.

We will be 5 weeks down east coast, 6115 miles from Naples, so it will be about 10 weeks from date of this before you get answer to any of your letters sent to Johannesburg S.A. Pass this letter to all the friends and folks, the Tallmadges should they desire to hear of us.

———

3. The Hehe of present-day Tanzania. They were a major source of resistance to German expansion, overwhelming a German expedition in 1891. Spellings of this tribe's name vary in the Burnham letters.

Blanche Burnham to Rebecca Russell Burnham
Letter is a copy in Rebecca Burnham's hand

> On board the *Reichstag*
> in the middle of the Red Sea.
> March 1, 1893

Dear Mother,

I am going to try to write a long letter this time but may not be able to finish today for there is a very strong wind and the little white caps are coming, but I have not been sick for five days so maybe I can stand a little rolling of the ship.

You need not feel very sorry for my being seasick for even on the Atlantic I was not sick like going over to Catalina. But I cannot sit up. Have the headache and can't keep food on my stomach. Of course I feel miserable but the last five days have revived me. These days have been nearly perfect, and I never saw anything like the sea was yesterday. Just like soft billowing folds of blue crepe. It looked as though a person could easily walk on it. We have not seen land for two days.

It is considerably wider here than when the Israelites crossed it. It is as blue as any sea now and the stories are contradictory about it ever being red. The guidebooks say it is red sometimes but not often. The first officer on ship says that sometimes when the wind is from the land it blows great swarms of grasshoppers out over the sea that makes it look red especially when they drop into the water.

I think I told you in my last that Fred was the first one on board to see Africa at Port Said. I wish you could see him. He is so happy and contented. I am so glad we came even if it never amounts to anything, for Fred's life ambition will have been gratified. But everything we hear is very favorable, and we are so sure it is the country for us that I believe it will be so. Tell Judd to begin to save his money for Africa.[1] Would it not be strange if you should all come here someday. Stranger things have happened. Who would have believed 9 years ago tomorrow that you would all be sitting in Pasadena. One thing is certain. There are a number of places in Europe that are as lovely as Pasadena, so when we become bloated aristocrats we could spend our winters in Africa and summers in Southern Europe. . . .

---

1. Judd Blick, younger brother of Blanche Burnham.

We are nearing the equator now but it is deliciously cool up on deck. The whole ship is covered with awnings. Well, it is the middle of the P.M. now. The wind is straight in our faces. The waves are small so I am all right. Roy is wondering if Uncle Jack's boat could ride these waves. He speaks of you all very often.

March 4. Well, I spent our wedding anniversary in bed. The pretty little white caps that I wrote about turned into angry billows 15 to 18 feet high late that day and a full blown monsoon raged for sixty hours, but the sun was shining, clear blue sky and a steady wind always blowing in one direction, north to south. It blew against us so we could not make fast time so we are just 24 hours behind time. I think I have written you that we have 200 Soudanese soldiers on board. They had a tough time. They are living under awnings on the lower decks. Some of them were very seasick, but they seemed to take it good naturedly. They were floating in water most of the time. Finally they put some of them on the upper deck, and even then they were frequently drenched. A very heavy monsoon for the Red Sea, the captain said. Of course Fred and Roy were all right so was I as long as I was lying down, so you need not think of me as being seasick. I managed to get up yesterday long enough to see the waves. No mistake they are grand when the mighty deep is in commotion.

It is quiet today and I am glad of it. We came through the straights of Babel Mandel this A.M. and stopped at Aden Persia, but as we are 24 hours late, not time for us to go on shore. . . .
Your loving,
Blanche

———

BBB to Blick family

Indian Ocean
March 8, 1893

My Dear Ones,

Oh such a lazy life as we are leading now. March 10—There you see how lazy we are, for I could not stir up enough ambition to write more than ten words, but today I am very smart. Mr. Williams told me last evening that we crossed the equator at six this morning, and you know that that has been one of our dreams, so I was up at half past five. They could not tell exactly for it is now 7:30 and he says not quite yet. We have had considerable fun over the subject. He says that it will give the ship a terrible bump as we go over and that old Neptune will come on board and shave every one with a barrel stave. He fixed a string across the spy glass this morning and then told us to look that the equator was in sight. I suppose it must be hot on the land of course but out here on the ocean we have a delightful breeze all the time. Some of the state rooms are very warm but we are very fortunate in having No. 1, and it has a good sized window opening toward the front of the ship, so we have a good breeze all the time. We wear our woolen underwear all the time. Not as warm as some of Pasadena's days but then as I say we are out on the ocean. Day after tomorrow we land at Tanga and the next Zanzibar and there we can tell more about the tropical climate. They say that there is plenty of fruit at Zanzibar, bananas, pineapples, &c. I hope so, for the warm weather makes us crave fruit. We shall lay in a supply for ourselves for fear that the ship does not. They have so much meat, I am tired of it. Do you want our bill of fare for yesterday? It is about the same with a little variation every day. Seven A.M.—coffee, tea, rolls and buns. 8:30—Breakfast—steak, chops and ham, boiled potatoes—2nd course and plates knives and forks are always changed, black bread, brown bread, white bread cut in very thin slices. You butter one of these and make a sandwich with either of two kinds of baloney sausage. (I do not know how to spell it.) And then we have raspberry jam. We take the jam and once in a while Roy eats a sandwich. Tea with that meal but not coffee. 12:30 Luncheon. Stuffed sausage, sauerkraut, and boiled potatoes or some kind of a stew in place of the sausage and kraut or meat curry and rice. 2nd course: some kind of salad, sardines, raw ham, canned beef and baloneys and cheese. Take your choice. Water to drink. 3:30—Tea, coffee sweet breads and mixed cookies. 6:00 Dinner. Soup, some kind of meat, boiled potatoes, carrots, turnips, kraut or horse beans, another kind of meat and a dish of sauce or a compote of fruit as they say, then a small piece of cake and an orange or nuts and raisins and coffee. Plenty of it and well served, but awfully monotonous and the beef is getting tougher every day. You know we must have something to grumble about, and the potatoes are always boiled. What would I give for some of Mother's baked beans and a piece of pie, two things we have not tasted since leaving home. They are purely American dishes. The French made the most delicious puddings but the Germans only make a very small thin cake. Nothing much to write about on shipboard, but I know that you like to hear the little things just as I do from home.

March 11—The captain just told me that we would pass a mail steamer tomorrow and that if we would give our letters to the purser he would take them on board for us, so I will finish my letter today. This will be the last letter we can mail until April 1 when we reach Natal or a few days later from Johannesburg because all the mail from Zanzibar down the coast goes by the western coast. So make up your minds that we are all right and that you cannot hear from us for three weeks and maybe four. Got up so early yesterday that I had to go to sleep before dinner time. They were fooling me for we did not cross the equator until 11:30 A.M., and now we are in the country of the Southern Cross, although it has been in sight for some time before we crossed the line. These are perfect days: the ocean is so smooth and blue and indigo. The ocean is full of fish. One day we saw a hundred or more porpoise. They were right alongside of the ship, and every day we see thousands and thousands of flying fish. I did not know that they could fly so far. Yesterday A.M. one flew the wrong way and came over the ship side. Roy was much interested in examining its wings. We see quantities of jelly fish and at night the water all around the ship is full of phosphorescent life that reminds me of the water in the Bay of Naples. . . . I will hope that you will all see these wonders for yourselves someday. I wish you could look down on the lower deck with me this A.M. A great big black is giving out the rations for luncheon. They have a sugar barrel full of boiled rice, and he gives a big wooden ladle full to each person. They try to stand in line but there is considerable confusion nevertheless. Such a variety of dishes as they have and they spat the rice down with their hands. As soon as he gets his bowl full of rice he passes down to the hard tack blanket and gets his portion of hard tack. It is all spread out in little heaps on a blanket. At night they have some kind of meat or fish with their rice and I think bread instead of hard tack for breakfast and supper. The soldiers are drilled every day. Such looking soldiers dressed in *all* sorts of garments. At Dar-es-Salaam they will be uniformed and it will be in coats and pants.

Now these men either wear long night gowns and if they can get hold of an old vest or coat they wear that also. Their clothes are of all colors. The women wear a gown of some dark color mostly, a band around their foreheads (some few wear the veil over their mouths) and a mantle thrown over the head and across the shoulder. Even the little girls have their heads wrapped up. The men wear a Turkish fez or a gay bandanna wrapped around the head. The females have their finger nails stained and wear bracelets, anklets, rings and some have an ornament in the side of their nose. All except the little children have their cheeks marked with long gashes and cuts. It does not take *any* stretch of imagination to believe that they are descendants of orangoutangs and yet there are one or two cute looking little girls with their bangs braided into pigtails and ornamented with bright strings and brass rings, chains of beads, corals and shells around their necks and little bracelets on their wrists and ankles. We will land them day after tomorrow. Poor things. I wonder how many will get killed. There will be a thousand warriors when they all get together. The Wahes kill all the caravans which pass through their country, so the Germans are going to take their country. That reminds me of what the captain told us about Cape Guardafui which we passed a few days ago. Will write it after luncheon. The wind blows up here on deck but it is warm down in the salon. Do not let father attempt to read this or he will scold about my poor writing and it does look more like hen's scratches than ever this morning.

4:10 P.M.—Saw a school of dolphins about an hour ago. They came so close that we could see their eyes. Oh! I forgot to tell you that our black passengers' legs look just like turkey legs. Does it not seem strange. We are thinking about supper and you are not out of bed yet. Twelve hours difference in our time. We crossed the sun's line, as the sailors call it, today. At noon the sun *was directly* overhead, rose exactly in the center of the east and will set exactly in the center of the west. Don't you wish you were with us. I do. Oh, yes, I was going to tell you about Cape Guardafui. The sailors call it the graveyard of ships. Four ships have been wrecked there in the last four years and a number before that. A fierce tribe live near there and they killed all the passengers and crew of the first three boats but were afraid and sent the survivors of the last ship to Aden in their boats. There is no lighthouse there. The captain says it would require an army to keep one. As you will see by looking on the map all vessels change their course at that point. There is another point just a little ways south of it which in the night or fog which generally hangs over it is mistaken for the cape. They make the turn and run ashore. Not many lighthouses down here. But there is one at Zanzibar, so we will wait there tonight and go to Tanga in the A.M. Mr. Williams just told me that maybe we would take the little steam launch and go up the river for a picnic while the ship was taking on cargo. We have a lovely little steam launch on board the ship. I do hope that we will. We are only a few miles from the coast now and it looks very fine. Plantations along the coast and thickly wooded mountains back of them. The timber looks very large. We will have a chance to see the tropics now with the dense vegetation which I have always wanted to see.

I wonder what you are doing these days. . . . Roderick is doing very well with his lessons. We bought a little globe in Paris for him. He can trace our route exactly. He sends love and kisses to *all.* He talks about you so much and so do we.

Adios my darlings.

Your loving Happy B.

We hear different stories about the English East African Co.[1] One man from Africa says six months enlistment gives you the choice of 3000 acres of land wherever you choose in their possessions. Mashonaland, where we are going, belongs to them. Fred thought that it was two years enlistment. We will find out all about it and if good Judd might come over when Howard comes if he wants to do that.[2] Thought I would tell you anyway. It may not amount to anything at all but it is an immense big country and not all desert by any means. You know that we cannot live without scheming.

B.

---

1. British South Africa Company.
2. Howard Burnham, FRB's younger brother.

FRB to Josiah Russell

Off Coast of Zanzibar
March 13, 1893

Dear Uncle,

The sea mail closes at 12, so I will just have time to write a little of our landing at Tanga. Our arrival was announced by the booming of an antiquated cannon on the turtle back and as we were to discharge cargo all day the passengers had use of steam launch for a frolic on shore and such a shore as it is. Huge mango trees 10 to 12 feet thick at the base and spreading like a live oak making a wonderful shade. Thousands of coconut palms, tall graceful trees, forests of bananas and a thousand shrubs, trees and plants of which I know nothing. A pretty harbor with an island in the middle and the mangrove trees living right in the ocean waters and bearing oysters made the assertion true that this was the country where oysters grow on trees. A few miles back of the fort and bay is a rugged range of mountains 2000 to 3000 feet high. I should have liked to explore them at once if I had the time and no one in the post seems to have any idea of what they are. The whole scene was perfectly tropical and beautiful. A different world entirely and life and all its surroundings looked at from a standpoint so utterly different from anything we ever knew or saw before. The natives, fat, smooth, black fellows, serve as boatmen, stevedores and even as a boat, for everyone has to be carried on shore on the back of a big black sitting astride his neck and holding on to his wooly head to keep your balance. It was altogether comical and novel.

Mrs. B. rebelled at this black craft for landing but as the water was deep it was ride or walk so I induced two of them to cross their hands on their shoulders and in a few moments she was ashore. The German officer, a very pompous and sedate man, lost all look of dignity astride the neck of a huge grinning black even though he persisted in full regimental and gun, a monocle and a pair of field glasses for he was going to pay his respects to the commander of the fort and had the dignity of the emperor to hold up even if on the back of a nigger. The second officer, a happy go lucky cuss, jumped overboard and holding his gun aloft walked ashore greatly to the astonishment of the blacks. But in the coming war I will wager the second officer will be worth a dozen of the first in a hard campaign. Our missionary also went ashore with a lot of hymns which he had translated into Somalia or the native tongue, also a big camera and tripod for shooting the mission buildings. They had the bell rung and service for the blacks (13 attended) assisted by the local missionary. I did not attend the service but went to a grand powwow of the natives and heard for the first time the weird sound of the tom-tom and the original darky melodies. It was rather pleasant music, though monotonous. There are very many kinds of blacks, the Soudanese soldiers on board are very tall wiry fellows and slim as rails, but the natives of Tanga most of them are wonderful men in physique, straight, broad-shouldered and the backbone deep sunken in knots of their bodies, a dark brown and a few of them jet black. There are 4000 blacks in Tanga, about 40 whites and quite a sprinkling of Hindoos or Banyans, a fine looking race with smooth clear olive skins, thin noses and large black eyes and head, shaped like the whites. They are mostly traders. An ivory caravan had discharged a fine lot of tusks here and one lone camel was solemnly pacing up and down the beach. Queer patient dumb sort of beast they are, capable of carrying an awful load and having such a water tank that he ought to drink beer. He could run such a close race with the Germans on board that I would be tempted to bet on him, but I might lose. A good part of our cargo is beer, but we have one missionary and 240 Soudanese soldiers to help civilize the ignorant blacks and initiate him into the intricacies of our Christian civilization.

And here in Tanga under a German fort two long strings of blacks were sent out to handle cargo with iron collars round their necks, connected by chains. I asked the officer if they were not slaves. *Oh no*, but we put the chains on to keep them from running away, and one was a boy not over 14 years old. For an African or Arab to do this would be slavery but for Germany or England it is not. For my part I fail to see the fine distinction. No doubt my mind is too much befogged by Yankee ideas yet. But why not call a spade a spade. We have the cheering intelligence that at Zanzibar there is a revolution on foot. The Sultan is dead ("Long live the Sultan"), so a German man-of-war is going over with us. Tonight we land our Soudanese soldiers who go to fight the Wahe. The Wahe have killed one expedition of 97 whites and 120 blacks, and one of 100 whites and 240 or thereabouts blacks so the chances of these fellows ever seeing the Soudan again is slim, but they are

Mohammedans and to die in battle gives them the 7th heaven direct without the tedious passage through the first six. So again the cross and crescent fight side by side in a conquest. An unholy war.

We will soon be in Zanzibar. The captain says this is the 3rd time he has been here at a Sultan's death. He says the English poisoned one Sultan but thinks that was of no moment and that probably British gold hired a native to put a pill in the food of this one.[1] Surely this is another world in politics as well as everything else. Even the stars and heavens are entirely changed. The cold winds are from the south and hot ones from the north, the cattle no larger than sheep, the goats with roman noses, the sheep with black heads, very little wool and huge tails, the chickens about the size of a quail. Then the huge camel and elephant, the tremendous plants and huge trees. The sea life is all different, its shells strange and beautiful and fish the same. Life is a succession of surprises to one who cares for nature.

We have one cockney on board who never was outside of London and by it all things are measured. Life to him is about as follows, *Naples* good macaroni and cool beer. Rome ditto, Cairo *poor beer* but good brandy and soda, Pyramids too blasted hot to see; went to see the review of English troops instead. Fine lot of men, big casino and dancing girls, more soda and brandy. Suez wretched, absolutely nothing to eat or drink. Tanga miserable beer, very warm, no ice, etc. He is a great specimen and just why he is going to Africa he don't know himself only to get a few diamonds and some gold if it is laying round handy.
Good bye in haste,
Fred

———

BBB to John Blick

Delagoa Bay
March 26, 1893
My Dear John,

Here goes for the last letter on shipboard and I am not sorry either. Let me remember, Fred wrote the last letter to Uncle Josiah

1. Great Britain placed Sultan Hamid Ben Thwain in power after Sultan Ali Ben Said's death.

Blanche Blick Burnham in Africa. From *Taking Chances* (Haynes Corporation, Publishers, 1944).

describing our trip to Tanga and my ride on the negroes' backs. Such a shiftless country, too lazy to build a wharf or even carry a plank out a few feet but then the blacks would not have anything to do. You have to pay six pence to be carried on shore. When we went back in the evening the tide was higher and our own boat put out a plank by which we climbed into the boat. I tell you it was a novel thing being carried through the water that way, but we will have a great time landing at Natal. It is always *very rough* there. A covered surf boat comes alongside and we have to be put into it in a basket like the cargo is. I don't imagine that it will be much fun. Of course I shall be seasick but thank fortune it will only be for a few minutes. Will write more about it if it is very horrible. From Tanga we went to Zanzibar but only to leave the mail and take on some coolies to unload the cargo at Dar-es-Salaam our next stopping point. We left one of our passengers at Tanga, two at Zanzibar, and four at Dar-es-Salaam, besides all the Soudanese soldiers. Dar-es-Salaam is a very pretty place and oh such quantities of fruit at all these tropical places. Vegetation is so plentiful. They do not try to raise anything, just pick the wild fruit. I wish I could tell you all the varieties. No wonder the blacks are a lazy people. What is the use to work when all you have to do when you are hungry is to go out and pick fruit. Such pods as the little nigs have. Why little Fred's is no where. The coconuts are lovely trees and every tree is loaded with fruit. It tastes so fresh and sweet. The fine apples are delicious, beautiful lemons, guavas, bananas, mangoes, plums, cashews and heart apples. I do not know half the names. The oranges are very good but they eat them before the skin turns yellow. They are only good then for a few days they say. Cloves are the chief source of wealth of Zanzibar, but oh such a filthy dirty town as it is. All the streets are so narrow. Two people cannot pass carrying umbrellas. Miserable set of people, ten prices for everything that you want to buy and nothing to be had but fruit and native clothing. Regular fever hole but all the places on the coast in the tropics are that. This Delagoa Bay is the worst of all, but it is a beautiful place, red bluffs, green trees, green grass, wide streets and very pretty houses. It is a Portuguese possession. The old citadel over 300 years old still standing. They are building a railroad here from Delagoa Bay to Johannesburg. 170 miles is completed but there are 500 yet to build. We are not going on shore. A

number of Italians came with us to this place to work on the R.R.
Miss Judd, an English girl 19 years old from Bombay, India, came
on board at Zanzibar with us. She is going to Durban or Natal to
marry a civil engineer. He has been here working on this R.R. but
has had the fever and has given up the job but has another position
in Durban. He is going on down with us. Miss Judd is a very pleasant girl but not healthy. Port Durban or Natal, one and the same
place, is *healthy*. It will seem good to see a place which is pretty and
healthy also. The country is *so pretty*. This is Sunday and we will be
in Natal Tuesday, A.M. We leave here tomorrow morning at ten.
Such a lot of nationalities as we have had on this steamer. From
Zanzibar to Mozambique we had one hundred Sikh warriors from
India under Lieutenant Edwards going into the interior. They are
fine looking men well uniformed in tan colored garments. They
wear the largest turban I ever saw. It is a piece of tan colored cloth
at least 2 yards square and bound round and round the head. These
were the picked soldiers from five regiments. Have all seen several
years service and have also served out of India, almost perfect
shots. They will do some fighting. They have some queer habits,
only drink consecrated water and carry their own food with them.
If a foreigner looks at them preparing their food or touches one of
their dishes, they throw the food and the dish away. They are
Buddhists. We have also on board 65 Banyan or Hindoo merchants
and their families included. We had eight missionaries from
England with us for a few days. Seven of them were under 21 years
of age and certainly did not look strong. All going to the same
place. Everyone says that at least six of them will die. There was a
ninth one but he got the fever in Zanzibar and has gone back to
England, wise boy. They went up the Zambezi, the same route that
Lieutenant Edwards went with his Sikh warriors.

So you see that we are making the acquaintance of all kinds
and classes. Every little station has its own money. A rupee is one
shilling, three pence or thirty cents but it takes 120 coppers as
large as a two cent piece to make one rupee. Pretty small divisions
of money is it not? A rupee will keep a native a long time. They are
a jolly set most of the time. We have a regular circus every once in
a while when they are loading or unloading cargo. While waiting
for the next consignment they will sing, clap hands, dance, imitate
animals, roll each other in blankets and all the while the perspira-

tion will just be rolling off them. At Zanzibar they did everything by music. They seem to need some incentive to help along the work. We have had several never-to-be-forgotten scenes. When in port they always work until midnight. At Zanzibar we had a steamer right along each side and was taking cargo from each. Such excitement as we had those two nights. You know each ship has its own electric dynamo so they can turn night into day. Speaking of electricity makes me think of the Suez Canal. Every ship passing through there at night is a blaze of light, so they will not run into each other. There are certain rules about right of way. We had to tie up a number of times to let others pass and these again we would pass. We passed twenty in all in the canal. It is eighty miles long. No ship is allowed to go faster than 5 miles an hour, otherwise the waves would soon wash the banks away. We sailed through miles of sea weed yesterday. The ocean is not so blue here, not so deep. Mr. Marston caught a dozen catfish today. We had some for supper and they were very good. One of the boatswains here Roy says looks like Uncle Jack, and he does somewhat. Roy wants me to tell you that he is one of his best partners. I tell you he has a happy time. He gets everything that he even expresses a wish for. A boy in London gave him the body of a sail boat. It has been rigged a dozen times. Now it is a German steamer. I think it has had six coats of paint. Paint is plentiful here. The captain keeps him supplied with sweet chocolate which is tied with red, white and black ribbon, the German colors. So he has plenty of flags and streamers. He wants to send this one to Uncle Jack for his boat. Be sure and give it to him.

March 31, 1893—Well here we are in S. Africa, really and truly and more astonished people you never saw than we are. We anchored outside of Natal at 6:30 Monday evening. The ocean looked smooth but oh such swells. It was an awful night, first bumping against one side of the berth and then the other. However, we managed to live and what was of more importance is get dressed the next morning. A surf boat came out and part of our passengers went ashore but they would not allow us to take any luggage on board and as usual Fred *had to see a man* and swell clothes were necessary so we decided to stay with the *Reichstag*. A pilot boat came out at noon and at one o'clock high tide we went over the bar and into the harbor. No trouble in getting through the customshouse. Did not open a single parcel and we were glad of it for we have to pack often enough as it is. Durban is a beautiful place. Our hotel is about two or three miles from the wharf. We came up in fine double-deck street cars. Fine wide streets, good sidewalks and such pretty little homes under the big trees. So many new varieties of trees and so many of them. Everything is green now. The rainy season is about over but we have just had a little shower. You do not know how good it seems to see white women and children and plenty of them and healthy looking ones too. There are 10,000 Europeans here in Durban. It seems very much like Southern California.

I am very tired from our long trip and Fred says that I look very peaked and thin. It seems so good to be on terra firma once again that I just want to sit and hold my hands. I will write more in a few days. The man that Fred wanted most particularly to see has gone up the coast and will not return for two or three weeks. Fred can busy himself very well here and thinks it worth while to wait, so we have sent to Johannesburg for our mail and will rent furnished rooms tomorrow for a couple of weeks. We are so hungry for some American cooking and just what we want. It is very likely that Roderick and I will remain here for several months until Fred finds some place in the interior which he likes. Cannot tell yet. May wait and go up with Howard. Fred is in love with Durban and bound to find some place and make money. . . . We went to the ship this P.M. to tell them good bye. The officers were so kind to us. The ship sails again tomorrow at 3 P.M. There are a number of children here at the hotel so Roderick is happy. There are some queer customs here and some queer people, but more of them in my next. . . .
With love from all,
B.

———

Blanche Blick Burnham to Rebecca Russell Burnham
Durban Natal S.A.
April 9, 1893

Dear Mother,
I thought that I would not write again until we received our mail from Johannesburg, but we either have no mail there or else

the post master does not intend to forward it to us. I have written so many letters without a word from home that it is getting rather monotonous simply telling you our experiences. But what cannot be cured must be endured so here goes for another letter. Fred has gone to see a man just down from Fort Salisbury, and I will write until he returns and then we will discuss plans again. We spend hours doing that anyway. The Steamer *Africa* is due tomorrow and if Col. Warton does not come on that he will not come for several weeks, and we will not wait for him. We are still at the Clarendon Hotel. We came on a Wednesday P.M. and then came Good Friday, Saturday, Sunday and Whit Monday and Camp Tuesday so that there was not a store or office open during that time except the native stores so we could find out nothing about a house. Rent is very high and we concluded it would not do to pay a month's rent and go to all the bother for a week or two. We like it here very much. Mr. and Mrs. Arnold are such very pleasant people and there are two very nice ladies boarding here. We have very sociable times. Have had several delightful rides in the Clarendon trap as they call the carriage. Oh it is such a lovely country. The roads are macadamized for miles around the city. The hills and the bay and ocean. Really and truly it is far more lovely than Pasadena. The grass never turns brown and the trees do not lose their leaves. It never frosts here. We went to the Botanical Gardens yesterday. I never saw such a variety of shrubs and trees. Will send you a leaf of one particularly pretty one. The flowers are yellow, the leaves at the end of the branch are white and the others green. It is a very large place. The park overlooks the bay and is naturally cared for but not much artificial. They have a race track, cricket grounds, lawn tennis, &c. The town garden is two blocks opposite the town hall. A very good public library and public baths. We went one day last week and are going again tomorrow. Everything is fine, except the bathing suits. They are cotton and the ugliest things I ever saw. Gentlemen and ladies have separate days. I expect that accounts for the ugly suits. The churches are so numerous that they cannot be counted. No natives are allowed to live in the town proper except the servants. They have big barracks built for them just out of the town. There is not even a dirty alley in the town. A person is fined if he does not keep his place clean. Scavengers come around three times a week and all refuse is burned. That is why it is so healthy here. Here comes a rickshaw. They are little two wheeled phaetons with a canvas cover and drawn by a native. You ought to see some of them run. They make pretty good horses. I noticed one the other morning drying his shirt on the shafts and his trousers over the top of the rickshaw (he did not have any passenger and also had on another suit). Some of them wear tufts of feathers on their heads and toss their heads just like a spirited horse to make their feathers show off. They charge 1½ s. per hour down here and 2½ s. up on the Berea. Oh yes, there is a big salvation army here. It sounds and looks quite homelike to see them. Every child under five years has a nurse and such helpless children as they are. This is not a large hotel but there are fourteen servants. This is the dull season. I do not know how many guests they have during the season which soon commences. Have only had from 15 to 20 since we came. Two missionaries left today for Umtala. They are going a different route. We will see them when passing through there. They are going with a better idea than the missionaries that came down on the *Reichstag*. They are going to teach the natives to work and care for their bodies as well as their souls. They are taking a lot of seeds with them and are going to have a farm. The natives there raise nothing but rice and corn. Oh such lazy people. One white man is worth about four of them. They are pretty well covered here but we have seen many that were not. In all of the upper coast towns the little children go entirely naked, and I expect they do here out in the country. Roy was terribly shocked at first and says that he will never go that way. He is having a delightful time here. There are two children about his age and he goes with them and their nurse. The bay is only a block from here. They were wading yesterday morning and fishing this morning. This P.M. they went for a drive and saw the navy volunteers coming home from their Easter encampment. He thinks their uniforms are *lovely* and wants one just like them. He is wearing his linen sailor suit with its blue collar and cuffs today and looks like a little sailor. I was so sorry in London that I could get nothing but sailor suits but do not care now for that is all little boys wear down here. He sends you a sailboat and a schooner.

I had only written one page when Fred came back this morning. We sat on the verandah and made plans for our trip upcountry until lunch time and for a couple of hours afterwards. Then went for a walk and got home just in time. Had a very heavy rain storm with thunder and lightening. Struck our telephone wire and made quite an excitement but injured no one. We were in the dining room and did not see the flash, but several people saw it. The air still feels sultry and there are frequent faint flashes of lightening so we do not think that the storm is over yet.

I have had to have a tooth filled since coming here. I should like to tell Dr. Small about it. Fred went over first to make the appointment for me. Such style as he puts on. He told Fred that in England they only acknowledged dentists from two colleges in America, Harvard and Ann Arbor. Fred told him that Dr. Small was a Harvard man. He, like all other dentists, praised the work.

Such a chair to sit in, glad I did not have to sit long. My feet were swinging about a foot from the floor and my neck was breaking. He said he had an American chair at Maritzburg but that the people were afraid of it. It had too much machinery. I had to smile. He rather resented it and said I must remember that the people here were not used to all new innovations as we Americans were. Whenever I had to rinse my mouth he either held the cuspidor or else I *jumped* out of the chair and went to the table. He *did* have one of those treadle machines but scarcely anything else. The first day he cleaned the tooth with that machine and put some medicine in to see if it needed any treatment for the nerve. Next day some more medicine, next day put in the silver filling like it was cotton and the next day burnished it with a small wood file. I said it did not feel smooth so he filed away with a smaller file twice again and said that was as smooth as it could be made and that it would wear smooth. Maybe it will *in time* $1.87½. Patients were always waiting but no wonder when he took four sittings to fill a very common cavity in a double tooth. It is rather a new thing here. More teeth are extracted than filled and everyone takes chloroform or gas.

It is raining again. This letter cannot start for home until Wednesday, so I will leave it open and maybe we will get some letters before that time. Fred is writing to Uncle. I will not send a letter home at least if I do I will not repeat so exchange letters please. Love to Etta. Roy sends you love and kisses.
Lovingly,
B.

————————

FRB to Josiah Russell

Durban
April 9, 1893

Dear Uncle,

The mail to Johannesburg we ordered sent down here, but it has not come yet and we may not get it until we get to Johannesburg two weeks yet. I am waiting here for the arrival of a Col. Warton to make arrangements for the opening up of some gold mines and general exploration of interior. But would have liked to hear how the other side of the world is moving and home news before writing again. Durban is one of the most beautiful spots of earth I have ever seen, and I have seen several. It is built on a crescent-shaped piece of land the convex side being the shore of a fine bay, the concave side washed by the Indian Ocean and having a fine beach and heavy surf. A semi-tropic vegetation creeps close out to tide water and the country rising in great terraces back to the summit of the Drakenburg Mountains gives the whole scene strength and great beauty of contour. . . . The town is the most de-mocratic I have yet seen. The corporation first of all owns the land (the essential thing). As the town grows and more lots are needed for building, the town grades the street, lays a train, extends the water mains, and then offers to the highest bidders lots of about 100 ft front on long time 8 years at 6%. And the money goes into the general fund instead of any one individual pocket. . . . Plenty of hotels, schools and churches. Business houses close Saturday noon and at five weekdays. All English holidays are observed and some colonial. The people are wealthy and have no slums or very poor although this is a harbor and shipping point for the whole colony and part of the Dutch Republic. Property values are about the same on main streets as Pasadena. Up on the terrace the villas are very splendid and ground worth from $30 to $100 per foot. And about two years ago they had quite a boom here and are hoping for another as soon as the R.R. is pushed up to the Rand gold fields when it is predicted the seventeen thousand population will double every fortnight and all the upcountry people come here for health and to spend their wealth. The gold fields are still producing won-derfully and new ones are being found. This is the land of gold sure enough. And it is also a land capable of sustaining a great European population. Cape Town is already sending fresh fruit to the London market, grapes, peaches, pears, &c, but not at the same season of year as Cal. hence no competition. Stock growing here though is a risky venture. So many diseases, caught from wild game it is claimed by some, but fatal just the same, horses especially. Cattle die from a lung disease and only the humble burro can be relied on to open up the upcountry. And still farther north one can only get along by using the saucy nigger as a donkey. But I am going to take up mules, donkeys, and horses and nigs if need be so nothing can stop me till I reach the land of Ophir. A few years now will see a R.R. into the heart of this country, probably the British flag from Cape Town to Cairo will wave without break of possession. This country is as different from California as Cal. is from Iowa, but yet it is a grand country. I will probably cast in my lot here. There is more room, a better chance, greater possibilities. But more of the country bye and bye. . . .

We leave Durban for Johannesburg. Two weeks on trip and from there we go north to the Zambezi River, 1000 miles through a wonderful rich country, from all reports, but I will write you of it as we progress upcountry. After seeing Europe I am ready to tackle the frontiers again and help build a new empire, but when I want a new world of ideas I will drop over to Rome, Paris and London. I tell you Uncle we will have to do Europe together yet. We would enjoy it. I will go upcountry, get a big grant of land, open up a mine and you come over to London. I will meet you there say 3 years from now and we will take in everything and you come on down to Africa and we will elect you district judge. So you can get a chance to wield an influence in the coming great commonwealth of the world. I think mother would be best pleased with a villa in the suburbs of gay Paris. The young stock of the family could come down to Africa and on its great tablelands find room to expand, but I have a lot of work to do tonight so will have to draw this to a close. I have to refit two set of harness. Blanche is much disappointed in not getting a letter from mother or her own folks but there must be some enroute and we will catch them in Johannesburg which will still be our address. You can look for another letter in about two or 3 weeks after this unless I should happen to get one if enroute.

Hoping we will all meet again (in Europe)
I am as ever
Fred

━━━━━━━━━━

BBB to Blick family

Seventy-five miles north of Durban
April 24, 1893

Dear Family,

It puzzles me very much to know to whom to address my letters, and then I cannot remember the last one that I addressed. But please do not get vexed because my letters are for each one of you separately and individually and collectively. Now that question is settled. A few days after my last to you in which I grumbled because I had received no letters, one came from Mother B., Madge and Jack and home. I cannot tell you how glad I was to get them. Mother is mistaken about there being only one steamer a month. There is only one from Germany but there is one *every week* from England to Cape Town and mail comes by rail then to Johannesburg which is just below the 26 parallel and ⅓ the distance between the 28 and 30 meridian. It is nine years old and has a population of 40,000. Greatest growth has been during the last five years owing to the big mining camps in the Rand Hills. Geographies and the outside world know very little about Africa. The country of Natal is beautiful. Johannesburg is in the Transvaal and that is a Dutch country. I suppose that is not in the postal union and that is why you have to pay so much postage. Have you had to pay extra on our letters. They told us it was the same as to England because Natal is in the union. I do not know about the Transvaal. We left Durban at 11 A.M. April 16 and stopped 3 days in Maritzburg. The roads are good but there are so many hills and mountains. Durban is at sea level and we are 5000 ft above so you see it is up and down. Our donkeys, Doc and Ta-ra, the leaders, and Ah Sin and Ti Wink, the wheelers, are very good travellers. They are trained to be driven here instead of packed. Our buckboard is just like the old one except that it is wider back of the seat that way and has the grain box fastened in front of the dashboard and a tool box with a sloping top for our foot rest. Everything is very convenient. We sent our trunks, big valise and

100 lbs of groceries by freight to Johannesburg, so we only have two valises, bedding and provisions with us. Splendid grass for the donkeys and we buy mealies (corn) along the road for them. We are having a good time. Have a mattress of coconut feathers (made from the covering of the shells) which just fits the buckboard, so we have a good bed. Have bows over the back part and a big flap which we fasten to the dashboard at night. Had a driving rain and hail storm last evening but we did not get a bit wet. Oh dear, the days are so short. We ate a cold dinner today on purpose so that we could write a few words. We will be all right but you must not expect many letters because we cannot take time to write. Donkeys are not the swiftest animals in the world but we can beat the ox wagons. No one seems to know what this horse sickness is. Horses fed on green food are more apt to have it, so it is concluded that it is something in that food. The cattle have a lung disease. The horses die very suddenly before you know that they are sick. We wanted to be sure and had no money to risk in horses. Will need the burros in prospecting. This disease only comes every few years. Fred says we must start on our journey again . . . . Tuesday noon. While Fred is making the fire I will write a few minutes. The wind blew yesterday P.M. and all night. We were chilly driving but snug and warm in our "ever moving home" at night. Cooked a good supper. Boiled potatoes, fried bacon and made gravy and had our first frying pan bread. It tasted good. We have bought all of our bread so far as flour is rather scarce. Green wood will *not* burn and dry wood is hard to find. We use *miss*, as they call it here, which is plentiful at the outspanning places.[1] You can guess what it is. It makes a good fire after you get it started. Better fuel upcountry they say. We are going to have roasting ears for dinner. Have had them twice before. We were told that the first 276 miles of our journey would be rough and over mountains and I should think it was. The roads are good but hilly. Have just come down a fearful hill and pulled up a more fearful one a mile in length. But we will be over the worst in a few days. We walk up all the hills so we have walked fully half the distance but we sleep well and have famous appetites. The stay in Durban did me good. I weighed 120 when I left. Fred has found some blue gum wood and says that we will have an old fashioned fire. We are under a beautiful blue gum

1. Outspan—to camp, to remove the yoke from oxen.

grove. Roderick is gathering fuel. He is very well and happy. Fred is satisfied and says that Africa will be our *home* but remember you are *all* to come sometime. Oh, I did not tell you that we had a foreloper or boy to lead the donkeys to Maritzburg. He could go no farther and we could get no other so we are alone now, and get along a great deal better. We cannot speak Kaffir and they are so slow and stupid that Mess was more bother than he was good. Doc and Ta-ra and Ah Sin and Ti Wink are getting used to travelling together now and guide very well. We only make 15 miles over this hilly country but will easily make 20 after leaving Charleston or Sangs Neck. Our foreloper was a jet black boy of 17 from the Clarendon Hotel kitchen. He could speak a few words of English. He was very tony dressed in some soldiers cast off uniform of blue trimmed with red and a brown derby hat, of course he was barefooted. I guess he thought it strange to see us working. I never saw such a lazy people as the whites are here. Cheap servants make lazy people but it takes about four blacks to equal one good person. I wonder if the tropics will make us lazy (Now don't smile). I mean Fred. Well I have had to stop three or four times since commencing. I only wash dishes once a day. We have such a fine set of cooking and eating utensils, white and blue porcelain. It is cheaper here than in California. Had a fine folding reflector made, so we are well fixed. There are so many things to write about that it worries me. We are keeping a diary of each day and will send it to you sure. After leaving Johannesburg the stage only runs once in two weeks. A great many people are going up to Mashonaland so we are in the fashion.

Friday—April 28 and my letter not finished yet. I must mail it tomorrow. We are so busy that time does not hang on our hands. Begin trekking[2] at 7 A.M., outspan at 11 for three hours, then trek from 2 until 7, eat a cold supper and are ready for bed. We cook a warm breakfast and at noon I wash the breakfast dishes, cook dinner and wash the dinner dishes and so far we have always had something to do about the outfit which kept us busy until two. I write our experience in a little journal as we are jogging along. Rather crooked scratches but I will copy it and send to you sometime in July. Fred is going to write a chapter on natives next Sunday.

2. Trekking—to journey or travel.

We are going to rest all that day but have plenty of work planned. A great big bull team just passed. They drive nine yoke of oxen here and have a foreloper who leads the oxen and the driver walks by the side of the team and uses a whip with a 10 ft stalk of bamboo and a ten ft lash. It would have been an interesting sight to you to see them go up this rocky hill. They had to rest the team quite often. The foreloper would whistle and hold up his hand for the oxen to stop and the driver and herder (the third man) yelled, shrieked and groaned until it sounded like a blood and thunder tragedy in a third class theatre. I expect they were cursing the animals. They drive four hours, outspan for four, and so on. This foreloper wore a red shirt, the driver a girdle of foxtails, and the herder a coat, shirt and pair of trousers. Another team of four yoke of oxen passed here this noon. A young man with two young wives. One of them was foreloping and the other riding on the load of pumpkins while he did the driving. The foreloper wore a low necked dress which did not reach to her knees. She had four or five bracelets on each ankle, knee, wrist and above her elbows. Both the women were very plump and well built. But more about the natives in our journal. Roderick amuses himself making boats out of corn stalks and wishing that Uncle Jack was here to make more for him. He always wants Aunt Grace when he sees flowers. He is helping Fred harness the donkeys. Does it not seem strange to get such old letters. I am so glad to get them, but I am always wondering what you are doing now. Write again Jack, no letter can be too long for us. Your letter may have been stale when we got off the boat but it tasted good nevertheless. We enjoyed Madge's too but hope her liver is in better condition now. But never mind Madge. You will all be here sometime and won't we be happy. You must wear glasses Grace or you will ruin your eyes. You must write a little every few days and that will not tire you. [letter incomplete].

———

Roderick Burnham to Aunt Grace Blick

Johannesburg, Transvaal
May 19, 1893

My Dear Chum,

I was so glad to have a letter all my own and now I am going to tell my mamma what to write for an answer. Yes I picked the

maiden hair ferns and here are some more that I picked on a rocky
hill near Colenso in Natal, S.A. I see so many pretty flowers and
wish you were with me to help pick them. One day I saw some
lovely big red flowers like those in Mr. Clark's garden up on the
hill. These little black native herders have a short whip with a long
lash which they can crack just like the big bull whackers. The other
night we passed a big transport wagon bogged down in a big mud
hole. They had to unload the wagon, unhook their six span of
mules, put them in the lead and seven yoke of oxen on the wheel
and then it took all day to get the wagon out. The African black
bird has white strips on its wings and white on its breast. We saw
eighty-five big vultures sunning themselves after eating a dead ox.
They are not a bit afraid and we drove right into the flock. They
were all gray except one which was black. I saw a funny one with a
great long bill and told Papa to look. Just then it stood up and it
was a big wader four feet high. The ravens here have a white breast
and white collar. The crows, Mamma says, are like Uncle Joe's
Toby. At a store we saw a pet crane that would come to his master
and would not fly away. I am going to have one someday. When its
master stroked its neck, it would make that queer noise like all
Sandy Hill cranes. We saw a big gray snake, but it was dead. We
have one burro named Doc, that is very hard to get to cross water.
Papa is going to buy him a whip made of hippopotamus hide like
the oxen drivers use and then I am going to have his old whip lash.
In Johannesburg on the Rand there is a mill every 200 yards. I
bring up the donkeys in the morning and help Papa to harness. I
like them all but Ah Sin and she will kick once in a while.
Charleston was a wretched little town, not nice at all. Papa bought
a bamboo whip stalk there. Before that he used to have to get a
wattle stalk and they would break as soon as they were dry. I can
make very good ships now, for I was on another big ship coming
across to Africa and was with the sailors a great deal of the time.
When we were crossing into the harbor of Natal, we had to have a
little pilot boat to pull us in. The Hindoos on our steamer went on
board another boat and had to be swung over into it in a big basket
over their heads with a door in it. I saw some monkeys in the
cemetery at Durban. They would sit up in front of the grave stones
like they were reading them. We outspanned alongside of a stream
one day and I fixed up my boat and sailed it and I waded. I saw a

lot of frogs sitting in a row in an old shaft and there was a dead one in the water with its mouth open. If we have any big rivers to cross, we are going to hitch the buckboard on to the end of a freight wagon and swim the donkeys. We will ride in the wagons. I like to camp and am not tired of it yet. Papa and I went prospecting one day on a little hill and found little pebbles of quartz in common rock. We saw a little scorpion too. The hills here are just covered with little mining dumps. We outspanned near a whole lot of shafts and all the deep ones are full of water. In Natal we saw lots of fat cattle but near Durban the ticks were thick on them. I saw a little live snake this morning and it ran out its tongue at me. Our donkeys are named Doc, Ta-ra, Ah Sin and Ti Wink. Ti Wink is the stoutest little thing you ever saw. In Natal we saw lots of ant hills, then we didn't see any and now we see lots of them. In the zoo in London we saw two big polar bears and two brown bears. The brown bears were playing and running up into the corners of their cage and turning around as quick as lightening. As soon as we got into the mineral country we saw lots of ledges. There are lots and lots of corrals built of stone for the sheep. The plains are just covered with them. I found a lot of fine feathers in a hole near the side of the road. We got enough to make me a little pillow. Papa says some wild fowls must have molted near there. I would dearly love to see you all and am pretty anxious to get settled down and have all you folks come across and we will have such jolly times. We are going to have a great big pond with an island in it and a little bridge. We will have some little play boats like I saw in Hyde Park in London if we can't have a big boat big enough to ride in.
Chum Roderick

—————

FRB to Rebecca Russell Burnham

May 3rd 1893

Dear Mother,

Still trekking into the heart of Africa and still in a glorious looking country though very queer up here on the tablelands. The grass is just turning brown and away on the Drakenbergs we can count over a dozen prairie fires, but they do not burn as fierce as in Minnesota. But the sunlight is yellow and the earth has that queer

ghastly look you so well remember. In some ways this country reminds me of Minnesota. We expect little change in scenery after
we cross the Drakenbergs until we reach the Crocodile River.[1]
Then we will hit forests and timbered park like country again. We
are camped near a native kraal, and one big black has just passed us
dressed a la white man and wearing a sweltering ulster while just
down the gulch a lot of children are playing in the sand without a
rag on them and they are not cold either. The weather is lovely,
much the same as California and such a valley as lays open before
us would turn a land boomer green with envy, rolling, grass-cov-
ered, fertile, well-watered, and only a handful of blacks to enjoy it
all. We pass many bands of angoras and often say what a pretty rug
this one or that one would make for you. Some are grey, some
black, and most pure bloods—white. Plenty of cattle and all gentle
stock as the blacks herd and milk all the cows. There is the making
of a vast empire here in Africa and it will not be many years before
Cape Town and Cairo will be in touch by rail.

Roy has been standing on top of a great ant hill flourishing
my big whip. . . . these ant hills are great. They look like hay cocks
all over the country but do not seem to bother us at all. We camp
among them and they do not come above ground at all, but they
say they are liable to sap the foundations of buildings, &c. which I
do not doubt as many of the hills contain two tons of earth
brought up from below. We will be very glad to get our mail at
Johannesburg. After that it will be 2 months again before we can
hear a word. You can say to any of my Pasadena friends that I am
on a big trekking expedition to the heart of Africa and that it takes
months to reach us. There is no use trying to tell them where we
are for one or few of the places are on any map at all. We are keeping a kind of journal which when we reach Salisbury we will forward home for all of you folks to read. By the by, we are going to
take a grant of land in the upcountry, thousands of acres, plenty of
grass, timber and water, a young paradise in fact. The black parts
with his estates much the same as the American Indian, and I know
now what the Spanish grants did for every Californian that held on
to them, even the poorest. I will not finish this letter this camp but
we have some great schemes to work out here and speedily at that.

1. The Crocodile or Limpopo River was the southern boundary of BSA territory.

I like the country so far and I know pretty near what kind I am going into. So there is no question of my *ever* returning from Africa farther than to Paris or Rome. Just take the world easy a little while and we will all meet either on the banks of the Zambezi River or the boulevards of Paris.

We are now crossing the Drakenberg range and passing through the country the Boers and English fought so for—and well worth fighting for it was, a beautiful and peaceful country it is now and covered with fat sleek looking stock. It is not so cold but that blue gums and century plants grow and around nearly every ranch house can be seen the silver leaved maple and weeping willow so the tree life does not seem so strange as on the coast. The air is still smoky and the great peaks of the Drakenberg loom up like clouds above us. We pass great bullock outfits that would draw a crowd in Los Angeles or the U.S., 18 head of cattle to each wagon and a black driver with a whip 25 ft long. Tis amazing how he swings it but he does and the cattle ante for its crack like they were invited to a free lunch and a band. The ranch houses are nearly all of stone and iron, very solid, and some of the bridges across the streams cost $100,000. England builds for more than a day. We cross into another country tomorrow, A Republic of South Africa (Dutch). It is about as large as Germany and France together. Natal is about as large as Oregon and ought to support a much larger population, and some day it will. We expect to reach Salisbury in 10 weeks, maybe in 9. We have some big rivers to cross and part of the time will have to keep fires all night to keep the lions and leopards from eating up our burros. I will have a chance to get some big game including crocodiles and hippopotamus. Will send you a tooth, tis finer ivory than elephant tusk. There are plenty of elephants also and a few zebra and rhinoceros. Roy has gone out to interview a Kaffir herder, but as they cannot understand each other it will be a one-sided visit. We will get our last glimpse of R.R. and civilization tomorrow except as we touch at Johannesburg. From there we will turn north into the wilds.
Yours as ever,
Fred

[Letter continued by BBB]
Dear Mother,

I see Fred has told you about the camp fires to keep the lions away. I did not intend that you should know that just yet. But he

likes to frighten people. There is not the slightest danger for *us*, but the lions do sometimes get the stock if fires are not kept burning. We are getting to like our burros very much and will take care of them, so do not lose any sleep over us. We meet so *many, many* teams now and will more after leaving Charleston the end of this R.R. We have such good times planning for our future in Africa. It seems so strange to have Fred talk of anything permanent and not be thinking that he *must* accomplish so much within *such* a time or have to *meet a man*. It is a new existence for us and a happy one. . . .
Much love,
From all to all
Blanche

———

BBB to Phebe Blick

Johannesburg, Dutch Republic, S.A.
May 20, 1893

Dear little mother,

This letter is for *you* and how I wish that you could read it for yourself and answer it too. . . . I am all right—only did you ever know me when I did not like to be with you even when I lived as close as in the Park Hotel. We used to be back and forth two or three times every day then, but never mind Ma, we will yet live that close together and within five years Fred says. You know what you told me the day I came away when I asked you if you would come to Africa if we like it and sent for you. Do you remember you said that you had started to follow us and would keep it up. You ought to hear the air castles we build almost every day about that time. Fred, the generous soul, he does not know what the word selfishness means, says that one of his greatest ambitions now that he is in Africa, the dream of his life, is to find a mine big enough to send for all of my family, his and Uncle Josiah if it is a good country and work can be found for the young people. This was his own suggestion and you may be sure that I seconded it. Never a day passes but what we mention it in some way. Although we are great to build air castles, you know that Fred has generally achieved everything he set out to do except making great wealth and there is more chance for that in this new country. He does not seem to want such fabulous amounts any more and really talks about settling down without a trip out of Africa until Roderick is sixteen when we will take him to some school in Europe. We are going to have a farm although we will not farm much of it. You can get 3000 acres for a two years enlistment, or by paying $200 for the surveying and then $60 a year rental. If we can find 3000 acres near the mountains and with timber and a stream we are going to buy one of the Chartered Co. next year, providing that we like that part of the world. If not there are other places in Africa. Of course we will do nothing *rash* but Fred says in Africa we are bound to live and to be perfectly contented. We must have all our people around us. We will not care then what our neighbors are like. Do you know with our different talents we could come pretty near running a little town of our own. We will all live close together, Ma right next door to me. Will give each of you a piece of land but of course you can buy 3000 acres apiece if you like. Now don't laugh at this scheme. It affords us lots of pleasure to plan it and stranger things have happened. I expect Howard will be here by the time this reaches you. Judd must come as soon as there is an opening for him and John must come as soon as he has gone to a mining school. Then the rest will have to come if we all like it and are successful.

Sunday P.M.—I know father would dearly love to have a 3000 acre farm or would that be land enough for him. They say that everything will grow up there. Oranges bear in five years from the seed, which is two years ahead of Cape Colony. I believe that I told you in my last exactly where Johannesburg is, but did I tell you where Ft. Salisbury is? Cannot get the map now but will leave a blank line to fill out. As near as I can make out Salisbury is in latitude 17°45′ S. and longitude 31°30′where Johannesburg is in latitude 26°15′ S. and longitude 28°55′. By wagon road from Durban to Johannesburg is 422 miles and from here to Ft. Salisbury 800 miles so you see we are only one third of our distance. Salisbury has an elevation of 4960 ft. and a very good climate—we hear, also that there are 800 people in the town. We are bound to see for ourselves anyway. We were just one month in coming this distance less six days, and a great deal of the country was mountainous. We keep the Drakenberg all the way to our right on the road up and they say that the roads are good. We have to have some of our things taken up by freight, $7.50 per hundred. It starts with a train of six wagons tomorrow at noon. We will start at the same time. Fred saw a lot of boxes going up for an American he knows because they had come across on the Cunard line. I hope that there will be and we hear that there are some Yankees in Mashonaland. While we have seen countries that are just as pretty—if not prettier—now I can just hear you all talking—but wait until you have seen these places, there are no people like our own Americans or Yankees as we are called here. We met two of them last Wednesday going south with a cart and four donkeys. They knew us at once but thought that we were from New York. One was a Boston man and the other from New Orleans. They have been here twelve years. We stopped and talked for half an hour. It seemed so good to see them, the first genuine Americans that we had seen since leaving New York. But I suppose that we will like the English better on closer acquaintance, for we liked the Arnolds of the Clarendon, Durban, very much after the ice had thawed and Jack's people we liked at once like they were our own, . . . Fred bought a good gun yesterday so now we will have some game to eat. We have seen so many kinds of birds. There will not be much chance of any larger game without going off the road. Fred is planning for some hunts when Judd comes. But by the way, has Judd the African fever? It is a great country. It would amuse you to hear us talking about our farm. . . . You know our farm is to have running water, timber and not be flat country. How do you like the prospect Ma, don't it make you want to come? This is Sunday evening and writing this way helps me to imagine that I am lying on the old lounge in the kitchen or having John or Kate comb my hair while I am talking to you. Won't we have plenty to "clackety clack" about. . . . I am wearing the brown dress that I made last Christmas. It has shrunk so much that it is just the right length for camping. I had to rip it off the belt and put some gathers in front. I have some congress gaiters so do not have to bother with buttons. Wear a wide sailor hat and that beautiful cloak of mine. Will finish the whole outfit this trip. Roderick has worn his blue suit almost constantly since leaving home, but I had to patch the seat yesterday. Can start in on new clothes in Salisbury. My tan color dress skirt wore off so around the bottom that I let it down and put a row of brown braid on something like Hercules, two inches wide around it. I wear it when I go into a town, and my brown felt hat. I have worn that so much I will have a lot of sewing to do when I get settled but I have a machine. I may have to turn dressmaker some time. It is a Singer, Jones Patent hand sewing machine. There were three of them in the hotel. Used here much more than the foot machine. Mine is new ($11.25). I have sewed some and like it very much. It will be worth three or four times as much in Salisbury and I always need one, but do not expect to buy any more dresses for five years. Have cloth for Roderick's suits too. We hear fearful tales of the prices of things up there but that is the case with all frontier towns. But that is an English country and as soon as the route is finished in from Beira, which will be within a year, things will be cheaper than here in the Transvaal. They charge such a duty. Bacon and hams are a shilling per pound in Natal and 2 shillings here. Flour is 16 shilling a C wt in Durban, 24 here, and 60 in Ft. Salisbury. Butter is 3 shillings a pound here and eggs are 4 shillings a dozen. All fresh meat .12½ per pound. But there is plenty of money here. Fred is writing a business letter to Uncle Josiah now but will write a letter on Johannesburg in a few days so I will not say anything about the town except that I do not like it. We have a very nice camp a mile or two out of town and right on the edge of a lovely little lake or pond rather. Roderick has fine times and the donkeys are having a good rest. I do not want to brag but really there could not be a better boy than he is. He is absolutely no trouble and is as cheerful and happy as the day is long. He whistles, sings Ta-ra, Clementine or Georgia, makes boats and whips, jumps on and off the back of the buckboard playing that he is conductor and talks and builds air castles about our home that is to be. For the last three days on the trip he spent most of the time prospecting and bringing Fred specimens. Fred takes a great deal of pains to explain and always looks at every rock he brings him. They left me with the wagon one noon and went prospecting for over an hour. For the last two weeks we have only trekked from seven until eleven and from two until five. We write up the journal at noon, wash the dishes, cook and eat dinner and wash the dishes again. Your days are getting longer now while ours are getting shorter. Oranges are raised near here. We have had some frosty mornings but on the whole very pleasant weather. It will be warmer after leaving Pretoria. Do not have to walk much now but do so from choice so that we walk several miles everyday. We are perfectly well and such appetites as we

have. I weighed 120 the day before I left Durban but I must weigh more than that now. My chin is decidedly double and my dresses are getting tight. The wrinkles in front of Fred's ears are going away. In fact we are regaining our youth. But my joints are still stiff and I do not like to jump out of the back of the wagon. Roderick saw me stepping down on a box one day and said too bad that Mamma was getting old, but the next morning while we were playing horse we ran a race and I beat him every time, and I can throw rocks into the streams farther than he can. Fred laughs and tells him that his Mamma may be getting old but that she can still run faster and throw farther than he can. He is sound asleep now. You would laugh if you could see us now. When on the road we go to bed at dark but we want to write and mail these before leaving Johannesburg. At night we unpack the trap, put the boxes under the wagon and make our bed in it, roll down the curtains at the back and pull down the flap in front and there we are and here we are tonight. The boy is asleep, the lantern is hanging from one of the wagon bows. Fred is sitting on the machine box on the bed and I am sitting on an inverted pail. The seats got rather hard so we have cushioned them with our pillows. It is ten o'clock now. . . .
Oceans of love.
Your loving daughter,
B.

———

BBB to Rebecca Russell Burnham

Johannesburg, S. Africa
May 22, 1893

Dear Mother,
. . . You are right in thinking that we are a long way from home. Roderick asks so many times, "What do you suppose that they are doing now." . . . I have just put the bridle on Doc and Roderick is riding him around camp. He says that he just *loves* Doc. Our donkeys are all good and so gentle. Had a little trouble in making Ti Wink learn his place in the team but he is young and had never been driven. I expect you have felt sorry for us driving these donkeys but you need not for as Fred says, "It is not so bad after all," and then we are in Africa which sweetens everything.

They guide easily, pull evenly, and take no more persuading than mules and not as much as oxen. We have averaged 17 miles on the trek so far, 422 miles in 25 days, and for the last two weeks have only driven seven hours a day. We are so glad that we haven't oxen for the grass is so short now. Too bad that there is horse sickness here or we would have had horses or mules and could have gone faster but then a month or so longer is not much when you expect to stay in a place and make your home. We are glad to see that you have the African fever for if we do well we want you all here. I wrote in mother's letter about the terms on which 3,000 acres could be leased. Last evening a gentleman told us that the Chartered Co. were now offering land at nine pence or about .18 cents an acre. Last year it could be had for nothing and next year it will be higher. A great many are going. We will buy some land if the country suits us and we can get the kind we want, but Fred says we are going to have a stream of water running through our land for we have had enough dry camps in America. We will dam it and have a pond. Roderick wants to talk a little *anyway* every day about this pond and the wonders that we will have on and around that pond. Fountains, islands, bridges, big boats, little boats for him and Fred, ducks, water birds, cranes, &c. and &c.

There I had to stop just now. Roderick came up for me to put him on Doc's back again. He had had to get off to pick up his whip. I had him lead Doc up to an ant hill and then he got on by himself. We want to astonish Fred when he comes home because he put Roderick on the donkey last night and he was afraid to sit up straight. He has been riding for over half an hour now and thinks that it is fine fun. He can inspan[1] the donkeys except putting on their bridles, and I expect Fred will teach him to do that soon. You ask if he is growing. I should rather think that he was. He is plenty large enough for sleeping three in a bed. Writing that word makes me think of Howard's remarks about our wedding anniversary. How we laughed over it and could imagine hearing you laugh when you read that ambiguous sentence. Thank you for standing up for us. You were always good to young people. "We are not as young as we used to be" but intend to grow younger in this wonderful country. We remembered Fred's birthday, the hap-

---

1. Inspan—to break camp and trek, so called from placing animals in yoke.

piest of his life because he was here. Howard will be twenty-three in a few days and is not Etta's birthday in this month?[2] Will spend Roderick's in Ft. Salisbury. Suppose we will have to eat our dinner out of doors on that day if we do not go farther than ten feet so he can call it a *picnic*. He was speculating on Christmas presents the other day. It is so nice to be able to write something not about ourselves. Ego is getting monotonous. I am going to take your letters in order and answer them. Here goes for the first dated Feb. 17 and sent to Hereford. It was waiting here some time for us. We enjoyed it so much because in reading all of our letters the first evening it got mislaid and I did not know that we had it until in looking over the letters yesterday I found it opened but unread. Fred does not care about having his letters published. The parts to publish would have to be carefully selected. Too bad that you gave cholera a thought. We did not, not even enough to mention it in our letters. Although we learned that our ship had had cholera on board during the epidemic and we were even quarantined for fifteen minutes at Mozambique. . . . I cannot get letters enough and I shall be alone for a month or more when we get to Salisbury because Fred wants to go prospecting before the rainy season which begins the last of October. We expect to be there two months from today, May 23, which will be July 23. We have been much interested so far but that interest will intensify as we near our goal. How I hope that we shall like it.

. . . All the country that we have come through is healthy and we have only a little strip of unhealthy to pass through but it is perfectly safe during the dry season. Only bad during the middle and latter part of the rainy season. Not a stick of wood to be had is true in some parts of the country especially here in the Dutch Republic, but they say after leaving this we pass into the prettiest part of S. Africa. If it is any prettier than parts of Durban, Natal it must be beautiful. But we shall soon see for ourselves and then we will tell you. Yes, the hills this side of the Drakenburg are brown on account of the frost, but we have brown hills in Cal. during the summer. We will get into a warmer country after leaving Pretoria. Our country must be quite tropical but the elevation 4960 helps. We hear that the climate is fine. That sounds like repetition but I

2. Etta Kenney, FRB's aunt.

can not remember all that I write each time. Johannesburg is a mining town and maybe a little like an American mining town but it seemed all English and Dutch to me. It is certainly all rush. . . .

Fifty years is not old. We will all live forever in Africa so just hurry up and get over your hot flashes so you will not go up in a sheet of flame when you cross the equator. But pshaw, it was nothing to Arizona or Daggett. Of course on land there the heat is different—and more dangerous, but it was delightful on shipboard. A little warm in some of the cabins at night but we had the coolest cabin on the ship. . . .

Answer to March 31—You have been thinking of us as in Johannesburg for a long while but we have only been here five days. Were going to start for Salisbury—800 miles—yesterday but it was the Queen—quick may she die—Fred says, birthday and the teams we are going with could not be loaded and Fred could not buy our supplies. The English stores close for the Dutch president's birthday, so the Dutch close for the English queen. More English here than Dutch. We are unfortunate in getting into places on holidays. We are going to travel with six or eight teams direct through to Salisbury. They will carry several passengers. One of them, a young colonial, ate supper with us last night. Fred thought that we would start by four this P.M. but it is now 3:30. . . .

Letter April 6—Am so glad that Howard succeeded in getting the Alvord money. Doubt if we would ever have received it if he had not gone to Pasadena. Oh, dear. I hate to think that we will not get another letter for two *months*, but shall look for a dozen then. After that we will get our mail regularly. Grace wrote to Roderick so he answered it. Will have him write to you soon. I read his letter to Fred and Fred is very proud of it. I did not help him at all, just wrote as he told me. I want you to read it. Fred is coming now and I have written all of this except the first page today and I am really tired. A rocking chair would feel quite comfortable just now. . . .

May 26—Oh, I forgot to tell you that Fred came home at 4 P.M. Tuesday with the startling news that Johannesburg was liable to be quarantined at any moment for small pox. The natives there have had if for sometime. You should have seen us throw the things on the buckboard and start. Had to go through town and pick up some boxes of groceries, tent &c. and drive out of the city limits.

We are safe and have not heard whether the town is quarantined yet
or not. I said that last Monday was the queen's birthday. It was a
mistake, was some religious holiday and Wednesday was the queen's
birthday. Dozens of teams passed us in the morning full of picnick-
ers and we saw some coming back in the evening, too intoxicated to
sit up straight. We only drove out a few miles and then unpacked
and repacked so that we know where everything is. The teams that
we expected to come with concluded to wait for more freight and
will not leave until Saturday, if not quarantined. We were afraid to
leave our supplies with them so only gave them the trunk and big
valise to haul. We have 800 lbs on the buckboard besides ourselves,
but are going slowly to Pretoria (40 miles) and will there buy two
more stout donkeys, about as cheap as to send freight. I have
changed my mind somewhat about Johannesburg. We were on the
edge of town next to the reef and at this time of year the hills are
brown, but on driving through and looking back it is really pretty
and has great chances for improvement. Some pretty residences,
trees growing and some fine places on this side. Fred says it is much
more solidly built than most mining towns. It would not be as bad
to live there as I thought, but it is on the continental divide and the
wind almost always blows. Plenty of excitement and all kinds of
people. These last few days are like the *perfect winter days* in
Pasadena. It is a pleasure simply to breath the air and walking up
the grades to ease the donkeys is just fine and we build air castles all
day long. More trees on the hills now so we think that this is the
prettiest part of the Transvaal. It is time to inspan now.

May 27—Howard's birthday and may he have many, many
happy returns of the day. . . . Oh yes, by the way, I have forgotten to
tell you of something very important. A cat came to me in Africa.
We were driving along one day a mile or more from any house
when I heard the meowing of a kitten coming toward us. Stopped
the donkeys immediately and found a poor little half starved kitten.
It came right up to me and I put it into the wagon. Fed it and carried it with us until we came to the station house and then gave it to
a little coolie girl. Wished that we could take it with us but Fred
thought 1000 miles was too far to carry a cat. We are in Pretoria
now, the capital of the Dutch Republic. Roderick is taking a good
look at the cars for they may be the last he will see for many a year.
We thought that the R.R. only came as far as Johannesburg but it

comes to Pretoria. Have not seen enough of the town yet to tell you anything about it. Fred has gone to the market to look for donkeys. I hope that we can get away today. Please send me a little piece of black court plaster to mend my umbrella with. They never heard of such a thing here. Had letters from Madge and Uncle J. last Tuesday. They have the African fever too. We wanted you all to get the fever but supposed that we would have to write a great deal. It is a very happy surprise to see how easily you have all caught it and if we are only successful you shall all come and we will end our days in the new Utopia in the heart of Africa, and won't we be happy, says Roderick. The country is getting much prettier. Have been neglecting the journal to write to you so must stop and post it. What do you think Roderick called the suburbs of Johannesburg? The lining. We had been admiring some sunset clouds with silver and gold linings. One day he said that Ta-ra's tail did not come down as far as her back knees. He does not think that the English and Dutch are worth much. He is always saying, "In America we would do so and so or have it *thus* and *thus*." No danger of Roderick forgetting his grandma Burnham. He sends lots of love and kisses to you and Etta. Fred has written a descriptive letter to Uncle this week. Hasn't he been a jewel to write so many letters and so have you.
Adios for this time,
With much love
Blanche Burnham

Fred says publish the letters if you like but make careful selection of parts.

———

FRB to Josiah Russell

Enroute to the North
May 24th, 1893

Dear Uncle,

Just where I left off in my last letter I have forgotten, so if I repeat please excuse. I think we were just climbing the mountains bordering Natal and passed the most famous peak or rather table mountains in S.A. The famous Majuba hill where the Boers scaled the mountains in [the] face of a force of British regulars under the command of the Gov. of Natal and defeated them, killing the commander and capturing the stronghold.[1] The monuments on the battlefield do not bear the usual tribute of praise and eulogy bestowed upon dead warriors and in fact the cowardly defense made does not deserve a monument. But fighting a horde of spear armed natives was a different thing from being attacked by a company of whites and especially expert riflemen like the Boers, for it is the first civilized warfare English troops have been actually called into action in since the days of the Crimea and they were not prepared for it mentally. From this great terrace the Republic begins and covers a rolling prairie country well watered and splendidly grassed, crossed by a few streams and some low ranges of mountains just enough to break the monotony of an absolute plain, but no timber. We of course were crossing in the winter and the grass was brown as the nights are frosty and some of the time it blows keen and hard from the south like Kansas. But barring the luck of the Irish it is a fine country. At some of the farms we saw large groves of blue gum and wattle trees. The later are valuable as ornament looking like our acacia, and the bark is valuable for tanning leather, but like most new countries they export the hides and the material to tan them and buy back in a pair of rough shoes the price of two hides and the bark thrown in. Wheat, corn and oats as fine as any country I ever saw and cattle by the thousand yet standard stock in every winkle (store) is canned beef, condensed milk, canned butter, beef and mutton, scotch oats, and flour from India. Why this is I attribute to two reasons. A scattered and not united people covering a vast domain yet fairly bustling with custom houses and local jealousies. Second the vast capital and skill required to compete with a, say, modern meat cannery like Armour. Bye the bye, the Boer farmer can buy a Syracuse plow for the same price a New Yorker can (Protection), and Blanche bought a sewing machine to ship upcountry at less than American prices yet it was a Yankee machine and had been freighted round ½ the world.

Well lest this page savors of the past campaigns of Harrison vs Cleveland, I will describe as well as a page can the camp of Johannesburg. Of course a general description is written for every paper and publication in the world of any note and probably a dozen

1. Battle of Majuba Hill in 1881 during the First Angle-Boer War.

or more have fallen into your hands ere this. But to know the writer as you know me enables you to discount the statements just right to the exact truth. It is a most interesting camp, a mixture of Boer Johnny bull and a sprinkling of Yankee. Nearly all the mining machinery and many of the superintendents are Yankees, and California is well represented by her products as well as her mining men. California dried apricots (25% duty) and canned apricots 1 & 6d can, Los Angeles tomatoes 1 & 3d can, California rock crushers, Washoi picks, pine boards 4d per ft and California brandy, but, alas, not a California saddle, only the miserable pads and little steel stirrups from which one is expected to raise the seat of his pants sufficiently high to show daylight at every stride of a rough bobtailed trotter. Tis English and quite good form, and the fashion is aped by the Kaffirs who work in the mines and earn about $15 per month and often blossom out in full English rig, and for a day or two be quite a gentleman, in his own opinion. I saw one Africomaniac who had a bobtailed horse and good bridle with four reins, a cane and whip combination, a two-girthed pad, but no stirrups. He had a plug hat, eye glass and ulster white shirt and collar, but at the waistline civilization stopped, and the bare black legs of the native Kaffir supported this embryo lord, but he mounted and rode round and round the great square giving to his body the proper English bounce, and this without stirrups which to me was the astonishing part of the performance. The Kaffir's life on the great square is a study all of itself. They are great ox drivers and the way they can swing a whip is amazing. The stock is of bamboo 15 ft long and lash the same, though some drivers will swing a lash 5 ft longer than the stock. The best lashes are a single thong of hippopotamus hide with a popper of finer hide neatly spliced on. The team generally consists of 9 yoke of cattle and except on well beaten roads these are led by a boy. The wagon is a broad bedded solid built affair and should last a lifetime made of this colonial wood for what wood there is in this country is wonderful hard and tough. They load light and travel fast for oxen (15 miles per day) and generally travel in company, 3 or 4 or more teams, and have a night herder. They travel 4 hours and then outspan or camp four hours so at any time of night when near the freight roads one may hear the swish of the long keen whips which sound like a nail hurled crosswise by a good thrower, and as the Kaffir is by nature a boisterous and noisy being nothing delights him

more to while away a midnight trek than to swing that terrible whip
and give voice to a series of yells, groans, and fiendish screeches that
would put a band of coyotes and Apaches in the shade. The noise
made by a train crossing say a rocky hill would break the best
phonograph Edison could make. The creaking of the brakes which
are put on the back of the hind wheels and set by turning a crank
from the tail board of the wagon, make noise enough to wake a village alone but to this add the shrieks of the drivers, the whistle of the
whips and the lowing and bellowing of the cattle and creaking of the
loaded wagons. Needs to be heard to be understood, but after the
trek a rest, and from a pot of peculiar construction and having 3 long
legs he quickly gets his rations of mealie meal (corn meal boiled into
mush). This pot of mealie mush he can renew easily and his dishes
are easily washed by licking his fingers, or if he is very tony he will
use a mush stick. His belly full he sleeps an hour or two and then the
African traits loom up strongest. They will, when all alone, dance
and go through the strangest contortions and motions with every
part of the body, whirl round and round till giddy seeming to enjoy
the sensation, laugh and sing, groan, roar, and shriek, in fact act like
a crazy person. That a savage should do this when alone way out on
the veldt and on food that would make a white man weep shows that
happiness is not denied to the heathen, even if they do not have the
privilege of paying taxes and reading the daily paper. The great
square in Johannesburg was a source of great attraction. The keen
Caucasian gold hunter, the wily coolie as near like John Chinamen
as possible, the shrewd Jew and happy go lucky Kaffir driving in the
long teams of oxen for his Boer boss who stolidly smokes and
barters, hardly yet realizing the changes now sweeping over his
beloved land where heretofore wealth was reckoned by the number
of acres of land he owned and a bullock was the small change of the
country. But he was sleeping on the greatest gold field in the world
and allowing to lay idle splendid veins of coal and other minerals
much the same as the old mission Padres shipped their hides and tal-
low from California in the olden times. The Boer is an interesting
character, hardy, strong people, very old fashioned and slow, yet
lovers of freedom and haters of British oppression and kings in general. They have demonstrated that the Caucasian thrives in this part
of the world and the Boers never mix with the blacks. All the white
race is pure, though many of them are very illiterate and far from the

neat industrious ancestors direct from Holland. But his slowness would drive a Yankee wild. The English are slow enough especially the colonial English, but they are lightening compared to the Boers. His dread of innovation has allowed the foreigner to grasp the gold mines and many other productive industries, and from the Rand alone over $20,000,000 per annum are produced, nearly double the entire output of California and one town of 40,000 is the center of all this wealth. The Rand is a tremendous belt or reef of sandstone conglomerate several hundred ft. wide and carrying three main pay streaks, which vary in width from 2 to 10 ft and the conglomerate and sandstone between, carries a little gold and in places in years to come will probably be quarried out en masse and milled, but at present mining is confined to the 3 main pay streaks. The length of this vein is tremendous. It has been traced nearly 60 miles E. & W. The dip is south about 60 degrees on an average and it has been explored to a depth of 900 ft and is still richer in the lower levels than before though not quite so free milling. The gold is extremely fine or floury and seldom visible to the eye or even a strong glass. The ore is treated the same as in California except that for this very fine gold the cyanide process seems to be a perfect success which as yet it has not been in California. I believe mining claims are small and sidelines are boundaries so there is a mill every few hundred yards along the reef and deep level mining has just now a big boom, but the time will come when the great companies will consolidate and work on one grand plan. Coal is easily obtained 30 miles away. Lumber is imported and very high so all buildings are made of iron. Masonry and filling will largely take place of timber underground. The roads are perfect, the town and reef laying in some low hills about as high as those back of Los Angeles, though the altitude of the place is several thousand ft. The town is quite a mixture of American mining camps and English colonial. Saloons, dance halls, and chapels are hopelessly mixed, the dust is awful, the wind hard, and the traffic on the streets enormous though now back of the town and under some protective hills they are growing blue gums and orange trees and building pretty homes. It is altogether a rare city, different from any other on earth, a black diamond in fact and full of contradictions.

. . . Pretoria is about same population as Johannesburg, 40,000, and it seems queer that a republic could exist surrounded on all sides as it is by England's possessions. In fact the English in the republics[2] outnumber the Dutch already but strange as it may seem they want to run the country, naturally at a faster pace then the Dutch but are most of them as adverse to giving it over to the English as the Dutch themselves. What the more progressive want is a union of all the South African states and some genius of a statesman who can heal all local friction and petty jealousies will unite in one great free country this last corner of earth that remains open for settlement and that can for a few years at least do what the United States did for so long, offer homes for all.

Here can be found all the natural conditions that made the U.S. what it is today and a much more even climate. Its coasts are deadly, but so are our southern coasts except in the middle of winter. There is one drawback, the old settlers soon dropped into the idea that a white should not work. Black labor is cheap and if it does take 5 blacks to do one man's work what of it. The result is most of the work is poorly done. While in the early days of the U.S. republic everyone had to do his own work and it made a strong self-reliant people, even if they were inclined to boast, for I find the Afrikander daunted at things that an American pioneer would think of as commonplace. To illustrate, one settler who had been here 10 years said to me there is no use starting north for two months yet. The grass is all right but the Limpopo River cannot be forded. I say, is that the only difficulty? Yes, he says, and quite enough. I told him I would swim it. He says what will you do with your wagons and freight. Make a raft, I said. He smiled as if expecting that answer from a newcomer and especially a Yankee. My dear fellow there is not a stick of timber nearer than 15 miles. I told him that that simply meant one day's haul of one big wagon and that the empty water casks would be used as buoys for the running gears, and the sideboard be made into a sweep, and cross I would. And I have already crossed the stream that drowned many of the troops in the Boer war. He seemed somewhat nonplussed at the proposition but as I had crossed one impassable stream no doubt the blamed Yankee might cross the next. The blacks are but little help except to herd and drive oxen. They are like children deliriously happy or in abject fear if danger is about them, great braggers when far away from a trial of nerve. . . .

2. Transvaal and the Orange Free State.

We are now at the quaint and rather pretty town of Pretoria. It reminds me of Santa Anna in many ways except the prices of horse feed, hay, green barley $80 ton, oats $60 ton, corn 2½ cts per lb, oats 3 cts. These prices rule for about 4 months. Yet the Boer farmer thinks he has an immense field if he has 3 acres in forage. The wild hay, indifferently and carelessly cured, sell for about ½ oat or barley. Vegetables scarce though easily raised. Potatoes 4 cts to 8 cts per lb, onions same and other things in keeping. One man near Johannesburg is making a great fortune. He put in this year 150 acres of potatoes and marketed every one at 3 cts per lb. But the country is being rapidly filled up by gold hunters and tradespeople. The same as the early days in California. It has only begun to settle with people who intend to stay within the last two years. . . .

Adios for a time

Yours as ever

Fred R. Burnham

———

BBB to James Blick

Three days north of Pretoria
June 3, 1893

Dear old daddy,

I think that it is time that some of your short but precious epistles were answered. . . . How are your trees especially the new ones? Did we ever tell you about the guavas (lemon) that they grow in Africa. The trees are as large or larger than our big peach trees on the old place and the guavas are the size of lemons. The trees were simply loaded with them while we were in Natal and didn't we eat quantities of them. It is not the right season for loquats, but we have seen many beautiful trees. Ask Grace if she remembers the time by a great effort I managed to eat a half of a small banana. While I was in Durban I *averaged* half a dozen every day. But they have a different taste from those that we get in California. They are *fresh*. On "our farm" we will have plenty of loquats, guavas, bananas and everything nice. You cannot imagine how anxious we are that we will like the country, do well and have you all over here. Yesterday we were talking about home and I happened to say that you would be 60 years old next November, Ma would be 53 and Mother B. 51. Fred jumped up in his seat, flourished his hippopotamus whip and yelled, "Get up donks. That makes me think how time is flying. No more loafing." He spent hours planning for the future when you are all here with us.

Monday, June 12. Have not had a chance to write one word since June 3rd [continues in FRB's handwriting] and now declares she is out of the mood and I must finish. We are now trekking through as lovely country as it is possible to find in many a day. A big range of hills on our left (west) and a reedy river full of water birds on our right and the slope, along which the road runs nicely timbered and well grassed, looks like a great park. The trees are not very large, more like the timber back of Clinton[1] but as to the varieties I am all at sea. Some look like blue gum, some oak, willow, ash, locust, &c. &c. We name them according to their different appearance. One bush we call the barbed wire. There are a dozen varieties of thorny mimosa, resembles mesquite of Arizona, and some lovely hardwoods that the Kaffirs make knobkerries[2] of that would look like ivory and rosewood. Yet as lovely as this is now with its wide expanse of valley and dim blue ranges of mountains ahead of us, the storekeeper said we would see a still better country north and far more beautiful. We are crazy to see it. I wish you and Judd were here for a day or two at least on this river Nyl (Nile). There is a kind of water buck or antelope that takes to the water and dives like a hippopotamus, in fact is a regular fish. It takes 3 men to hunt one. One holds a station on a bend and one each side beats the reeds down and drives, otherwise one may wade round a week and not get one. They are fine eating, have beautiful horns and hide and weigh 200 lbs. We will cross into a belt of fever country tomorrow. It seems the inland fevers of Africa are about the same as those of the early settlers of Indiana and Iowa, a shakes pure and simple and in the summer one must keep away from the low country. Of course at this time of year one can go where he pleases as tis dry and warm lovely in fact in every way. Lots of game, grass, timber, water and pleasant. And plenty of room to swing the cut without being in the way of a neighbor. The Boers in this country hold it much as the old Spanish grants were held in California. Each man or head of

1. The Blicks were from Clinton, Iowa.
2. Knobkerries—a native club.

family holds a little country of his own. 2 or 3 thousand acres of high veldt (prairie for summer residence and pasture) 6 or 7 thousand acres for winter residence and pasture on the bush veldt, and in the winter he inspans a herd of cattle to a great ponderous house wagon and treks into the veldt with his entire family and goes on a big 3 month hunt. It is a peculiar life and has many charms I will admit. So he is not entirely to blame when he sees the restless gold hunter coming into the land that he always considered his own. Drop us a line again when you can spare a moment and we will talk over the details of everything when we meet on the 30000 acre veldt farm of the spoofs in Mashonaland.

Yours as ever,

Fred

BBB to Grace Blick

In a pass in the Waterberg Mts
June 14, 1893

My Dear Grace,

I have a few minutes before it is time to make the bread for dinner. This is our day of rest although it does not happen to be Sunday. I generally wash and mend on this day but today have only cleaned my kitchen and provision boxes which is no small task. It seemed such a luxury to lie in bed this morning. Did not have breakfast (fried quail, frying of pan bread and coffee) until nine o'clock. The days are so short now that we have to be trekking before the sun is up, and eat both breakfast and supper by the light of the campfire or the lantern. We trek seven hours and rest three at noon. I always think that I will have time to write then but such appetites as we have would astonish you. You would not complain that Fred was fussy and ate nothing now. We do nothing but sleep, cook, eat and trek, and we make puddings, pies, cakes, roast birds with dressing, make pot pies &c. We always think of father when we have a pot pie. Had one a few days ago made with a parrot, pigeon and plover. The pheasants are larger than a spring chicken and delicious. Have all the birds that we *can eat*. It is the style to go off on a hunting trek every winter in this country and we have planned many a delightful trip when you are all here. I know how you love camping. It will be two months on the 17th since we started and we are not tired of it yet only getting anxious to see what Mashonaland *looks* like. We have been passing through most beautiful country for the last week and yet we are told that Mashonaland is far lovelier. Fred wrote mother a descriptive letter to be handed around so I will not repeat. Roderick found a knee bracelet of twisted brass wire for which some African belle is now lamenting. He wants you to have it so will send when I can get a newspaper. He helps pick all the birds and does it as neatly as I can. We put the feathers in his pillow. Bought him a little fox terrier last week. The native wanted four shillings but Fred told him that *he* did not want the dog but that R. had two shillings and no more and that he would give them for the dog which we finally got. Do not know where the native got her but she has certainly been a white man's dog. She had a very pretty collar. I think R. is as proud of that as he is of the dog. Of course he calls her Gypsy. She really has some sense if she did fall out of the wagon yesterday. Fred laughs at our making a fuss over her but he likes her too and she cares more for him than she does for R. or I. I do not see how she escaped as it was the hind wheel which ran over her. She moves around all right but does not care to walk much yet. . . .

With lots of love.

Your loving Sister.

B.

———

FRB to John Blick

June 14, 1893

My dear John,

I wish a big stout young buck like yourself was along with me now. You bet he would have an appetite when grub time came, and if your partner Razor or left bower Whiskers was here I could get good action on their surplus energies also, and I think Razor would grow an inch a day. If I had struck this country when young, I would have been big enough to have amounted to something in the world. But the kid is growing and I am working him 18 hours a day and have [him] herd the stock and chop wood while he is resting.

Well what I told you before about machinery holds good over

here and doubly so. Even in these wilds there are plenty of clerks and professional men (save good dentists), but a first class machinist and engineer can command his own wages. I will tell you a little business opening I saw here for a man with a little money and "savvy how." Timber is a fabulous price, yet we pass through bush veldt with the finest hardwoods in it and good roads and market for it as mining timber for the rough, and house wagon, and furniture timber for the best. Now the Yankees set up the cheapest most durable and portable sawmills in the world and a portable sawmill in this country is unknown as far as I have seen. Any good machinist should be able to set one up and run it but in Africa you could not get a man in 500 that could touch one.

Well Johnny if you were here today you could flop your lip over some johnny bread and beans and fried partridge and I will quit to eat your share and my own. . . .

Adios for the time.

Yours as ever,

Fred

FRB to Madge Blick

[June 1893]

Dear Madge,

You can say to those aspiring young men and to the foreman of the Throop[1] that if they want to go into cattle farming they must come and first learn the language (Zulu), then if used to the business at home they can surely win here as it is done on entirely different lines here. . . . But nearly everything one ever knew before has to be unlearned here. And if a man has the happy faculty of making himself a zero and learning from the start again he will in one year see things that are really profitable. But it is a great mistake to think they can come to Africa with American knowledge only and pick up a fortune in a few years and then return to America. One must come to stay. As to teaching it is not a very good country for that, as the English don't care a fig for education and look down on all teachers as about on a par with barbers and

---

1. Throop Preparatory School, now California Institute of Technology.

cigarette makers. But that will soon change for the better especially as the American element is growing and bids fair to be the controlling one here inside 5 years. But I am sorry to say a lot of so-called Americans are here who are a disgrace to any country. What we want is men who will work and who will stay in the country. There is coal and iron and gold mines and many other resources. There is also fever and much that is unpleasant. Yet I can see no difficulty but what is within the power of an energetic people to overcome. Doc Hammond[2] of the Hammond party takes dinner with us tomorrow. I knew him in Arizona in the old days when you and I were both very young and long before a silver thread had woven its mystic meaning into life [letter incomplete].

———

FRB to Rebecca Russell Burnham

> In a pass of the Waterberg Mts
> Enroute to the Zambezi
> June 14, 1893

Dear Mother,

According to our almanac it is Sunday for we are strictly independent and pay no attention to many of the conventionalities of life and we stop and call it Sunday whenever the spirit moves us. There will be no church today and no contribution box, however we will this afternoon take a Sabbath day's journey to the top of a rugged little mountain peak that rises almost a precipice above us, 1000 ft, and from it we will see many a man, a mile of grass covered hills and timber belts and blue ranges of mountain way toward the Crocodile or Limpopo River, and from the summit of this mountains I may offer a silent prayer of thanks that there is still left such a beautiful country and still free. I expected South Africa to be like Arizona, mostly dry and plains covered with thorny cactus and sand with occasional rich valleys made so by irrigation, and while much of the western part is probably that way it does not apply to thousands of square miles over which we have and are now trekking. A cool breeze is blowing from the south for everything is here turned bottom side up, and we have already

2. Andrew Hammond, American mining expert.

crossed into the tropic zone by going north and look for points of compass by looking south for the southern cross instead of the pole star. The heavens are strange and only the sun and moon seem like old acquaintances, and I am looking for the man in the moon to shave his whiskers or do something queer. Every hour of the day shows up some strange and unnamed bug or flower or tree and we name them according to their resemblance to some well known king or from local or personal characteristics, but one familiar pest we find is the tick. Every once in a while we hit a patch of them and then I have a picnic, but strange to say they don't bother B. Fleas are scarce. Poisonous snakes are a good deal like the California rattler. They are here but nobody seems ever to get bit by one except in some tradition 10 or 50 yrs old. Nevertheless they are dangerous, I have no doubt, but not so bad as the kind men often get in their boots in this as well as our own country.

This is a great mineral country and hardly yet prospected. Ledge after ledge untouched and many of them rich, waiting for the magic sound of the iron horse to make the country as it has already done the Rand which produces $2,000,000 every month. Miles and miles of hoists and quartz mills, the greatest gold camp on earth. The products of Africa should be as diversified as California and more so. . . . The winter climate corresponds to California's only it is dry, like the season of 86–7. But the summer season is rainy instead of dry like California, so there is no dust and dry hills, but plenty of rain, averaging 30 inches and some years 40. It comes in heavy storms with thunder and lightening but no winds. The mountain scenery is not as rugged as the Sierras. It is more like New Mexico and northern part of old Mexico and the coast ranges of California. Natal is much like the Contra Costa hills in March and many of the valleys remind one of the Santa Clara and San Jose country. The Transvaal is an independent republic, so is the Orange Free State, both Dutch Boers. The latter is very much like Kansas and the southern part of Transvaal is like Kansas and Indian Territory, but the northern part is very beautiful. Plenty of lovely timber. Some of it looks like the timber back of Lyons and much of it looks like Old England only lacking in roads and other earmarks of civilization such as saloons, insane asylums, tenement houses and wretchedly poor, with a few lovely stone castles on its bluffs and hills. I believe I told you in a former letter of a splendid English castle built on the banks of a beautiful swift river in Natal at a place called Howick. It was turreted and ivy-clad and worked in shades of red and gray stone, rough hewn and finely joined.

Our live stock are now ready for corn and stand in a semicircle around me watching this pen weave back and forth in its mysterious way from line to line, and Ti Wink feels so sorry for me he is shedding tears. They all send their love across the big ponds that now roll between us and hope that we may yet have a marble-halled castle on the highlands of the Zambezi with a big pasture and nothing to do for them but give the kid an occasional ride in a rickshaw. We are now getting more and more into the wilds. The savages have left off their gorgeous apparel and fine linen such as is shipped to Africa from the junk shops of London. Old wool sacks are as standard as black silk, and red soldiers coats as calico. Horse blankets and old ulsters are next in order of importance, and plug hats and red umbrellas form the principal articles of adornment to the black Apollos of the lower Transvaal. But up here a string of beads and a patch of leather the size of an old stove lid (and that is not size enough) suffice for most of them. The blacks are now streaming past our camp with baskets of corn and peanuts on their heads to market at a Dutch store 5 miles back where they will get salt, beads, wire, sacks (rum on the quiet) and jews harps, hoes, axes, &c. Queer people but a living is obtained so easy that they are fat and happy as birds in a tree top. I learned yesterday that there are some Californians up in the Mazoe gold fields. (I am going through there after I get to Salisbury.) It is here that one of those strange old cities of Africa are located whose early history and origin is lost long [ago] in traditions of the blacks. I shall explore its old ruins and will write you an account of them. The inhabitants were miners and worked gold as the ornaments have been found and I saw a ring beautifully carved that came from there. You would be delighted at the beautiful hardwoods which the natives work up into all kinds of useless ornaments and sick [sic]. One native tree the wood looks like lemon, another like ivory. It is as solid as stone almost. The hide of the hippopotamus is over an inch thick when cured and tough as whale bone and the plumage of the tropic birds would set a Parisian milliner wild with joy as he would have lady swelldom at his feet with bags of gold to buy them. Some of the birds are singers but so far have not seen a bird that comes up to the California mocking bird for song. So far the worst drawback I have yet found in Africa is the fact that horses are subject to a mysterious disease. Fat and in the best of grass they fall sick and die every season for about 4 or 5 months and so far without any known remedy. Some live right through without harm. This season about 10 percent around Pretoria died. Imported cattle the same. Native stock is tolerably free from disease. Nevertheless I shall have horses and let them die if they must, but I shall try the scheme of feeding on oats and alfalfa instead of grass and native hay. Native cattle are about the same as Texas stock but gentle as the natives handle everything and raise it by hand, but I imagine it would require about 5 cows to equal old Jumbo for butter, but as feed costs nothing that is all right.

Bye the bye, yesterday was dog day. Our full blooded sky terrier bull pup fell out of the wagon in the A.M. and again in the P.M. and got run over. Of course it cried. Roy cried. That made B. cry and Ti Wink weep silently and me cuss inwardly at the wasted fuss over dogs, but as today the dog is around on all fours slightly disfigured but still in the ring. All is well and the dog *may* have learned something, that I will not be stopped on my northward flight anymore than the *geese* and this particular geese is a Yankee geese and going to get there. . . .
Yours as ever,
Fred

BBB to John Blick

Brak River
June 22, 1893

My Dear John,

Just a week yesterday since I wrote home and in that time we have done some pretty good trekking. Started at seven the next morning and camped three miles the other side of Marabatstad [Maritzburg], the scene of an old mining excitement. I expect it is in your old geographies because it is marked *gold* on our map and Johannesburg is not. Some good mines around there but none working now. Some trouble about water rights. It is a sleepy little old place, only an hotel, two stores and three houses. I believe we left the main road there which would have carried us through Petersburg, the largest town (1000) of northern Transvaal. Very few towns of any size in the Transvaal, Johannesburg and Pretoria each 40,000, Heidelburg about 1000 I should say and Standerton a few hundred. Mostly stock farms and very little cultivation in the country through which we have come. The Boers do not seem to care for the luxuries of life and yet some of them are very wealthy. I think I wrote that Pretoria is a very pretty town with some really artistic buildings. A great many English in Pretoria. We were there five days in a lovely camp north of town. We call it Donkeytown because Fred was looking for donkeys to buy every day. We like the two that he bought very much and call them Chub, because she is so chubby, and Baby. But tell Grace that she would not be disgraced if Chub was named after her because she is an excellent donkey in every respect and we are very fond of her. We look quite swell with our six donkeys and we have something else which puts us in keeping with the country, and we are not stared at quite so much anymore since the addition of two more burros and a bed made of laced rawhide and swinging under the wagon. They drive such long trains here. So many have gone to Mashona with donkeys. They keep up so much better than oxen but then we feed them mealies. Roderick sleeps in the wagon and we on the rawhide bed. As I write this it seems as though I had written it before but you know what a poor memory I have and will pardon me. I get the journal and my letters mixed. Well to go back to Marabatstad, we saved fifteen miles by not going through the town. On coming to the winkle (store), where the two roads meet, we learned that within a mile the roads separated again, the coach road saving fifteen miles over the transport or freight road, but that water was sixteen miles distant and then thirty-two without water and there the roads came together again and separated, the coach going to Tuli, and a new road called the hunter's or middle drift went straight north meeting the other about fifty miles this side of Victoria. But on this new road you have to build campfires around your stock every night to keep the lions away and that teams always went in a company. There were five teams outspanned at the winkle and they were all going the lion road. We agreed to join them and meet here and here we are and have been since day before yesterday and in the meantime six more teams have joined us so we now number twelve teams, 19 white men and a lot of Kaffirs and dogs. I have seen three women and I think there is at least one more in the last wagon. There is one little girl about Mina's age.[1] Every wagon has several guns, one has eight so we are well equipped to meet the lions. Plenty of all sorts of game on the road and we expect to have some fun and rather hope to meet some lions. One Kaffir boy, aged ten, with whom Roderick is now playing. They say he is a good boy. Roderick is wild to play. Thinks he will like the little girl. You should have seen our donkeys as we drove up to the winkle. We thought for a few minutes that we would have a run away. Three tame ostriches were stalking around the place and Ta-ra and the Baby thought that they were going to be eaten alive. Fred had to get out and lead them. The birds are very large. The man brought them here when little chicks and turned them loose on the veldt several years ago. There are quite a number in the country now. A fine for shooting them. These three are tamer than Ma's chickens. Anyone can pet them. The man had four but a wolf or wolves killed one last week.

June 23rd—When we get our farm I am going to have a pair. I said the wagons all met here but we camped for a day or two four miles back at the first water and Fred killed a big rabbit, a brush partridge and a guinea hen. The first P.M. we have had three different kinds of partridges, the brown, yellow and brush. They are about twice the size of our quail. The guinea hens look exactly like the domestic ones. The first one Fred killed was as large as a big rooster. Delicious flavor. I have dried mint and sage and stuff the big birds and roast them in the reflector. Have had several big birds entirely strange to me. We sat around the campfire last night and wished for you and Judd. . . . Bright moonlight, campfires gleaming, men talking and laughing and Kaffirs singing and playing the concertina, and just before bedtime a big outfit pulled in from the north. You can hear them a mile away, whips popping, dogs barking and those queer indescribable yells, shrieks and groans, which are considered necessary to make the oxen move. R. almost always says when he hears them coming especially at night, "Don't you wish Aunt Kate was here Papa. Would she be *scared*." There are two little Dutch boys here at the winkle so this morning

---

1. Mina was the daughter of Homer and Linnie Blick.

the Yankee, Dutch and Kaffir are playing together and seem as happy as if they could understand every word said. I am glad that he has someone to play with even for a day. A wolf came right into camp last night and the dogs made a great fuss. I believe that they are what we call hyenas. Three colonial English boys enroute for Salisbury with freight for their father's store were in camp day before yesterday. They had four guns and shot at everything, good to eat or not. Poor shots, although they thought they were crack hunters. Fred wished that Judd was here to go with them. He would have astonished them somewhat. They were so boyish. They made me think of you boys and I liked them. They shot two monkeys and said the monkeys looked at them and moaned and cried like a person. They had to shoot several times before killing them. I know that you and Judd will wish you were with us for the next 250 miles, and just think when this letter reaches you we will be in Ft. Salisbury. Will not pass another winkle or white man's habitation for 250 miles, so it will be some time before you get another letter. Several Boers in our train. Most of the men speak good English but you seldom see a woman that can, so I am afraid they will not be much company for me but you know that that never worries me. I rather prefer talking to men but still I am glad that I am not the only woman. They only joined us yesterday and outspanned below us so have not spoken to them. But after this we will have to pull our wagons close together. We will trek this P.M. Only expect to make ten or eleven miles a day because the animals have to do all their feeding during the daytime. Some of the wagons had to be repaired today and shift their loads so the camp is very busy. The coach passed us the other day and it made me almost sick to think that almost for a certainty there were letters in it for us and we cannot get them for so long. But we did not want to risk losing any letter by having them sent along the road so they are all forwarded to Ft. Salisbury. The women who came in last night are just building a fire in a big ant hill which looks as though it had been used dozens of times. But I prefer baking in the reflector and we are going to have roast guinea hen for dinner and it is about time to make the dressing. Had to buy some brown denim or overall cloth here to make R. pants and waist. We sent most of our clothes up by freight and I did not keep enough out for him, but fortunately have my little hand sewing machine with me and it will not take very long. Shall try to keep my brown dress together but have had to darn it already. So many thorn bushes. I tell you that I am a famous walker now and know that I can easily outwalk Mrs. Kimball. Get tired sitting in the seat and love to walk. Only wore my gaiters about three weeks and have had the second half soles and heels put on the shoes I had made in S.F. [San Francisco]. Wish I had another pair like them.

None of the hounds here are as handsome as Bruce and they are such thieves. Study hard John and do not waste a moment. Does Judd want to come to Africa? We saw some quartz last evening which pleased us immensely and if we can only find a country entirely free from fever we will all be together again. . . . As ever your loving sister,
B.B.B.

———

FRB to Josiah Russell

Enroute to Mashonaland
June 23rd, 1893

Dear Uncle,

We are now in camp at Brackman River as the roads fork here one going by way of Ft. Tuli and the new one which saves about 80 miles travel goes direct to Ft. Victoria. Is this latter road we will take but as the country is wild and infested with lions and other wild beasts we have to gather in strong parties, so for several days the teams have been stringing on and now we have 12 outfits together and quite a little army of guns and can stand off the lions and, if need be, a tribe of blacks. Our cavalcade is over a mile long, very queer and picturesque. The weather is all that could be asked for, cool nights and not very warm even at noon. The country we now travel through is densely wooded with short heavy timber and a few mountain peaks loom up ahead of us. Just on our left is a great rugged mountain, looks very much like the Superstition Mountains in Arizona, and on the right is a peak like Commodore Peak back of Pasadena. I have just stopped for a moment to kill a guinea hen. They are fat and very fine eating and so tame they are liable to bite one. Have just tried out some of the fat for gun oil. A couple of boys in the train shot two large monkeys yesterday, but they look too much like humans for me to quietly take a shot at especially as they harm nothing in this wild country, and then suppose they were our ancestors. Who would want the sin of slaying them, or maybe they are the reincarnation of our great great great . . . grandmother and would have to do it all over again just from a whim of their enlightened and *Christian* descendants. There are also a few ostriches around here and plenty of bush buck and other game. 7 of our wagons are loaded with quartz mills to crush the ores already mined at Victoria and Salisbury. We have as a pilot an old hunter, a Boer. He is a character. Looks very much like some of the old style American frontiersmen. He took an active part in the late unpleasantness with the English[1] and lost one eye but is now the affable guide to that resistless race and pilots his former enemies into the finest country in Africa by his own say so and our hope so, for if it is finer than we have already seen then it must be fine indeed. Water hereabouts is rather scarce and we trekked 32 miles the last trek to this river, but it could easily be obtained by digging. We are now on the edge of the fever belt which is very dangerous here in the rainy season. 25 per cent of the people get a dose of it in crossing but at this time of year tis a fine country. Still it will not be in this 19th century at least settled by the whites. There are thousands of miles of uplands first that can be filled. We are the only Yankees in the train. There is one Dutch family. The rest are old country English or colonial English or old colony chaps as they are called, strong hardy people but law abiding. There are a few head of horses that have had that mysterious African sickness and lived, along with us and as tis like the small pox in the human (once only) they will survive in the Mashonaland country. Some young veterinary student who can inoculate or prevent this horse sickness in this country has the key to fame and fortune for aside from that horses do well here. So new and strange and different does it all seem in this country that it really seems as if I had two or more lives or lived in more than one world, Pasadena and its environs forming the capital and center of one. I should like to see the Stars and Stripes float over this fair land and see it settled and peopled by such men as builded the great

---

1. By "the late unpleasantness," Burnham is referring to the 1881 war between the Boers and the British.

Republic. Africa is so new yet that a national impulse is only just beginning to be felt. It is strongest in the Boers but as that clashes with the English it will never be overcome till all South Africa is independent of the Mother country and united in one great republic of its own, and it will be. The missionary element is the fort of the conservative and imperialist party who want Africa divided into concessions with a duke at the head of each and ruled by the English Bishops. Cape Colony is now independent and Natal struggling to be against the solid church of England element and at the last parliament gained a liberal majority, but only one vote, not enough, so declared at home, to give her independence, but it will come next year any way as the Mother country never refuses a majority vote if emphatic. The Dutch Republics of Orange Free State and Transvaal will then come into a union not as solid and binding perhaps as the American, but sufficient to loosen the strictures on commerce and trade, which is the only way that any modern government is nowadays oppressive, for so far as personal law and liberty is concerned you could not tell whether Stars and Stripes, Union Jack or the colors of Africa floated over you. Tis the horrid customs houses that choke you. Bye the bye we never got a paper sent us at all. They went to a big family of Burnhams in Pretoria and not to us. But I wish you would send me a catalogue of saw mills (portable) mostly. There is timber up north, hardwood mostly and yet on our train is mining *timbers* being hauled 800 miles on ox wagons to the mines. They know nothing of portable saw mills in this country and lumber is 25 cts per foot in Salisbury and big demand. A little portable mill would be a fortune. Furniture timber and wagon timber can also be had and would bring any price asked. Send the catalogue after cutting out waste advertisements by letter post to Salisbury. I must close at once.
In haste
Fred

FRB to Josiah Russell

June 24, 1893

Dear Uncle,

I have another ½ hour or so to scribble to you all and will continue on the political vein mentioned in yesterday's page.

All the country laying north of the Crocodile River and west of the Transvaal Republic extending across the Karoo and Kalihari desert to the borders of the German possessions of West Africa and Portuguese possessions and north to the Zambezi River was claimed by the Boers and by England. But the latter country while wanting it did not want to spend the enormous sums needed to show its protectorate rights by stations, troops, &c, &c. Yet did not want any other nation to have it and threatened war on the Boers if they trekked into the northern wilds. In the struggle between financial economy and political greed, the brilliant mind of Cecil Rhodes saw a great opportunity to satisfy the British land hunger and still allow them to hold tight the purse strings of the imperial treasure. He is a magnetic man with brilliant imagination, fine address and plenty of courage. He formed a company and drew into it many of the great names near the throne of England and obtained another of those liberal concessions which England often makes of other peoples possessions to her own titled citizens. It was called the British South African Company and was granted nearly the same privileges as the British East India except customs dues. Cecil Rhodes was and is the moving spirit and he at once raised a great expedition of 1500 white volunteers to go north and take possession of the Company's land clear to the Zambezi River, for old Lobengula[1] can raise 100,000 fighting men and did not recognize Cecil Rhodes. But by much adroitness and a show of great reserves of troops &c. &c. Rhodes managed to gain a footing in the north without shedding a drop of blood. It was as fine diplomacy as could be found anywhere and from nothing he gained first, the protection of the great flag of England to keep the Boers and other nations off, and with money contributed by the dukes and lords of England, some for national glory but mostly in expectation of the Dutchman's one percent, he got money to equip this little army, and from the power he showed and his knowledge of African character he got Lobengula to concede to him the entire rights to Mashonaland, which is a conquered province of Lobengula's, mineral rights and all, but has never yet got the great concession of Matabeleland. But the first step was accomplished and he spent £2,000,000 in doing it. Now his next is about as follows. Holding undoubted sway over all the country surrounding

1. King of the Matabele nation who claimed sovereignty over the region.

Loben he will make one hand wash the other. The home company has not yet seen a penny return and it is 3 years, so they will not put up, but having gained an empire they are in position to invite settlers on liberal terms and until the end of this year they will give to every settler 3000 acres of land and a mineral right covering 10 claims. 3 years residence gives the farm in fee simple and you are allowed to keep any white man as your proxy. This is the first year of heavy immigration and 4 million acres are already granted and 3 flourishing towns laid off and doing well. Victoria on the gold belt, which is undoubtedly one of the best camps yet found, Salisbury about 30 miles from another great gold belt, the Co's capital and built on a high plateau, and Umtala, mining and farming country at end of the coast. R.R. from Beira now building. Now there are in Mashonaland about 2000 whites. As soon as they get a little stronger or probably even now England would never see them destroyed by Loben's warriors and he inside of 2 years will have to do as thousands of other fierce chiefs have done, come under the Union Jack and the empire of Matabele will be open for all white races. Meantime Rhodes and Company have started the ball and can now sit down and let the whites work out the peace of the country without keeping up a garrison at private expense, and yet they can sell their broad acres at 25 cts an acre and get rich. One can not but admire Rhodes yet feels a little hostile to be under the government of what is practically a British syndicate. The upshot of all will be that in the charter it provides that the govt. has the privilege of buying the Co. out. The govt will do it and the settlers float a bonded debt large enough to make Rhodes & Co. 200 percent probably, but even then one should not kick or otherwise it might have been 30 years before the weight of population would have forced Loben to open the gateway of the north. This is my ideas to date of the company &c. subject of course to radical changes bye and bye.

I can think of no matters of business needing a word at present so will close hoping to give you definite news of the country at next writing.

I am as ever

F

BBB to Blick family

Seven miles from the junction with Tuli
July, I do not know what, 1893

My dear mother, father and all the rest,

It is a long long time since we had a chance to mail a letter but if nothing happens will mail this tomorrow. Well the lions have not eaten us *yet* and there are not so many on the main road, but we still will have to be watchful of the stock. We have written the little happenings of any interest in the journal which will forward as soon as we reach Salisbury. Have really turned it into a home letter.

The trip has been very pleasant and although we have seen fresh lion tracks and once within fifty yards of the camp we have not seen Mr. Leo himself, but one followed Fred who was coming in on horseback from building fires around a koodoo,[1] I do not know how that is spelled but that is the way that it is pronounced, which he had killed. His horse was very restless but it was pitch dark and he could see nothing, but they saw the tracks the next morning. They only went off the road to hunt for two days and in that time Fred shot a koodoo, two reed bucks, a dyker buck and a wild pig, total 1000 pounds of meat. We kept the horns and skins, the hams of a reed buck and of the pig and gave the rest away. The other four who went with Fred only killed a stem buck and a small reed buck. Says he could have done much better if he had only had a Winchester repeater. He killed two other buck the week before and we have had any amount of birds. He has quite a reputation and so wishes that he had a little twenty-two and that Judd was here. It was a great mistake not to bring guns from home but did not think that ammunition could be procured here. But Fred has written all about the hunt in the long letter journal, and I must now tell you of our new danger. The Chartered Co. owns Mashonaland but are bound to protect the Mashonas from the Matabeles who have just come over the border and killed 200 of the Mashona and are stealing cattle. Then the Mashona poured into Victoria for protection. The mounted police were ordered to drive them, the Matabeles, back over the border and in doing so killed thirty of them, the first time they have ever been killed by the whites and there is great excitement. Victoria, Salisbury and

1. Koodoo or kudu—large grayish-brown African antelope.

Tuli are in laagers or forts. Some returning teams brought us the news yesterday and said many teams had thrown off their loads and were going back as fast as they could. So Fred with three others went across eight miles to a telegraph station where these telegrams had been received. "If wagons (transport riders) are within five days of Victoria come, if not return or go into laager." That means fortify yourselves. But the last wire said, "Tell people not to be alarmed. Will wire anything fresh." Not the exact words but the right import, so we made a trek last night and here we are today. They sent back for news and also sent a wire to know whether it was safe to proceed. No news and the man waited several hours but received no answer. Grand council out around a big campfire but I do not know their decision yet. They have done nothing but talk of Matabeles today, and quite a number were for turning back this morning but by evening had decided to stay. Now receiving no answer has upset them again and I do not know how it will turn out. We are not going back anyway. It is too far and we would be just as liable to an attack. I do not know the exact number but we have at least twenty-five wagons and there must be forty or more white men and plenty of guns and ammunition. Have been getting arms ready all day. You should hear Roderick talking to the men. He says *he* is not going to turn back. We will *fight* and if they kill us we will die, that is all. He does wish that he had a pistol and could shoot. I am going to make him a cartridge belt tomorrow and also one for myself, for we may have to leave the wagons and go afoot before we get there. It is eighty-five miles from here. Fred is very proud of Roderick and says that he thinks he would stand right behind him and hand cartridges. We have a rifle, shotgun and six shooter. Do not all belong to us but are ours to use. Of course you will see accounts of the trouble in the papers and doubtless have ere this. We were not born to be killed by the Matabeles so do not worry any more than you can help. The Matabeles may not be ready to fight yet and it may amount to nothing this time, but thought it best to write in case fate should turn against us. We are all together and that is a great comfort. Some way I do not think that we will be killed. Remember the mail only leaves this part of the world once in two weeks and then they may not connect with trains and steamers, so it might be longer before you receive another letter. I will write at every opportunity so you may get several letters at once. How glad we will be to get your letters in Salisbury, but it will be a month or more before we reach there as we want to stop in Victoria a few days, and it is almost 200 miles of heavy sand from there. Beautiful roads now. We scarcely average ten miles a day or rather morning and evening because the stock have to be tied up at night. Some very nice people in the train and we have enjoyed the trip very much. Fred is attending the council and I am sitting on Roderick's bed. He is wondering if Grandma Blick is washing now and wishing that she could see his cartridge belt. He wants to wear it all the time like the men do.

Will send the next letter to mother. Lots of love to her and all of you. My dear little mother, I am sorry to cause you any worry but we will come out all right and we will all live together in Matabeleland which they say is much finer than Mashonaland. Good night dear ones with love from all.
Your loving daughter,
B.

July 25—I have found out the date. One day later and we are still alive and unharmed. Made a trek this morning and one this evening. Our wagons are drawn up in a circle, guards posted, guns and ammunition distributed. Mr. Molie, a gunsmith, had eight new guns which he has loaned for the service. No alarming news has reached us so shall push on toward Victoria. Two wagons have turned back and five more are on the fence. Good! Fresh telegram just arrived. "Road free for transport riders (freight teams). Private conveyance use their own judgment." They interpret that, that the company will be responsible for any losses so we will go ahead but take proper precautions. Will mail a letter at every opportunity. Now don't worry for as I said before, I hate to write this but one never knows what may happen and we thought best that you should know. Some way I do not feel alarmed at all and think that we will get through all right. They count me as a man if any trouble comes, and it makes me quite proud. Only one other woman has been with us but one more in the wagons which joined us a few days ago. She says that she is not a coward herself but is sorry for her little Annie. Would like to go back but her husband does not want to go. This news has braced them up and maybe the doubtful

ones will go on now. I am so anxious for letters from home. They
are the only things that make me realize that I am so far away. I
suppose Howard is on the road over here ere this. Of course you
will think about us but don't worry. That is our chief anxiety.
Plenty of excitement in our lives now. With boundless love. You
enter into all our thoughts and plans every day.

Your loving daughter and sister,

B.

———

BBB to Blick Family

Tokwe River,
Aug. 4, 1893

Dear folks at home,

Six years ago today we arrived in Pasadena from our visit to
Kansas and here we are in "terra incognita" and oh, such a long
way from California, and our little baby is a great big boy. He is
undressing now. We make his bed so that he can sleep during these
night treks. No moon now so it is not so pleasant trekking. Our
lives are full of excitement now and liable to be more so. Here
comes Fred and it is time to inspan.

Aug. 5—Yesterday morning a messenger rode out from
Victoria to tell us that a very unsatisfactory message had been received from the chief of the Matabeles and for the wagons to come
in. No immediate danger but best not to delay. And last evening
one of our passengers returned who had walked into Victoria. He
says that he saw the message from Lobengula and it was this. "I
have granted you nothing in Mashonaland except the mineral
rights, and if I get hold of you (Capt. Lendy)[1] I will cut off your
ears as I do the Mashona."

So Victoria and Salisbury are preparing for war. Have good
forts but are still improving them. Three big guns at Victoria and
they say 100 men can hold the fort easily. They have mounted police on the borderline who report that there is no massing of
troops *yet*. But the Matabele will certainly avenge the death of

---

1. Captain Charles Frederick Lendy was in charge of the patrol that killed several
Matabele during their raid on the Mashona.

those thirty, three of whom were petty chiefs. The question is *when*. This is my third letter since leaving the lion road. I wonder if you have received the other two, one I addressed to my mother and the other to Mother Burnham. You may of course never get this. We will be in Victoria tomorrow evening we think. We do not like to stop there in the fort for we do not know for how long it may be and during the summer months Victoria is not as healthy as Salisbury. Our mail is in Salisbury too. Our bullocks (I speak of those belonging to the parties with whom we are traveling) are very poor and it is *impossible* for them to haul the transport to Salisbury. So parties from Victoria meet us tomorrow and guarantee to land the transport in Salisbury in twelve days which is very quick time. When we reach Victoria we will decide whether to stay or put *all* of our goods on the big wagons and go along with them. Dread the fever more than we do the Matabeles. There are not enough whites to take the aggressive, so all we can do is to hold the fort, and if we are besieged volunteers will come from below and there are 600 trained native soldiers 35 miles from Tuli and 80 miles farther Kahma[2] will send 15,000 warriors. And here we are trekking along as unconcernedly as can be. Africa is a queer country and its people are queerer. The country that we are passing through now is very pretty. One of the men shot a sable antelope, 500 lbs, a few days ago and this morning Mr. Couright shot a water buck, 400 lbs, so we have plenty of meat. The antelope is delicious. We cook the steak rare as we do beef steak. Only two drawbacks to this country. Fever, but that is not every place, and *appetites*. We eat 90 lbs of flour a month. You will hardly believe that but it is the solemn truth. When we stop trekking we certainly will not eat so much. Wouldn't we like some of your grapes, peaches, and apricots now. But we will have fruit here in a few years. Will write more tomorrow. Fred is drawing up a will for me to copy. Holographic wills are acknowledged in Cal. and we are in a wild country and if anything should happen to us the court would get everything we have. Should have done this before leaving home but did not realize where we were going. In case of my death of course it reverts to Fred, but if he does not survive me the Fullerton ranch or the proceeds of its sale go to Roderick and the

---

2. King Kahma, pro-British chieftain in Bechuanaland.

Maylin St. property to Mother Burnham and Howard. In case of Roderick's death, and if the Matabeles kill one of us they will kill all, the ranch and the Maylin St. property are to be divided *equally* between mother, Howard and you, father. If there is any money collected from the Clapp note Fred has divided that between Uncle, Madge and Homer. We do not want the lawyers to get anything and do not see how they can now if there is no squabbling among you. I made objection, thinking that mother [Burnham] might feel a little sore at your getting so much, but Fred said no, because we had already given her the El Dorado St. and N. Pasadena lot. He considers the property as much mine as his. Will send the papers to Uncle Josiah as he has all the other papers. Fred has written to mother so everyone understands. All this sounds serious. Of course we do not want to die but realize that there is some danger. But someway I feel confident that we will all see you again. Still, coming to such a country we should have done this before. Oh, I must tell you what Roderick said this morning. We had heard that no dogs are allowed in the fort and Roderick has been very much concerned for fear Gyp would starve. Fred said he would shoot her but R. did not like that idea, so when we were eating breakfast this morning he said, "I tell you what I will do. I will cut a hole through a big piece of meat, tie a string on to it and fasten it to Gyp's collar." Pretty cute we thought. Did I tell you that he wanted to sleep in his cartridge belt the first day that he wore it.

Aug. 6—Well we expect to get near enough to Victoria tonight to find out what is going on there. How I wish it was Salisbury and we could get our mail. We are not homesick but we would dearly love to see you all. We always would but now more than ever. All is peace and quiet at home, but it will be so here some day. Some are going down into Gazie Land[3] 110 miles with the cattle. We may go there but will tell you our plans as soon as they are decided. The weather is simply perfect and has been all the time. Like your loveliest winter weather.

Wednesday—and they say the mail is closed. Will try to send these down by passengers. We were misinformed about the mail. Have been here two days and I have been sick with the headache. It is fearful here. Broiling hot sun, wagons drawn so close together

3. Gazaland.

that the hubs touch. The report is now that troops will come in from below and go into Matabeleland from Tuli so that Victoria and Salisbury will have to lie in laager for months. We are going east into Gazie Land with some parties to hunt. Think we will more than likely drift back to Johannesburg until Matabele is open. Will come up with the troops. May not hear from us for months but we will be all right. Oceans of love. Will try to get mail from Salisbury if possible.

B.

FRB to Josiah Russell

Aug. 5, 1893
Tokwe River

Dear Uncle,

Everything is being done in a terrible rush. The machine guns are training on the surrounding veldt and all men under arms and in laager, so whether this holographic will will now hold in California I can't tell, but it may serve as a guide to any settlement that may be made of our property, and carries with it untold volumes of love which we bear for all the numerous members of our family. What little we still possess we feel should go among those who have the greatest hardships in providing this world's goods. And to the strong and young and able we send only our love and knowing that only a matter of a few years and we all must meet on common ground. We are going to try and cut our way east from Ft. Victoria through the Matabele country[1] and from there pick a safe road into Transvaal and come up with fresh troops to fight Lobengula. This is a land of gold and even California in her palmy days did not exceed this for rich veins. But there are hostile nations to conquer and fever belts to avoid but Matabeleland is high and healthy. I shall try and get a runner into Victoria with a longer letter to you all but may fail. Goodbye and endless love.

I am as ever
Fred

----

1. Actually, east of Fort Victoria was Mashona country.

FRB to Rebecca Russell Burnham

Aug 5, 93

Dear Mother,

As we expect to be besieged in Ft. Victoria this may be the last note for a long time from any of us as the Matabele war will be quite a little fuss, old Lobengula being able to send 80,000 men into the field. And of course if the Fort falls you will get no news till we all *cross over.* I have little to say as to our present condition. We are having exciting times and I enjoy it. Roderick is brave and carries a belt of cartridges ready to hand me any instant and he won't flinch for anything. Only the other day when a woman was telling B. how the Matabeles killed before her eyes the Mashona boys and cut out their tongues, he said, I wonder if they would do that to me. This is a beautiful country at this season. We expect to come out of the war in good shape and join the first trek into Matabeleland, the finest in all Africa. B. has made her will so that you and Roderick and Howard are secure and if Roderick should go up the flume with us the property goes to you ⅓, Howard ⅓ and ⅓ divided among other members of our family. So with boundless love, appreciating the dangers by which we are surrounded, yet confident of success
I am as always,
Fred

Fern Spruit[1] 12 miles from Victoria Aug 5th 1893
Roderick sends love and says he can be a soldier anyway if a small one.

BBB to Madge Blick Ford

16 miles east of Victoria
Aug. 12, 1893

My dear Madge,

No telling whether this letter will ever get mailed or not but I will write and trust to good luck. Was too late for the mail in Victoria, which is very uncertain anyway, so gave them to an Amer-

1. Spruit—a small stream.

ican friend who will start with a special stage for Johannesburg today (20 days) and promised to mail them there. Such troubled times looked for here that we thought best to make our wills, which we did and sent to Uncle Josiah.

. . . We reached Victoria Aug. 7 and found no fresh news. People are just waiting and fortifying the place and some think that the Matabeles are doing the same. The general impression is that troops will be brought in from the Transvaal by way of Ft. Tuli and march on the Matabele Capitol. People seem to have recovered from the first scare and some teams are leaving. Still the town is full. There is scarcely space to pass between the wagons and inside the fort it is thicker still. Not a tree to break the glare of the sun and it is good and warm now in the middle of the day. What will it be in the summer time? The Chartered Co. only pay the volunteers five shillings a day and rations. Absolutely no business going on and provisions steadily increasing in value. I have not been sick a day on the trip but the first hour in Victoria saw me with the headache which I have had ever since. The last few days before reaching Victoria were very hard on me and the last day Fred had a severe headache from indigestion, the second in Africa, but was all right the next day, and I am better. There is not a bit of feed for the stock at Victoria, so Mr. Saunders, a very pleasant young fellow about twenty-two, started east on the 9th with two wagons and the oxen belonging to seven. We put *all* our luggage on one of these wagons and are with him. Will go east until we find *good* feed for the oxen between 40 and 60 miles if not farther. Have to go very slowly on account of the oxen. The wolves have already killed one and four have died. Fred and Mr. Saunders went out hunting this morning. Killed two young koodoo and Fred wounded a big bull at 500 yds. Looked for him a long time but could not find him. The big rocks around here are gray and the grass a light brown and the koodoo is a betwixt so they are very hard to find. They have gone out after them now with eight oxen and a brush sled. I have washed towels and an apron, baked a pan of bread and boiled a pudding, suet and dried peaches. Thought that they would surely be here by this time (3 P.M.). Can't wait any longer. R. has had a piece of bread but I have eaten nothing since breakfast.—There we had a cup of tea, some bread and a bit of roasted bill tong (jerky). It is delicious. Here they come with the trophies and they are beauties.

Sundown, and we have just trekked the long distance of one mile, but two of the boys bring in the news that the grass is burned so far ahead that we cannot possibly reach good grass tonight, so we have outspanned and the boys are dressing the bucks. Magnificent stream Roderick says there is just at the foot of this hill, and Fred reports beautiful valleys in the mountains and big streams that fall in cascades. Ideal places for homes but not entirely free from fever and we do not want a home unless it is. Fred says this is a *wonderful* mineral country, the best that he ever saw, and Matabeleland is reported as much richer and healthy. We did not go to Salisbury (168 miles of sandy road). Our donkeys would have been completely worn out, no good grass near and we would have had to stay around the fort for months maybe. So we will stay out here with Mr. Saunders for a month or six weeks, then go down to Johannesburg by this east road or by way of Tuli if the Matabele are still quiet. Then we will come into Matabeleland with the troops if they do not come during the fever months, as there is some low country to cross. If they do we will wait until the country is thrown open. Have written to Howard in Johannesburg and also telegraphed him to stay there. It would have been better if he had not started until we knew more, but of course we could not foresee this war. Would have been almost in Salisbury had it not been for that. I wrote *there* to have our mail sent down to Victoria, care of Mr. Cumming whose oxen are with us, and he will send them out to us by the boy that we send in shortly for news. I can hardly wait for the letters and should like "The Times" to hear about the World's Fair but we never expect to see them. It is getting cold now. I wonder if you are having warm weather now. You must be getting Jack breakfast now and is my little Glady awake. Don't let him forget his Aunt B. and ask him what he wants me to bring him from the black man's country. It is too dark to write any more. . . .

Aug. 16—Melosi 40 miles from Victoria. Latest news, 1000 men are going into Matabeleland the middle of next month. 150 from Salisbury, 250 from Victoria and the balance come in by way of Tuli. Will carry 9 Maxim guns. Each man is to be furnished with a horse, guns, ammunition and rations. Terms—no pay but 6000 acres of land, 20 mineral claims and half the loot (mostly cattle), officers and men share alike. Fred will go. We will stay out here as long as possible and then I will stay in Victoria until summer or go

to Johannesburg to Howard. Will wait to see how the cat jumps.
Am perfectly well now. Will commence another letter home to
mail when possible. Mr. Saunders is going in today. Oceans of love
to all my dear sister. Kiss Glady.
Your loving sister
Blanche

━━━━━━━━━

FRB, probably to Josiah Russell(fragment)

[Circa September 1893]

. . . Fearing things have gone wrong and my luck changed I
shall take military service with the Chartered Co. and go into the
war. I will go in an independent troop as scout and get as pay arms
and mount, rations (when possible) ½ of the spoils and 6000 acres
of land, 15 mineral claims and 5 alluvial. It will be a hard and desperate service but full of adventure and a chance to see unknown
lands for which in spite of the long trek I still love to see more. In
fact, I am infatuated with Africa. It is grand in size and life, is full
of possibilities and not carried on in such a hammer and tongs way
as in California. There will be 5 Americans, hardy restless nervy
men they are, who will be in the scouts.[1] There will be only 20
scouts and a total of 1000 men. We expect to begin the campaign
in 20 days. Probably it will be 50 though before we really cross the
border of King Lobengula's country and have our first fight with
his ebony soldiers. The tactics of Lobengula are defensive until the
rainy season so we must beard the lion in dry weather on horseback and not flounder through swamps surrounded by blacks in
wet season. Matabeleland is one of the finest countries in Africa.
Corn, wheat, rice and all semitropic products grow well. In fact
this country is all one could ask (Mashonaland) timber, beautiful
streams, flowing over rocky beds, fine climate to all appearances,
undulating and wooded, with some abrupt mountains and picturesque granite buttes. In fact lovely to the eye. Soil extremely
fertile. Just the country I thought, as I came through Providential
Pass, to stay in and help build a commonwealth where the cry of
"work or bread" should not be heard. But one thing failed me on

1. Bob Bain, Pete Ingram, Tex Long, and the Posselt brothers.

close investigation. I find that part of the year there lurks the awful fever, not the deadly sort, unless helped on by hard drink or natural proneness. But nevertheless not good enough to settle in after living in Pasadena and seeing Naples and Durban. But Matabeleland is *claimed* positively to be free from it and still rich and beautiful. A mission station of 16 yrs is fever free and they have turned over the soil and have orchards, gardens &c. If this be so my 6000 acres is worth about $1.00 [per] acre the moment peace is declared. Mineral rights about the same. However this is counting too fast. Should Matabeleland and westward prove healthy there is little doubt of my driving my pegs in its fertile soil. If unhealthy I shall sell them and still hunt through the unknown wilds for the spot that suits me.

. . . Long before *this* reaches you I hope all the financial troubles of June will be only a memory. . . .

. . . I think I can get a good start in this country by next year. But at present the hazard of a scout into Matabeleland seems most alluring. Trading with the natives is very profitable and I can make an easy living with a good rifle. Bye the bye, find out if a finely dressed lion or leopard skin would sell in Pasadena and would it need to be mounted. I will send you one and go halves on proceeds. They are worth from £5 to £10 each here according to condition. . . .

As to the ranch, I suppose $5000 net is a good price for it but I am so fearful that the temptation to draw on funds will eat all up that I had as leave let the ranch lay. Tis like your old farm in Iowa, a kind of anchor. I do not need any large sums to invest in Africa, if I cannot win with my hands and skill I cannot with money. In old countries money is essential but here the man with a few hundred is about as likely to win, say in 3 yrs, as the man with several thousand. If you have sent the 1000 by this time that should do me for a long time. We returned from the Gazaland road a few days ago learning the whites are to take the aggressive before the fever season. We never got a copy of Times and are hungry for political and local news, World's Fair, Cleveland, &c. &c. America is here what Australia is to us. There are now here in Fort about 250 soldiers, about 20 families, a wedding party at garrison tonight, and Blanche will get chance to air her Paris gowns for first time. We expect war to be over in 4 months. These blacks fight in masses and come in thousands, often at night, and if defeated will after about two fights surrender. The border tribes may require guerrilla war for 6 months longer. They use guns but mainly rely on the assegais[2] and weight of numbers. Lobengula is a crafty and well-posted black and is said to be adverse to fighting the whites but will have to please his bloodthirsty army. . . . We are now in a strictly African hut just under the brick wall of the Fort. It is shaped like a candle extinguisher, thatched roof, mud walls, and floor made of ant heaps and cow dung (really a smooth floor strange as it may seem). We have two big tents but the hut is far better. Plenty of savages, black shiny fellows very closely allied to the monkey. In fact it is a question whether the savage has not deteriorated from a respectable tribe of monkeys. These are the Mashonas (meaning filthy) which the Matabeles have for years raided and enslaved and in whose defense Exeter Hall[3] is to be roused if possible to sanction the movement of whites in conquering the Matabeles and incidentally gobbling up their land while we spread the light of Christianity (with gatlings and maxims and trained scouts).

I leave tomorrow to visit the ruins of an ancient African city and will write its description in my next. . . .

Yours ever,

Fred

———

FRB to Rebecca Russell Burnham

Victoria, Mashonaland
Sept 1st, 1893

Dear Mother,

It will be a long time without a letter from me when this reaches you, however the journal is a dozen or more in one and is to be yours after the family have had a chance to read it. We will send to J. S. Blick and write them to give it to you. We have no copy of it so hope it will not go astray. We are now returned from the Gazaland road as news came by runner to us that the Chartered Co. was going to take the aggressive and force the fighting and they are offering great inducements in shape of land grants

2. Assegai—a short spear used for stabbing rather than throwing.
3. Exeter hall—headquarters of the British Aborigine Protective Society.

and mining concessions. I am going to the war, and ere this reaches you we will be fighting the dusky hordes of Lobengula to decide the possession of Matabeleland. . . . However an active war is far preferable to garrison life in a fever country, and I was retreating out of it rather than pass in my checks inside its brick walls. But now we are to advance. 1000 men in arms. 250 from this fort, 150 from Salisbury and balance from Ft. Tuli and the Dutch Republic. It seems a small force to go against Lobengula who it is claimed can raise 80000 men. They fight mostly at night and come in thousands. They give no quarter and will get none. They have guns and some modern ones also but rely mostly on the assegais and weight of numbers. For the benefit of your missionary friends I will give a slight review of the true situation here.

England, in the rush for empire between the Christian nations to prevent other nations getting this part of Africa, gave it away to a company composed of her royal dukes, lords, &c. She gave an empire to which she had no shadow of claim and sanctioned the granting of a Royal Charter to perpetuate the power of the English nobility and try and build in Africa a dominion where no white man dare clamor for a vote or say so in the affairs of the country, everything being done by appointment and no appeal. The pretext on which the first white men came into Mashonaland was to open (friendly) relations with King Lobengula, made him handsome presents, 2000 stands of rifles, 2,000,000 rounds of ammunition and other Christian tokens of sincere friendship. For this concession Mashonaland proper was to be given the Chartered Company for its mineral rights alone. To the Mashona, whose country Lobengula had traded off, having learned that much from his Christian friends already i.e. trading off what his neighbors owned. To the Mashonas the Co. promised a millennium, the gospel and freedom from their lifelong oppressor, Lobengula, but at same time they allowed King Lobengula to collect his taxes. Now to the whites the Company, having for nothing acquired what they now owned, they gave farms and mineral concessions and collect taxes as though they were the English government themselves. So the country is now owned by the Mashonas, claimed by King Lobengula in the hands of the Chartered Co., and supposed to be under the British government. Out of this muddle but one result can come—*war*—and as greed is at the bottom of all it would have been far more open and above board to have simply invaded the country at first and told King Lobengula the Mashonas and whites we take this because we want more empire and have the strength to uphold our claims. But that is not the way of England or English diplomacy. She has given her word to the whites to open up all central Africa that we may trade and settle in it. To the Mashonas she has said we will take you under the shadow of our wing and the Queen sheds tears as she says her evening prayers at the wrong the Matabeles have imposed upon you. You shall know the oppressor no more. To the Matabeles she has said we only want to establish *friendly* relations and be allowed to exchange courtesies and eventually mix the noble blood of your house with our own nobility and so sail down the stream of time one lovely blended race of every shade from brindle to sorrel and pinto. As to our wanting your land, *impossible*, did ever an Englishman rob a neighbor (unless very much weaker).

To the Christian nations she has said we claim only a little colony at Cape Town and a few other small possessions, but of course we do not expect you to interfere with our sphere of influence which includes all that unknown region north of the equator, also all the known and unknown region south of the equator. All else we generously give as an Englishmen always does to you all and hoping you will not quarrel over this vast domain which we leave to you but rather join hands with and help shed the rays of the true Christian civilization until by the God above assisted by the Home Government and advised by our gracious Queen the whole world shall know the true light. (Please sing God Save the Queen and take your hat off while you sing.) Under all this bombastic talk of civilization remains the one fact that to the victor belongs the spoils. Lobengula conquered by and holds his scepter by strength and by greater strength will he be conquered and at this stage of the world's evolution the Caucasian in spite of his gloss is a mighty fighting animal and a little blood stirs him stronger than any race in the world. The battle fire is strong here in this fort. The recent fight and killing of 30 Matabeles has only whet the appetite and the cry is Matabeleland and never surrender. So fierce is the feeling that for amusement the men get up prize fights, dog fights, chicken fights, donkey fights, anything so it fights and King Lobengula is as sure to lose his empire as though it were already gone. Suppose he kills this 1000 men. It would but advertise to the world a bigger fight and thousands of Caucasians would come. Tis useless to try to stop the peculiar phase of conquest that will soon bring all savage tribes under the iron heel of the white. Prayers and tears and petitions and even money will not prevent it and tis better so. (Missionaries cut but little figure in the final end. Sometimes they hasten the country into the white man's grasp. Sometimes retard it a little.) In the fever belts the negro will reign supreme, so no fear of his extinction, in fact he increases in bondage more than in savagery in spite of his proneness to absorb every vice of the white and carefully guard losing any that he previously had. We are now to invade King Lobengula, and the garrison chaplain was last Sunday likening these Christian soldiers to the crusaders who invaded to spread the gospel. The next morning on the gate of the fort was a splendid drawing of the apostles to spread the light into Matabeleland with various bible quotations. Some wag had it down fine and Apostle Capt Lendy of Volunteers, Apostle Capt Wilson of Artillery, Apostle Chief Scout Burnham, &c. &c, and a picture of the cannon loaded with bibles and tracts to forcibly put into their thick skulls. This is the way and means of converting the Matabeles. A mission station of 16 years standing has only converted 3 Matabele, so tis now time to throw off the mask and capture the land by strength and hard fighting. All these things have been gone over with again and again in our Indian policy and we are the same as the English in our greed and breaking of treaties. Up to date, Christianity has for the black in Africa done nothing. If it has sown the seed, I fear it is a long time sprouting, or maybe the gifts to the cause of the heathen were tainted by a secret hope for big solitaire diamonds in heaven later on.

The great hunter and guide, Selous,[1] who has been so lionized in England is enroute here and I will have the honor of serving with him in the coming war. He is a little sawed off wiry chap very nervy, a splendid runner, very much of a gentleman, a dead shot, and very popular with the men. To part of the world we will be Apostles of civilization; to some freebooters and land pirates; to the Matabeles murderers and invaders; to the Mashonas what a lion is to a jackal, the giver of offal and stray bones hence wel-

1. Frederick Courtney Selous (1851–1917).

comed not loved. To the historians in later years we will but prove the continuity of evolution in the year 93–4. To the young and adventure hunting, and secretly that strain runs far into the life of many more men than one would at first believe, we will be considered lucky in falling upon stirring times. Some romances can take our dreary marches strewn with the bones of our dead oxen and horses and dotted by the graves of those of us who fell, our desperate fights in dead of night, our lovely camps beside swift rivers and among blue mountains the plains dotted with noble game, the earth a paradise, the solitary scout cut off from his command and selling his life as dear as possible, the lovely girl in the garrison who is in love with the capt., the grand country conquered by a handful of men, that countless thousands may settle in peace and quiet, the buildings of an empire on our smoldering bones. All these things flash before me as I write this my last letter to you before I am off to the war. But let the world class me as they choose murderer, apostles, pirate, invader or what not to you I am always Fred

I will write next week to you and home.
B.

━━━━━━━━━

BBB to Blick family

Victoria, Mashonaland, S. Africa
Sept 8, 1893

My dear family,
    . . . Sept. 9, Sunday evening and I am fearfully lonesome. Fred went out to a camp six miles west of here with Mr. Cumming to lead the cattle. Left this morning and will not come back until tomorrow. How can I ever stand it when they really go to the war and then added to the loneliness will be the suspense and anxiety. I tell him that if he gets through this alive he shall never go into another. Why *do* men love to fight. I cannot keep him out of this without making him lose his self-respect and be thought cowardly, and you know he would rather die than have that thought of him, so I cannot say much. He assures me that he was never born to be killed by a negro, and so I believe him most of the time but not al-

ways. How I wish some of you could be with me. I cannot even have Howard. No need to bring any more of us into danger. I might join him in Johannesburg, but the road is not perfectly safe, would have to go as passenger and without Fred, and I dread the long trek down and back again into Matabeleland. I will be nearer Fred if I stay here. They expect to march in within a couple of weeks and that the campaign will not last over two or three months and then we can go in there. Well enough of this subject, although it is all that interests us here. I have written six pages in the journal today which we will send off in this mail. Will send to you. Better get the family together and read it aloud and then give it to Mother Burnham. She will keep it for us as we have no copy and are very anxious to have it saved. Roderick will enjoy it when he is older. I am not going to destroy any more of your letters. Destroyed them all in Johannesburg except one from Madge and one from Uncle which we received the last day and read on the way out. Those were the last letters for three months. I kept them in my little handbag and read and reread more than a dozen times. Had such a big bundle on our return from Gazaland and then the next mail brought two from Uncle, one from home and two bundles of papers from Mother Burnham containing my ostrich feather and Roderick's birthday remembrances. He was so pleased even if there were holes worn in the false face so that it would not blow up and the puzzles were broken. He guesses that it was to be a pond with fish and pond lilies. I have told somewhere about his birthday in Africa. . . .

Monday evening. We got hungry for sweets today so I made some peanut candy. Fine success. Am afraid Fred and Roderick will have the nightmare if they eat much more. We have no fruit whatever that is fresh fruit, but vegetables are brought in once a week. Very nice but a nice price also. Lettuce 1s6d per dozen heads. Tomatoes [word indecipherable] a dozen small ones. Small but solid cabbage 9d &c. Meat 9d per lb. Mr. Cumming's boys and Mr. Couright returned the other day and our larder was enriched by a guinea fowl, about five pounds of fried reed bucks and fifty of fresh roan antelope. Am drying the latter today. It is too warm to keep long. We have rented a hut which have described in the journal. It is very cool and comfortable. A couple of cane chairs and a cot were in the hut. Use the cot for a lounge in the daytime and

Roderick's bed. Carry our rawhide frame outside and with a judicious stowing away of boxes for cupboards and tables we have room to swing the cot. Cook out of doors of course. Your home must begin to look like a picture and I am so glad that father should have a lovely yard and mother a finished and so prettily furnished a house. We will have to find a paradise to ask you to leave such a beautiful home. Fred is very hopeful and seems to have utterly forgotten all his past except his love for our relatives. . . .
Your loving
B.

Blanche Blick Burnham to Madge and Jack Ford

Oct. 24, 1893

My dear Madge and Jack,
   . . . I heard from several sources two or three days ago that Fred was distinguishing himself. That he had killed five Matabeles out of six shots. This morning a gentleman brought me a short note from him. Said that Fred wanted him to bring me two assegais, a shield and a pair of Matabele ears but he could not possibly carry them. I was *very very* glad to get the note. It was an unsealed note so I suppose he did not want to brag but I guess that report is true. Here is a copy of the little note. "We march at once and I get this in with Mr. Lloyds letter. We have had two fights. Main, Lynch, Dunn and I attacked an impi, killed twelve and captured 200 cattle. At ten o'clock we (the scouts) all got into a hot fight and killed ten more but Forbes lost one man. Everything OK and in good shape. This is a lovely country."
   You see the scouts are always in advance of the column. The column had had no fight as yet. Maybe the coach has brought some news. My letter is seven days old. They were marching ahead as fast as possible. Dr. Jameson, the administrator, is with our troops. There is another column coming in from the west and one from the south. They must be very near together now. The captured cattle were sent here. There are at least 100 men here, 27 women and I do not know how many children. The greater majority sleep in the fort. Mrs. Nelson and I have held out thinking home was more comfortable, but every day I would hear of others

going in to sleep, so yesterday I concluded that prudence was the better part of valor and made arrangements to sleep there. Captain Arnold thought our trap was too small and kindly loaned us his wagonette, small covered wagon. We were very comfortable last night. I think I have already written that I had had the buckboard and a box full of my best things taken into the fort. Mrs. Nelson has a little girl two years old, a son thirteen and then she has two black boys working for her. She thinks it is too much bother to go back and forth with the baby. Of course we could have tents and live in the fort entirely but the heat would be unbearable during the daytime when our thatched houses are *very* comfortable. Mrs. N. is *mad* because I have gone into the fort. She can come too but she will not. From what she has said I know if there was an alarm in the night, if I did not go over there, kick that stupid Richard into consciousness, help get the baby ready and follow them up to the fort, she would tell every one that I was a coward and deserted her. That is what she thinks now, I suppose. She has an awful tongue and thinks she is one of the most ladylike women in existence . . . but she is very kindhearted and I am sorry that she feels this way about my going to the fort. She said as I had left her alone at night she hoped I would in the daytime. I merely said, "All right Mrs. Nelson," and have not spoken to her all day. I am not used to such treatment and do not like it. Captain Arnold told me yesterday that he was very glad that I had decided to come into the fort and he wished everyone else would. They would have enough to do to defend the fort without hunting up those who slept outside. They have a very secure place to put the ladies in case of an attack. We do not really expect an attack unless the Matabele get the best of our forces but still you never know what may happen. We have only three foot pickets on the western edge of town. They rely mostly on the Makalaka[1] to bring us news. They cannot take the fort so do not worry about Roderick and I. Imperial troops are sixty miles below the Limpopo and are ready to help if necessary. Fred is so confident of coming out that I try not to think too much about it. . . .

Mr. Bowman gave Roderick seven painted pictures of U.S. warships, so each one of those has to be copied several times. He is

1. Blanche evidently means the Mashona, who were porters on the expedition.

as fond of ships as ever and looks forward to the time when he can
sail them with Uncle Jack. . . .
Your loving
B.

Kiss Glady.

━━━━━━━

BBB to Blick family

Victoria, Mashonaland
Nov. 2, 1893

Our dear ones at home,

Fortune favors you this time. I wrote all the news in Mother
Burnham's letter and posted it Tuesday evening but Cecil Rhodes,
the great, is on the coach which waited for dispatches at Ft. Charter
and will not put in an appearance until this evening, and in the
meanwhile Capt. Hurrell, who took dispatches from here sometime
ago, returned yesterday from the column and brought me a letter
from Fred which I will copy leaving out the "lovey parts" which are
for my eye alone. I know you are almost as anxious for news as I
am. In mother's letter I said the natives had brought in the report
that Buluwayo was captured. Capt. Hurrell says it can hardly be
true for our column was not to reach there until today. Still, the
other two columns may have been doing something. Well here is
Fred's letter. "We are in the heart of the enemies country and fighting every day but so far have had but one night attack on laager, loss
about 100 Matabeles, one hundred of our blacks and one white, and
several wounded. Please mail the enclosed at once. We could send
but one letter, so I curtailed my own to give [Duncan] Dollar and
[Art] Cumming a chance. This is a wonderful land in mineral, hundreds of quartz veins and one ancient working I have already found.
There are no swamps and the grass is short and sweet though dry.
We have kept on high veldt all the way and the captive Matabeles
say there is no fever. We are 4000, 5000, 3500 feet high all the time.
Plenty of timber, much like the Gazaland country, and blue mountain ranges which of course we avoid as much as possible. We are
now within 35 miles of Buluwayo and last night could count 28
campfires of the enemy. We will have a big fight soon but don't

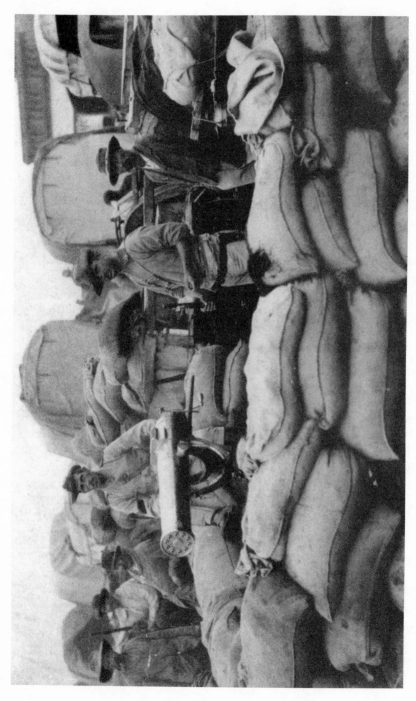

The Gatling gun supposedly used in the defense of Fort Victoria under the supervision of Blanche Burnham. From *Taking Chances*.

worry for the Kaffir can't shoot a *little bit* for we have only lost six men so far (except blacks). I have killed five Matabeles dead and wounded others to date. The last one I shot off my horse fair through the heart. They are not lacking in courage but can't shoot straight enough. We will have the country at our disposal inside 30 days. (You know how sanguine Fred is so take that 30 days with a big grain of allowance, but how I would love to believe it.) And you shall come on to Buluwayo with Dollar and Cumming teams most likely. I see a thousand chances to make money and I like the country fine. Tis a splendid cattle country and horses will live, which is good news you know. But our poor brutes are mere skeletons now from constant work and then they were poor when we started. There is a roar about the size of my letter and I hear the boom of our cannon firing on a big kraal as I write this note. The kraal is now in flames and the cannon booming. This is the chief's kraal that attacked Victoria and we will have a fight no doubt tonight from his regiment. I have a thousand tales of adventure to tell you and Roderick, comical, pathetic and exciting. All our past journal is dull and tame to what could be said of this trip into the unknown parts of Matabeleland. Hoping and believing you are in good hope and spirits and that when this reaches you Buluwayo will have fallen, I must close as we are to go to the front at once and the horses are being saddled. Evidently they need support for the guns, &c, &c, &c."

He seems in good spirits does he not? Mr. Clark has just brought me the news which was read out at parade this P.M. In that night attack there were 5000 Matabele, 400 of them killed, two white men, one missing and four wounded. They stood on their arms until the moon came up, then went to sleep. Their Makalakas were all out around the camp and when the Matabele made the rush those that were not killed were driven along with them in the rush and were killed by our men. The fight lasted from 4 A.M. until 6:30. They [Matabeles] say they are not afraid of the rifles but do not like to charge the machine guns. The next day three troops went out and killed 100 more and then next day Capt. Lendy took out one of the guns, shelled one of the kraals, drove them all out, set fire to everything, and captured some cattle. All around Buluwayo are regiment kraals, just the warriors, no families. These are what they have been attacking. They had captured some cattle but lost them in the night attack. Capt. Hurrell says this night attack was a good thing. Our men were beginning to think victory was too easy a thing.

How is your African fever now Johnny? Don't you wish you were here? Now I will answer some of your letter. Thank you very much for the interest you have taken in the saw mill. . . . So glad that you are going to take the same course of study. Tell Ray that we fully expect him to come over with you. I will be a mother to both of you and keep you from taking too many Kaffir wives. Read him Fred's account of Matabeleland. My hopes are away up again and we all will yet live together somewhere in the heart of Africa. No catalogues as yet but will doubtless put in an appearance in good time. Fred has described the Victoria saw mill in the journal. From previous letters you know that that young man's account of the fever is correct, but last year was an exceptionally bad one all over Africa. He is entirely wrong about our starving to death as I have explained at length in mother's letter. You made the mistake when you told him 40,000 in Salisbury. Fred said Johannesburg. Several hundred in Mashonaland. Not many families last year but there are 27 women and 37 children in Victoria and a great many more in Salisbury. I will send you a Salisbury paper. Tell that young man that we *did* get here with our six donkeys and never stuck in a drift or had to beat them up a hill.[1] I do not know whether we told you that they were afraid our boxes would get wet in crossing the Crocodile so we put most of our load on the wagons but the donkeys went through so bravely that we never offloaded a single thing for any of the other rivers. So Fred's raft stories did not come true. The rivers were low, fortunately. We did not have to pass through any fly belt, and there is none between here and Salisbury but there is between Salisbury and Beira. He must have starved his donkeys. We fed ours mealies. The Zambezi is way north of Salisbury.

. . . Seems to me someone asked about the ants. The white ants work in the walls and floors so that valuable things must be set up on bricks or boxes. But there are no ants to bother our food. Borers eat all the native timber so in all old houses you find things

---

1. Reference to a Pasadena man who was predicting failure and doom for the Burnhams.

sifted over with a yellow dust. Roderick wants to write to Chum so good night. With love much kisses.

Your loving daughter and sis

Blanche

———

FRB to Josiah Russell

Tati, Matabeleland
Nov. 8, 1893

Dear Uncle,

The last letter to you I think gave you the news of war and that I would take service with the B.S.A. as scout and get certain concessions of land, mineral rights, &c. I will try and give as well as I can the events as they occurred. The column left Victoria, 400 men with several Maxim guns and one 7 pounder and one Hotchkiss. We crossed the Shashi River on the 1st Oct. which was the border of Matabeleland and from natives learned that an impi (regiment) of the enemy were within 5 miles. We advanced slowly through a lovely well wooded country dotted with enormous buttes of granite of most fantastic shapes and the home of the Mashonas or slave tribe of the Matabeles. They build their huts under and in these enormous rocks and till little patches of corn, rice, beans, &c. in the surrounding valleys. We raided them for food supplies, goats, fowls, cattle. When they had them, and as we were fighting their lifelong enemies the Matabeles, they were told to charge the account to profit and loss, but so mild was our raiding compared to the Matabele that they took it as a joke and followed our column in the hundreds to live off the offal and get a chance to loot the Matabele if we should conquer. They are a cowardly, cringing, thankless lot of dirty beasts to say the most, lacking even that one redeeming quality with many savage races, courage. Westward on the watershed between the Zambezi and Crocodile Rivers, through as beautiful a land as ever an English army stole, we reached a mountain of iron used by the natives for ages to make their spears and hoes of. The trails leading to it could be seen for 30 miles. Here we were to meet 300 men and guns, Gatling and Maxims, from Ft. Salisbury, but the columns missed each other and heavy scouting was required. I was successful in finding the column and passing the camps of the

Matabele who did not attack the single columns as they should have done from their point of war. Five of us then took the trail of an impi driving a large herd of cattle. We followed them all night and at daybreak located them in a large valley not far from the iron mountain and knowing the columns were only a few miles apart. One man I sent back for reinforcements. Looking into the valley was an interesting sight. About 100 men were ½ mile in advance of the herd of cattle. We could see their shields and guns. About the same number were 1½ miles behind, while in the middle was a cattle guard of about 48, driving the cattle up the valley and into the mountains. I knew they would have them into the mountains before aid came to us, so made up my mind to attack and check them at any rate. Four of us rode down this mountain direct toward the soldiers in the lower end of the valley. They evidently did not think it possible for 4 men to attack them, for they are armed with the same rifle we carry. We rode straight for them until within 500 yds, then turned and went up the valley like a flash and before the cattle guard realized what was up we [were] onto them. We killed 12 in less than 5 minutes and they were so excited their bullets flew wild, while we hardly missed a shot. We rushed the cattle out of the valley but were attacked by advance guard. These we fought for some time but they recovered about 200 of the 500 head from us, we getting clear with 300 which were turned over to the column. Being reinforced by 10 scouts, we returned to the attack and again fought the advance guard but they suddenly brought over the mountain 1000 men and gave us volley after volley. Some of them are very plucky and one of their chiefs singled me out, coolly walked out of cover, threw down his shield and blanket, and began shooting at me. I dismounted, knelt on the ground with my bridle resting on my arm, and we both poured lead to each other at a lively rate. He was a fairly good shot, grazing my head and throwing dirt in my face the first and second shots, but skill and blood must tell and his shield and spears are now my trophy. But the situation was getting serious and we were forced to retire. We lost that day Capt. Campbell[1] and several horses, some slight wounds among ourselves. This was the opening fight with the Matabeles. From that time on I was in the saddle almost night and day more or less, fighting all the time but not in large force, crossing

---

1. Captain John Alexander Livingston Campbell, first white casualty of the campaign.

some lovely plateaus dotted with herds of various kinds of game and camping on the extreme headwaters of the Tok Lundi and other rivers of size which here are only little streams heading in park-like valleys. We are in a wonderful mineral country, gold veins and ancient works abound and many fine samples showing free gold were brought into camp every day. We raid and burn and destroy everything as clean as Sherman's men did in Georgia. On the River Shangani the Matabele made their first stand. About 5000 of them rushed on the laager about 4:00 A.M. and speared about 300 of our men, the (black watch) native contingent and recovered about 400 head of cattle which we had raided from them. The scene is hard to describe. The steady whiz of the Maxim, the shrieks of the speared men, blowing of bugles, shouts of officers and a perfect blaze of flame from our regiments into a corresponding blaze in the bush around us, horses surging on the picket lines and shrieking from wounds or snorting with fear, the boom of the 7 pounder and bursting of shells was a scene never to be forgotten. For we were in the heart of the enemy's country without hope of escape if whipped. The bush thick, the night quite dark, thankful we were for daylight when the deadly skill of our rifles and Maxims soon sent the enemy into the rocks over the hills with a seven pound shell bursting at their heels to remember us by. We killed about 200 men. We lost about 20 horses, 400 head of cattle and 300 men. We broke camp and left the bodies to lay in the bush for vultures and hyenas and a good place for some medical student to get a sample of thick skulls mixed with a few thin ones. Now the heavy work of the scouts began. Incessant tiresome creeping out at dead of night, riding and watching and listening, sometimes cutting our way through killing those in front of us and getting a shower of lead from those on either side. Two of us were 40 hours in the saddle and once entirely surrounded, but they wanted to take us alive (to torture) so did not shoot us when they could and we baffled them, for a heavy mist came up and we crept through the black circle.[2] They gave us up for dead at the columns. We rode within sight of Buluwayo and slept within hearing of the crack regiment of the king. We then made a desperate effort to get in communication with the army from the south under Lt.

2. A reference to Burnham and Bob Vavasseur searching for the Chief's Mountain (Intabas Induna) that marked the road to Buluwayo.

Col. Goold-Adams. We failed. 4500 warriors were in front of him and several thousand in front of our columns. But at a point about 10 miles east of the Chiefs Mountain the crack regiment of King Lobengula made their great rush. So insolent and egotistical were they that they refused the aid of other regiments and said they would show the white man what fighting was, and for the other part of Loben's army to watch. We had just formed laager on a little rising ground, the nearest timber being about 400 yds away. The native regiments formed up in this timber and charged in splendid shape and with wonderful pluck. Nothing but death could stop many of them, but under such a fire as we poured in a bird could not have lived long, and in a few moments the crack regiment was no more. Only a handful of them left. We killed 1000. Though from a vantage point to the west an attempt very nearly successful was made to stampede our horses, and only a few mounted men were holding 600 horses on herd. These came under a crossfire and let the horses go. Volunteers were called for and with the bullets throwing a cloud of dust about them they dashed through and by hard riding turned the herd toward the regiment's laager. We were safe, for had we been left on foot in this country. Tis very doubtful if this letter or any other of mine would have ever reached you, for the Matabele is a wonderful runner and uses both rifle, shield and spear. A bayonet is no match to his spear, but the swift movements of cavalry prevent his rushes and the deadly shooting of the white man and his machine guns finish him off. The bulk of the nation are very little above the average nigger in bravery, but the old Zulu stock of which crack regiments were mostly formed, had a splendid courage. Numbers of the Imbeso regiments hung themselves rather than retreat to their [indecipherable]. Next day we had more fighting and while the attack was being made on our right flank and answered by the 7 pounder and Maxim, 3 of us slipped out on the swiftest horses on the left flank, cut through the few men on that side and rode toward Buluwayo, the capital supposed to be 12 miles to our west. We saw few natives and had no fight but found the city in flames. All the storehouses of the king, ivory, hardwoods, ammunition, powder, &c. had been burned. We heard the explosion and saw a cloud of smoke and dust that cost $100,000 go skyward. The king had really abandoned the city 8 days before but did not fire it until he heard of the defeat of his regiments. Old King Lobengula is, for a savage, not so bad as he might be. He will not torture a prisoner (though his men will) and when he left his capital he left two white traders there with their entire stock of goods and a guard to protect them. But his burning parties were just going to kill them and had scared off the king's guard when we three rode up. Not knowing white men were alive in Buluwayo we came near shooting them for the enemy. Finding the situation critical, I sent two men to the column and I stayed to help the traders stand off the raiders till aid came which was just in the nick of time as they were gathering in the rocks above the magazines to clean us out next day.

Nov. 4th the column formed laager in the capital of Matabeleland. The war is not over yet for Loben with thousands of warriors is north of us, but tis the beginning of the end, and then as fine a country as it has yet been England's privilege to steal will be thrown open to the restless, ever-conquering white man. King Loben will probably be made a chief under British rule still but his cutthroat regiments will be scattered to the winds or gathered into missionaries' folds according to the point of view. That afternoon, Nov. 4, loaded with cablegrams, &c. I was given a chance to again win land and a little honor if I could cut my way through to Tati on the south, 125 miles. I had several close calls but am here safe and sound and expect to ride from here to Buluwayo with return despatches in hours and beat the record.[3] I shall bring B.B. to Buluwayo as soon as possible, for while all the buildings are burnt the whites will soon build more and besides the old site is not good being short on water and on rocky ground. The new town will probably be built near the king's private palace, a few miles from the present site and on a good stream of water. My principal companion in most of my hard rides is a California lad about 22 yrs old.[4] He has good nerve and is a fine fellow. The Chartered Co., by this master stroke in whipping King Loben, has probably prolonged its life in this country and certainly quadruped the value of its shares. Its terms to settlers and miners are much better than they were and opportunity for energetic men to do well is not lacking either in their service or on individual account. The country is free from fever, well grassed, timbered and watered. Tis crossed by sev-

3. Burnham carried the news of Buluwayo's fall and Lobengula's flight to the outside world.

4. Pete "Pearl" Ingram.

eral ranges of mountains about the size of the coast range, climate about same as Sonoma County on the plateaus, getting warmer as one comes to lower altitudes. At Hope Fountain, a missionary station 25 miles from Buluwayo, oranges, bananas, &c. do well, in fact tis Los Angeles County, but at Buluwayo the ice forms one inch thick sometimes. The rainy season is about 4 months and is heavy, Dec. Jan. Feb. Mar., 30 to 40 inches, but the rains are warm rains. It being summer all kinds of grasses do well and horses live after once being salted to the country. Cattle do splendid, also small stock. It would take pages and pages to tell a tithe of all that has happened in the last month or describe the strange life and country, but I feel you will eat porridge with us at our house in New Buluwayo and go out to my 20,000 acre farm a few miles off or go up Matopo mountains and inspect the workings of the 10 stamp mill.

Yours as ever
Fred

───────

Blanche Blick Burnham to Josiah Russell

Victoria
Nov. 20, 1893

Dear Uncle,

I was going to write to you this week, but received this long long letter from Fred to send to you. He and Pete Ingram carried the despatches which I wrote about last week to Tati. And while waiting there for answers [wrote] me two letters. I was envied by everyone for I was the only one who received a letter. While it contained no later news, it told details. Said I would hear again in about two weeks so am impatiently waiting. I am to write to him at Buluwayo. So much writing to do this week that this letter will have to do for all in California. I am trying to get all the old writings copied into the journal before Fred comes back. Have just finished copying his letter to you in the journal. Must write to Miss Cumming of Johannesburg who wrote asking me for any news that Fred might write. Her brother[1] is one of the scouts. Must write to Howard. I wish it would rain. The days are quite sultry. It looks

1. Art Cumming.

very threatening this P.M. Fred seems to be in the good graces of all the officers especially of Dr. Jameson, the administrator, and seems very hopeful of the future. Well I hope the Burnhams will soon be together in Buluwayo. I do not like living alone although Roderick is a great comfort to me. Time passes much pleasanter than I thought it would.

Tuesday P.M. Mrs. G. and I drank tea with Mrs. Clark and spent the rest of the P.M. at the tennis court. Wednesday P.M. shooting match between the burghers and volunteers. Ladies invited to drink tea, lemonade or ginger ale. The gentlemen drank something stronger. Thursday Mrs. G. was here, spent the day with her. Friday, Saturday, Sunday and today have been cooking, sewing or writing. The pastor here drinks like a fish and is a hypocrite, so the congregations are gradually falling off. Thank you for the paper clipping. Has anyone kept the articles copied from Fred's letters and how do you like the journal? Of course I am saving all the letters for him. Received mother's containing one from Howard which I will send tomorrow. One year ago and Roderick and I were at home. I cannot write a long letter but I am sure I could talk. Love to all your family.

With love,

B.

———

FRB to BBB (fragment)

November, 1893

I dare write not a moment longer. If you have no funds from home yet, you will I fear be short of funds to buy food to come in with, but the transport you need not pay, as I can arrange that at this end and any wagons going to Bulawayo will take you collect here. You see I am figuring on my not getting off to Victoria, for the war is not yet ended and Lobengula and 10000 men have run north but it is quiet at Bulawayo, Loben having burned his ivory stores, 2500£ power and 80000 rounds of ammunition and the entire town. 6 hours before Pete and I rode up we heard the explosions and saved the outside traders' buildings and rescued two white men. All things will be explained when I hold you in my arms again, for now I have tales to tell that would put Othello in the shade.

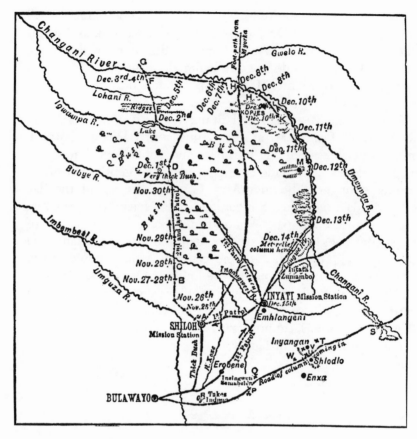

Map of the Bulawayo Campaign, showing the line taken in the attempt to capture King Lobengula. From *Scouting on Two Continents.*

I still have Roderick's letter in my pocket.
Goodbye love,
Fred

BBB to Rebecca Russell Burnham

Victoria, Mashonaland
Dec. 19, 1893

Dear Mother,

. . . Mr. Cumming arrived last Thursday and said that when he left, Fred had gone with a patrol to capture Lobengula. Did not expect to be gone more than two weeks and then Dr. Jameson had promised him a good horse to come immediately to Victoria. They must have had to go farther and the roads are very bad now on account of the rains. This going without news is very, very trying. A very sad Christmas it will be for me if Fred is not here but I shall not give up hope until the day is over.

Four men are in on leave and all are loud in their praises of Fred. Say Dr. Jameson says that if there were ten Burnhams, Lobengula would have been captured weeks ago. It is very pleasant to hear such things. Will tell you more in my next.

Yours lovingly
B.

Part II
1894
African Pioneers

Burnham (second from right, kneeling) and fellow scout Pete Ingram (far left, standing) pose for this photo taken right after the first Matabele war. From *Scouting on Two Continents*.

BBB, recipient unknown

Fortune has favored us as usual for while it rained every day last month and the roads were almost impassable, some of the teams ahead of us having to throw off part of their load and then pull out sometimes with as many as six span. You see this is an entirely new road, never traveled over until the column came in last October. One of our carts just now upset in crossing one of the little spruits, but no damage done, only a little delay. We are going to outspan anyway. Will be at our destination day after tomorrow and then for our first mining in Africa.

Did I write you about Fred's arrival in Victoria? . . . all of Victoria rode out in wagonettes, drawn by oxen, to a beautiful fig grove, for a picnic. The gentlemen had furnished all the provisions and hired them prepared so we were not all tired out with cooking. A beautiful lunch and lemonade soda water, ginger ale and stronger drinks without limit. All sorts of games and everyone enjoying themselves immensely. Running matches in progress when we saw two horsemen riding up. There comes Mr. Burnham said the magistrate, for he is the only man in the country who has that kind of a hat. Roderick's keen eyes saw him in a minute and with a cry of papa, papa, he dashed off down the road followed a *little* more sedately by his mother, and such a reception as the people gave him. He has made a fine record and is more talked of I do believe than any man in the column, at least by the Victoria people. They never saw such scouting, such daring and such wonderful escapes. But he brought sad news for Mrs. Greenfield. Fred, Mr. Ingram and Mr. Gooding were sent for reinforcements and were the only men who escaped out of the 32. Major Wilson was not going to send Ingram but Fred asked for him and so as it turned out saved his life. . . .

He brought a little Mashona boy, age about 13, from Victoria for my especial servant, but we had only been a few days on the road when met some wagons returning from Buluwayo and the boys told long yarns about fever and all the boys dying in Buluwayo. He wanted to go back but we told him we were not going to B. but when morning came he was gone. The next day we came to

Questerds kraal. Q. is a native commissioner. Bought some meal there and got another boy for me. The boy had to get his wardrobe ready so Mr. Q. brought him down to our camp in the evening. Mr. Q. ate supper with us. He had not sat at the table with a woman for six years. Said that many of the blacks at his kraal, my boy among them, had never seen a white woman before and were talking all the P.M. about me, how I was dressed, how I wore my hair, my hat and how fast I sewed. (I was mending clothes while waiting there.)

Jack [Ford] seems to insinuate that the ladies of our family are not quite so enthusiastic about Africa as they were before this black trouble, but that will all be settled before long. The old king is not captured yet but all the quartz part of the country is considered safe, so we are going in to open up this mine. Fred will write and explain the ways and means in a note to Homer. Our camp will consist of Mr. Ingram, Banes [sic; Bob Bain] and Reed (all Americans) and a host of blacks. I do not know Reed but you will remember the names of Ingram and Banes who formed part of our party for some time on the "lion road." Ingram has been Fred's chief companion on all of his rides and came back to Victoria with him but went on a few days ahead of us to take care of some transport at the mine for us.

[Portion of letter missing] . . . sometime in April so you need not delay writing on that account. Now I have scolded enough. You will think Africa has spoiled my temper, but you must admit that I have had provocation. I do not include you and Homer or Daisy and Joe in my scolding because your letters were unexpected but very, very welcome. Write again. I am so glad that you are doing well and like your little home so much. This country is not so beautiful as Pasadena because it has not the mountains, but still it is a very pretty country, especially at this time of year when everything is so green. It rivals Cal. for wild flowers. Roderick is so happy all day long. He walks most of the time in order to gather flowers. Keeps our tent (covered wagon) full. Twists the flowers into all sorts of shapes making everything out of them from an angel down to a tadpole or vice versa. Fred says as we are tadpoles in the first stage but wind up as angels, the wind up is far off. . . . The country is covered with trees but not large ones. We are getting away from Victoria before the fever season and if

Matabeleland or portions of it are free from fever it is a good enough country for us. We will make you a visit [following line inserted in FRB's hand] (as soon as I found a little empire or rather join the Rhodes scheme of a U.S. of Africa).

———

FRB to Josiah Russell

[Circa January 1894]

Dear Uncle,

I believe that this account sent exclusively to the [San Francisco] Examiner would be worth $200 or at least something; could you forward a copy to Examiner and send the letter on to Mother. I also want a copy returned to me here to put in our journal. So you could take this to some copyist and let them make a typewritten manifold. Send Mother one and one to me. Keep one and the other send to Examiner. I know they paid well for Mashonaland news, and maybe they might like a letter once a month or so from Africa if good, and the proceeds could go to Mother. I would send this to her direct but she may be in N.Y. yet. But it is evident I am not born to be killed by Matabele, although 3 out of 32 is a pretty small percentage to run on and picked careful men at that.[1] . . .

Yours of Nov 15th 1893 just at hand. I am just leaving Victoria for Matabeleland to open up some mines for Cecil Rhodes who is backing me. I have a big mineral and land concession extra as payment for the desperate services rendered the Co. during the war. Prospects bright. Rains heavy but will pull through some way. Have 4 big cargoes of supplies. I am still on the Co.'s staff and hold myself in readiness to take field at head of scouts if need be at any time. . . . Address us Buluwayo Matabeleland Africa. I will write much more on road. Send by black runner to post office 100 miles away. We will be midway between Victoria and Buluwayo, a lovely country. Yours as ever

F.

1. Referring to Major Allan Wilson's patrol. Burnham was one of the survivors of the massacre of December 4, 1893.

BBB to Linnie and Homer Blick

Forty Miles from Victoria
On the Road to Matabeleland
Jan 13, 1894

My dear Linnie and Homer,

. . . Now we have started for the mines, Burnham Syndicate, on the Gwelo River halfway between Victoria and Buluwayo. Our mail will be forwarded to Buluwayo and we may send in occasionally but one hundred miles is a long distance to go for mail. But we will be in Buluwayo.

My boy (no one except blacks are called boys here) is about seventeen, very grave and sedate and nearly falls over himself in his eagerness to do my bidding. Have to do a great deal of showing because I cannot speak the language. When I cannot make him understand, one of our drivers who understands English helps me. Machamcoola is a Maholi (a slave tribe in Matabeleland). He wears a leather apron in the back and a strip of blanket about a foot wide and one and a half long in front with a streamer or two of blue calico. Wrists and ankles adorned with brass and leather bracelets. In the morning and evening he wears a blanket and very gracefully too. Let one end fall over the other and tie the string around the neck. He has bargained to stay with us two months. Then he will go back for a visit and either return or another is sent if we please. We are all learning the language. They are going to inspan now so must close. Yes, we would like little Ruth's picture very much. I know that she is sweet and good. Roderick plays a great deal about Fred. Love to all the Blick family and I hope that there are ever so many letters on the road for us. Our letters are for all. Much love and kisses for the little ones.
Your loving sister,
B.

BBB to Blick family

Burnhams, Gwelo River
Feb 6, 1894

The dear ones at home,

 . . . Although it had rained every day for over a month we had a few clear days before our departure, and only two little showers during our whole trip. About 150 miles for we had to drive around so many valleys (vlays). The wagon we rode in never stuck but once but the other one stuck several times on account of young bullocks not knowing how to pull. The roads are impassable to heavily loaded wagons during rainy weather. We spent one day on the road inoculating the young bullocks with lung sickness. One of the oxen had this sickness so Mr. Posselt shot him, took the liquor (not the blood which would blood poison [lead to blood poisoning in the animal]) from the lungs, mixed it with water and poured half a cupful down each bullock, and that was the last of the lung sick. If any animal had it at the time of inoculation it would die but fortunately none of ours had.

 The Posselts[1] have taken up farms near here and have gone into Buluwayo to register. We arrived here Jan. 21. Have had several rainy days since then. Fred and Mr. Bain went into Buluwayo with the Scotch cart on the 23 and did not get back until the 3rd. Fixed up a pretty good camp while they were away. We sleep in the big wagon and use the front part of it for a storeroom. We are away up off the ground and perfectly dry. All my boxes and valises are in the wagon. Our dining room is a Company tent 10 × 16 with 5 ft. walls. A big wagon sail for an awning all over it so it is dry as well as cool. The three men have also a tent with a thatch awning. The cook house is thatched with canvas sides. Mr. Reed sleeps in the buckboard. The other men in their tent. Around these "buildings" we have good scherm [barricade] of thorny brush. We have a good sized paddock enclosed with brush for our stock at night, 26 oxen, 5 horses and 3 donkeys (and more coming). Will have some milch cows, beef cattle and sheep and goats (and chickens if there are any to be had at the Insukameni Kraal: where two of the men have gone for corn (orders from the Company). The corn stored in that kraal belonged to Lobengula but belongs to the white man now. The boys who work at the mine have a hut half way between the mine and our scherm.

---

1. The Posselt brothers, William and Harry, were the sons of American missionaries but were raised in Africa.

We have a colonial boy for a cook and he does very well. We eat in our own tent. They made me a nice big table and we brought chairs from Victoria. Mr. Cumming brought me a folding chair made of fine iron slats from the missionary station at Inyati. The houses at the missionary stations were *very* well furnished and so large and comfortable. But they were forced to leave them and will find nothing but the buildings if they return. First the Matabeles raided them, then a set of toughs who came up from below with [Lt. Col. Goold-]Adams' column, and now the hospital has taken anything that was left. They were beautiful places and are still reserved as missionary stations. Mrs. Colenbrander, the interpreter's wife, has returned to Buluwayo and is the only white woman there now. Fred did a good stroke of business while in town. No money in it but very convenient. Got Dr. Jameson to send native runners with letters from Buluwayo to Charter with our place for half way. Fred guarantees to see that the runners are looked after and go on their routes. There will be eight in all so there will be two here all the time. First ones are expected in this evening. Wonder if they will bring us any letters. They will stop here while those from Insukomeni will leave for Charter tomorrow.

Feb. 10—The runners came day before yesterday but had no mail for us. Almost too soon to get any as it was sent to Buluwayo by the long route. But will come now via Charter, in less than a week. Three runners came from Buluwayo. They are nearer pure blood Matabele and feel far superior to the ones Mr. Ingram and Mr. Cumming brought yesterday. They have longer heads and sharper features although the others are much sleeker and glossier looking. The blacks have not returned to the Insukamany [sic] Kraal but are still with Lobengula. So, Mr. Ingram went to the Mavene Kraal adjoining. The rain got into the pits where the king's corn was stored and it is all rotting. A great shame when food is so scarce. They managed to get 1½ sacks of ground millet, 2 sheep and four goats and also brought four men as mail carriers. This kraal had been raided while off fighting for the king by the Makalangas. We sent two carriers on to Charter. I made a mistake. There will always be four or five staying here. They do not like to work and wanted to do nothing while waiting here (a week) but sleep, eat and have someone to wait on them. Have always had slaves to work for them but they find that life will be a little different now. They had to make their own hut and have had to grind their own food. (Some of the corn and millet is not ground and the boys working in the mine must have what is ground.) Scoff (food) we must have for the boys if we do any developing work, so Mr. Ingram took the Scotch cart again with some trading goods and went to some other kraals.

Monday—Feb. 12. Returned yesterday with eight sacks of meal (and eight more bargained for and Johannes [Colenbrander] has gone after them today) and three boys. Eight more boys coming today. Have only been sinking two shafts. Will start more tomorrow. Mr. Ingram brought me a little boy about ten or eleven years old named Zonia. He is to stay at least a year and then we give his father a cow and calf when we send him back. They (people) say that when you make a bargain like this with their father that he tells the boy that he belongs to *you* and must stay and generally does. Then give them clothes to wear and teach them what white man's food and tobacco tastes like and they will come back to you even if they do go home in a year. Well I sincerely hope so for you no sooner get one taught to do a few things than away he goes. In Natal you enter into contracts with them for different lengths of time. They can be brought back if they leave you and you in your turn are *bound* to pay them wages, but there are no such laws as yet under the Chartered Co. I told you about Gundan running back to Victoria because he heard stories of fever and about my new boy Machamcoola. He was learning *a little* when a few days after reaching camp Mr. Ingram gave him an old shirt and a pair of trousers. He felt so proud then, especially when Fred gave him some hide to make sandals (he wanted to work at them all the time), that he burned the scones (baking powder biscuits baked on a gridiron over coals, delicious) in the morning and in the P.M. burned the beans. That was a little too much so he was sent to help build the scherm around the paddock and Tom, the leader for the big wagon which we do not drive any more, was made cook for the whole camp. He is a colonial, could understand and talk a little English so I soon taught him to make sour dough bread, scones and cook our staple articles of diet, beans, rice, meat, and make tea and coffee. He was quick and neat. The boy that herds the stock does the washing so I was having a very lazy time when four days ago Fred sent Paul, the driver of the big wagon, with ten oxen of Sir John Willoughby's into Buluwayo. (We keep 16 oxen belonging to the Co.) Tom wanted to go too said he had a brother in Buluwayo from Natal. So we let him go. They are no good when they want to leave, so now we have another new, raw boy. I always disliked to hear women talk about their servants, but ours are *black heathens* and all their little peculiarities are unknown to you, so I am sure of your interest and here is another little incident. The second day after we reduced Machamcoola's rank he came to the tent and with a most doleful look said he was Maningy, sick boss. Maningy sick. We thought he was shamming and Mr. C. suggested giving him a dose of jalap,[2] but it not being convenient gave him an immense dose of quinine (and such quantities as they take in this country). But the poor chap really had the fever and very bad too. Castor oil and quinine are the remedies. He would not eat for two or three days and then we *made* him. He said he was going to die but we did not propose that he should die here, so gave him beef extract, cooked cornstarch, rice &c. He was not *going* to swallow, but just stand over them and say piisa, piisa and let on as though you would kill them if they did not and you can make them drink anything generally. If not, a "hiding" will make them. He got so weak that he could not stand without the aid of a stick and got so poor it gave you the horrors just to look at him. He came from a very sickly place on the Shasi [sic] River. The fever had left him but he was still too weak to be of any use so sent him home on a passing wagon a few days ago with an order from Dr. Jameson for some cattle from his kraal. Have had to dose several others but they have been all right again in a day or so. How would you like dosing the negroes, Madge? We have two big boxes of medicine. There are two doctors in Victoria and also two in Buluwayo, and will very likely be one in this township next dry season. We expect this to be quite a place, but will wait a few months before building. It is 6,000 above sea level while Victoria is not 4000. I was well enough in Victoria but Roderick (I would not tell you then) had several attacks of diarrhea and had had it steadily for over a month when we left V. and had a very poor appetite. We had not been out of there for a week before he was perfectly well and is getting plump and rosy-cheeked again. He is so happy here and busy all day long. He is learning the language and can "boss up" the negroes and make them work as well as anyone. He flourishes a lit-

2. Purgative drug.

tle jambok (whip) and says "Subenza! Chacha now!!" (work—quick)
"Yah boss" they say. They seem to think he is very cute, but I will
not let him play with them so they consider him a little master.
Fred and I are too good to them and I expect we will be hum-
bugged many a time. But if we are too easy the other men are not.
All the old Afrikanders and old timers say the rougher you treat the
blacks the better they are and the more respect they have for you.
The old Boers are the best masters. Civilize and educate them and
they are spoiled, think they are as good as white men and become
saucy, cunning and thieving. It is a hard thing to say but no one
wants missionaries' servants. Still I do not believe I could be mean
to them. I wish there were no blacks in Africa. It would be a beautiful country. No I have not overcome my fear of them entirely and
there are so many in our camp now. Our tents are about ⅛ of a mile
from where they are working on the reef and whenever I am alone
here, all the men at the reef or off prospecting, I keep the loaded six
shooter where I can touch it with my hand. They do not come to
my tent except the kitchen boys, and the wild ones are respectful
enough. I do not get at all nervous or afraid but you know I always
feel better and easier in my mind when I have a six shooter. Are we
not gaining experience? Plenty of spice in our lives. But I am getting old. Feb. 25: less than two weeks makes me *thirty-two* years old.
I do not think that I feel any older except that I have learned so
much more, but the silver hairs are increasing in number rapidly
and some more crows feet around my eyes. But, wonderful to re-
late, my head is full of new hair and I have a regular fringe in the
back from ear to ear and—it is quite curly—not kinky. What do you
think of that for Africa? My hair came out on the road up here but
it is more than making up for it now. All the short hair I had when
in Pasadena has grown long and I wear it waved as I used to do.
Could not be bothered with curls on the trip so rolled it into a poll
and then it was so long I hated to have it cut again. . . . Fred says
you can get a Cook's excursion ticket from S.F. to Johannesburg via
London and the *west coast* for $272 second class. Good tickets to get
too. All the latter part of last season you could come from
Johannesburg to Victoria by ox wagon for from $20 to $50 and
Buluwayo is even nearer. But we must see whether this country is
healthy before advising Judd to come. We will stay this year but if
almost everyone has fever, even if we do not, as sometimes happens

the first year, we will go below before the next fever season. The coach makes the trip in ten days $150. But all the old traders say it is healthier so we will keep hopeful and Judd save up your money. We are certainly healthy enough now. Oh, Uncle has asked several times about the ants. Yes, you have heard exaggerated reports, but if the *white ants* get into your house they will eat anything, eat holes through brick walls. But we have been fortunate. Have not troubled us at all until last week. Mr. Cumming left a pack saddle on the ground and they ate all the padding. I have heard so much about them that I never set anything unless it is iron on the ground. All the wagons when left standing are raised a few inches by stones under the wheels. Almost everything is kept on the wagons and what few boxes we are obliged to keep in the tents are raised up from the ground. The only way to get rid of them is to follow and hunt their hole, then dig until you find the queen, a great big white grub. Kill her and that is the end of that tribe. They are something fearful if you do not use precaution. Then there are other ants that eat holes in the floor and walls. We have millions of big black ants here but they do not bother us much and help destroy the white ants. Then we have a bug smaller than a fly, called a borer, which eats *almost* all native timber and if your houses are not ceiled with cloth, they keep everything covered with a fine yellow powder. There are quantities of a bitter wild plum growing in this country and it is said if you boil these and dip the timber in the water that the borers will not touch it. And *still* we like Africa and are glad that we came.

. . . Tuesday Feb. 13 and a little confusion in camp. When the bell was rung for the miners to go to work only two (the new ones) appeared instead of nine. The others had gone before daylight. These two wanted to go but they came from the kraal where the cart has returned for the grain and were afraid to leave. Would like to go and burn their kraals but the government is too unsettled and we have no authority. Might get Dr. Jameson into trouble with the home government. While Fred was away this A.M. we saw a band of Matabeles, we could tell by the gleam of the sun on their shields across the river, driving a band of cattle. Our camp was evidently a surprise for as soon as they came within good sight they stopped a few minutes and then two turned the cattle off from us and drove them away on the run. Thirteen stood and looked at the camp and then followed. Not a horse in camp to follow them. Mr. Bain and Mr. Cumming took the only half way decent ones into Buluwayo Sunday and the three here are too poor to more than move and the ground is so soft. About an hour afterward we saw three more men going in the same direction. We heard yesterday that thirty Matabeles had returned from the king and are in a kraal north of here. These were surely more returning. Too big a country out here without a patrol. The blacks will soon get cheeky I am afraid. Fred sends in two runners tomorrow to carry the news to Dr. Jameson. We should have a small fort with about fifty men and a Maxim or two in this township. The Co. *intends* to send a patrol out here but the want of horses, and all they have are so poor, makes their movements very slow. Of course there is a good fort and patrol at B. another at a station 18 miles from there and another 50. But we are one hundred miles from any of these. We do not really apprehend any danger, but it is raining this P.M. so they are oiling up guns and getting ammunition ready. There are ten white men camped at the drift two miles from here and parties of two and three scattered all over the country. But I hardly think that they will attack the white men, still you never know what a "nigger" will do. They are only good when they are dead, and then they are best a long way off, and I wish the Chartered Co. had captured or better yet killed old Lobengula. They have sent messengers down to him and think that he will surrender as food is so scarce and his troops (so report says) are leaving him. So our adventures excite a little talk in Pasadena. Well it is a strange exciting and somewhat dangerous life compared with life there, but there is nothing like adapting yourself to circumstances. I do not feel in the writing humor this P.M. so will take a little nap while the men are all here in camp. With nothing to do the days are sometimes very long especially when Fred is away, and thank fortune, he does not expect to be away more than a day at a time anymore. The carriers have just come from Buluwayo and have sent others on to Charter. No mail for us. Will send this tomorrow. May write more but if not Oceans of love. Will only write once in two weeks I think and the next will be addressed to Mother Burnham. She must be home by this time.

Love, love, love.

B.B.B.

Wednesday Feb. 14 and still a short time to write before the runners leave. I forgot to tell you that Zonia (the pickinin) was taken captive by the Matabeles when he was only five years old and has been their slave ever since until this war broke out and then he ran home. So he can speak the pure Matabele. Another item I forgot. Fred took pity on the boys when it rained and was so cold that he gave them their blankets two weeks ahead of time and that is why they left. They solemnly promised that they would stay but only remembered their promise about four days. I guess it is as the old timers say, "You must not feel any pity for a black for he will surely take advantage of you." But it did seem hard to see the naked things shivering in the cold, and they can not make such warm huts now as they can in the dry season. It is not the loss of the blankets before their month was out for that amounts to nothing. It is the principle of the thing. Two of the men were going over to their kraal today to remonstrate with the chief and make him send more boys (we think that it can be done peaceably). But the staat [settlement] is eighteen miles across country from here and it not only poured all yesterday P.M. but rained all night and the ground is a bog hole. It is cold, windy and misting this morning. So we will wait until Johannes comes back with the cart and see whether he brings the grain and boys promised.

I suppose you have thought of us as melting and panting for a suit of varnish during the last two and a half months. We were never so happily disappointed in a country in that respect. We have not seen *one mile* of desert since passing Egypt and the climate is no warmer, *no* not as warm as in Pasadena, nor for as long a time. Have worn flannels all the time and slept *between* blankets. Like Pasadena, only warm from ten until about four P.M. We thought that the rains coming in the summer time would make the heat oppressive like Iowa and Kansas. But the rains are either cool or cold and the sun seldom comes out immediately after a shower. Sometimes it is somewhat oppressive before a storm. Have had very little thunder and lightening. The weather will be quite cold within a month. We are nearer the equator but the altitude is in our favor.

Uncle thinks it would seem strange to see the sun in the north. Tell him that that does not bother me much for although *I* never get lost, even in a city, I always lose the points of the compass. So it matters very little to me whether the sun is in the north or south. But when I go out star gazing I miss the familiar north star and realize how far away from home I am. The Southern Cross is all right but she wobbles around as Fred says and her center star is not visible, but Old Orion, always my favorite constellation, is here to remind us that we are still on the same planet with you all.

Fred had so many business letters to write this week that he cannot write home but sends love, and so does Roderick. He is stringing beads now calling them kings, indunas, boys and pickinins according to their size and color. It is wet out of doors so he is wearing a pair of his father's top boots and thinks he is quite a man. He is growing so tall and slim. No one would ever think that he had such a "pod" a few years ago. He could write you a letter but he wants to use so many words that he cannot spell yet. I want him to learn from the California books. So please tell Uncle Josiah and ask him for the money, or tell him to send, it does not matter which way it is done, the California Second Reader and Arithmetic to me at Buluwayo via Mafeking. It will take four or five months and he will be ready for the Reader at least by that time. I am teaching him from Appleton's Illustrated Numbers, you remember that little book, and he had a California First Reader. Had he better have a Geography? He *might* possibly go to school in Pasadena sometime. Please *be sure and have this done*. Carriers are ready to go now. What a splendid thing it is for Kate to have that scholarship. I wish someone would give John one.

Your loving daughter

B.

FRB to Josiah Russell

Gwelo River
Matabeleland
Feb. 17th 94

Dear Uncle,

Things do get wonderfully twisted in the press in spite of the rapidity of the telegraph &c. I will enclose to you another letter which if African affairs are of public interest would make them news agents anxious to get it.

More about the African War

Dear Uncle,

The clippings of the American papers adverse to this war are as nothing to what one rabid element of old England herself pours out. *Truth*[1] stigmatized us as land pirates, hired assassins and murderers of deepest dye, vile drunken loafers and everything else a subtle master of English language can command.

In my previous letter I gave you an exact account of things as they happened and how Ingram, Gooding and myself rode out of the death trap.[2] But now I will give you the several accounts of that day in December by the enemy, who have since come in and surrendered.[3]

The first actual account by a participant was given by a chief who lived on the Shangani River about 100 miles above the point of battle and said, "The king's orders were on Dec 3rd for Gambo, with 4000 men, and myself, with the other 3 regiments of the king, to attack the white impi at daybreak. The night being very dark and stormy my young men did not do as told and lay in their scherm to keep out the storm. Meantime, the white men took witch medicine and a few of them came out of the black night right to the king's wagons though hid in bush and talked but did not fight and went away. Our hearts were weak. But at daylight we got brave knowing the white men were few and we thousands. Some attacked the machine guns and when the induna with 35 men again rode up to the king's wagons being a long way from the big guns we attacked him and said we will see if white men are afraid to die. We fought them, they killed us, but we drove them back, their horses could not run. Our young men came up and rushed after them, but they got off their horses and killed many of us. Then we sent for all of Gambo's army, the white men going into the bush carrying their wounded and leading horses. We followed on both sides, but three men ran ahead on horses, a small man with big horse, some of my young men know him. He always rides at night and is the white induna's eye. We sent our best runners to ambush them. Some never came back

---

1. British anti-imperialist newspaper edited by Henry Labouchere.

2. George Gooding was the third man sent with Burnham and Ingram for reinforcements. All escaped the fate of the Wilson patrol.

3. A portion of this letter appears in a slightly different form in Frederick Russell Burnham, *Scouting on Two Continents* (Garden City, NY: Doubleday, Page & Co., 1926), pp . 202–204.

but the three got away. Now we swore to eat the hearts of all the rest and attacked the whites again. But they fought hard. Again we killed more horses and some white men ran to their horses and got on but a tall induna with big hat in his hand shouted to them and pointed to the men who were bleeding.[4] They all got off and tied their horses in a ring, head to head. I urged on my men to rush at once but the white man's medicine was very strong and my men fell. I could not get them to close up and rush. They said these are not men but lions with guns that never got empty. We now waited for Gambo and from behind the trees we watched the white men. They killed all the horses and dragged them end to end and tore up their shirts and tied up the wounds on each other. Many were dead. The induna carried the guns of the dead to the strong ones and laid the belts of cartridges with them. Then he took off his hat and the others stood up bare headed. They sang songs and some put their hands this way (crossing or locking them) just like they do in Victoria when the white man prays to his God for strong medicine. We watched but did not fight as we wanted Gambo's men and Gambo's men all came up and we shot and shot until we thought they were all dead but on creeping up several got up and shot us. They fought with the little guns (revolvers) and some put them to their heads and went so (snapping) but they had shot all at us and had to die by the Matabele spear, but the induna was umtagati (bewitched). We shot him with six rifles and he still fought us, a wounded man passing up to him a new gun all the time, but we got him at last and the wounded men who could not fight just put their fingers over their eyes while we ran the assegais into them. Ah, they do not die like the Mashonas. They never cry or groan. They are men. No I will never fight the whites again. They are not afraid to die. They are men."

On being asked what he thought when the white impis surprised them by a night march he said, "We did not know what to think. They did not kill the children or women and shot only a few young men who had rifles. We thought the white man hated death but I know it is not that. When *we* fight we kill everything, even dogs, unless we take slaves."

Another who was present at the end says of the white induna (Major Wilson) that he was the last man to stand up and that he

4. Apparently Major Allan Wilson.

was bleeding all over and no more cartridges to shoot, so a young warrior rushed up to him with assegai in hand. He stood still and looked straight at him and he put down his spear but raised it and plunged it into his chest and drew it out dripping with blood. The induna staggered toward him when he threw it into him leaving it sticking up in his breast. The induna then fell dead as he could not raise his hands to pull out the spear.

On being asked why they did not mutilate the bodies after the usual fashion, they said the white men died so bravely we would not treat them as they do the cowards (Mashonas and others). We stripped off the clothing only and left them behind their dead horses. Our dead we carried off (those who had friends) and they were very many.

Another said "tis no use wounding a white man. Hit in the leg he lays down and fights; in the arm, he shoots with the other, and he saw a white man with both arms flopping and bleeding, carry in his teeth a belt of cartridges to another man from one who was dead."

So much for the account of these men by their enemies. Now these men were not hired soldiers but volunteers who had business interests, homes and families in Mashonaland. They were England's real pioneers who built the brick and iron towns of Victoria and Salisbury and did not forget in the meantime to endow hospitals and churches, made them in fact peaceable towns of which any Englishman might be proud. They could not stand to have the tongues of their servants dried as trophies by the young warriors of a savage king living on their borders. They have taken this king's country as a result of the inevitable war that must always come between barbarism and civilization when the two come together. Lobengula could not rule under the flag in any material way different than under his own despotic sway.

Now Labouchere and his ilk are so very fond of asking questions, I should like to ask him a few. These men who perished were the very head and front of the volunteer force, and to them belongs most of the abuse heaped on them by the L.E.P.[5] Now how is it that these men, who until a few months ago were engaged in all manner of honorable business pursuits and numbered among them men whom Englishmen at home were proud to claim as friends and

5. Little Englanders Party, or anti-imperialist party.

countrymen, should suddenly turn out to be the scavengers of the earth and plunderers of innocence and on which every epithet applied to Attila the Hun is heaped? Is it not unusual for 1000 felons to act in unison? Can it be that the English colonist, noted the world over for carrying the solid virtues of his race into every clime, has in this instance carried unanimously only faults and vices?

If the crimes of Labouchere be no blacker than is written against these men for their parts in the Matabele war, he will wear wings like an angel. But if dismemberment of the British Empire be accounted a crime, he will be the devil's own and his wings resemble a vampire, for his forked tongue and unjust abuse has turned away the hearts of thousands of loyal Englishmen, and already one can hear on every side, "We will have independence or fight." And if he doubts our ability to do the latter, let him come and try too. As to the increasing American element in this country, tis needless to say to what party they belong and the party grows daily. History is making fast in this part of the world. A vast continent is before us and the howlings of a Labouchere will only recoil on him and his party in time.

Poor Capt. Lendy, on whom the vials of wrath have been constantly poured by Labouchere and his adherents, now lies under the sod at Buluwayo, his patient heroism on the retreat from the Shangani and during the time that our diet consisted of our starving horses will long be remembered by all of us who took part in it. Commandant Raaf, the most experienced Kaffir fighter in Africa,[6] lies beside him. [letter incomplete].

———

FRB to Josiah Russell

Burnhams
Gwelo River
Feb 18th 94
Matabeleland

Dear Uncle,

Your newsy letters are a great comfort to us and will be even more so now that the fierce excitement of war is passed and we set-

---

6. Commandant Pieter Johannes Raaf, whom many credited with leading Forbes's party to safety.

tle down to slowly opening up the country and incidentally making a living. You must indeed be passing through a crisis in the U.S. and I still think it well that I am not there. Have you seen anything since I left that I could have made a $ at, unless I joined a clique of schemers and then took chances. But in this wild country sans R.R.s and sidewalks and electric lights and organs, libraries and churches the buzz of the world is spent and we produce in a way sufficient for our needs and really it is strange how little a man really needs to press the button for all the luxuries of the 19th century; but when once among them we all feel the need of them and will barter our souls to obtain them. But of course ere long we will have in these wilds the flesh pots of civilization, and instead of a Matabele War we will have that constant industrial war in common with other countries.

We must have churches and jails hospitals and mad houses— the drink evil, the social evils and all the rest. But if one can busy themselves by building only the churches and hospitals and does not get ensnared by the ever present badness, life is worth living and savagery is better done away with. And now the track of the white impi is burned into a well beaten road and mines are being pegged off, a townsite is laid out. On our ranch last week I laid the matter of mail service before the administration in such a way that they at once established a weekly service between here and Mashonaland and some of the late hostiles are now carrying the mail under H.M. flag. As to my mining ventures, tis of course too early yet to speak. We are sinking shafts although it is now the rainy season and the air seems saturated with moisture all the time in fact. It rains on the slightest provocation I ever saw. Those rainmakers should come over here. They could get a shower for every explosion. Am not sure but explosive language would bring it on. We have had 40 rainy days so far since Nov. 9.

So small is the supply of writing papers, must write on this vanity stuff on both sides, put it on a piece of white cardboard or it can hardly be read at all. There is no paper in Buluwayo. The accounts of Matabele slaughter are of course somewhat exaggerated but we killed a great many, 600 to 1000 and at Imbembeze, probably 600 on the Shangani campaign, total perhaps of 2000. Without machine guns it would have been madness to come into this country. The Matabele have the same guns we fought with and plenty of ammunition, but they are not crack shots else every scout would have been killed as enough of them have fired upon me to kill a hundred men and make allowance for misses besides. All rot about Lobengula allowing ants to eat gun stocks and if so his clever slaves would have restocked them. They do wood carving and some quite neat iron work. I have visited their iron mines and crude smelters but unless we get coal I don't see their great value.

The government lays out all townsites and saves the land to the town. In this instance they have laid out a radius of 4 miles. Lots will be sold at auction and the fund so raised goes to make improvements. Later on another tract will come in and be sold in the same way and finally after a town is once solidly started the balance of the reserve is leased and not sold outright. From this fund hospitals, roads, sewers &c. are financed. Have just stopped to doctor up a black. He is my ox driver and quite an important personage. His big black foot is swollen and I told him to make a pot of mush and that I would put some medicine on it. He said all right boss. No kill em boys. Me give him mush in the morning. So I shall only put in a handful of salt to counteract his gout. But really the boys would never notice a little thing like that as tonight they are gorging themselves on ox entrails and leave the clean quarters hanging on the posts outside.

I think on business matters there is little to say, . . . I will send power of atty as soon as official life in these parts permit. Officers will be appointed soon. Guess farmers [in the U.S.] are as usual between hell and deep sea. . . . There is too much to say to write and you will have to drop over for a year or two and see life as it is on the underside of the world.

Yours as ever,

Fred

———

FRB to Josiah Russell

[Circa February, 1894]

To Uncle Josiah

. . . I have had the honor of F.C. Selous acquaintance. He is a true nimrod and a credit to his race. He and I served in same capacity in the late Matabele unpleasantness and my first meeting was under the tent of Col. Goold-Adams in command of the imperial forces for whom he was chief scout. I had just succeeded in passing through the regiments of Chief Gambo and brought the news of the movements of the volunteer army and fall of Buluwayo and written and verbal instructions from Dr. Jameson to Col. Adams. Selous was then wounded but able to be about. He is one of those men who do not disappoint you on meeting, and should he come to America, as I think he will, and to the coast don't fail to see him. I think the Americans will give him a cordial reception as we as a nation admire nerve and spirit. You will find nothing of the cowboy or bravado about him but an educated earnest man. The next time I met Selous was when about 100 of us worn and ragged and starving were carrying our wounded and guardedly creeping back from our expedition after the king in which we had lost our bravest and best men. He galloped over a ridge to us and called, "Reinforcements mile and one half ahead. Cecil Rhodes and Dr. Jameson both with them and grub now cooking for you all." We hurrahed for the grub, Selous, Rhodes, Dr. Jameson and in fact for everybody, ourselves, our poor horses, our brilliant rescue.

There was a great time that night but alas most of us were hurt by its very profusion and many had to go to hospital, I among the rest. Too sudden a change. A diet of horse meat and surrounded by hostile savages, then suddenly welcomed by friends, waited on like babies. We, like them, ate too much and several died from nothing else. There was gathered in Inyati a strong contingent of England's best blood, not titled, but potent for her upbuilding or national disgrace according as they choose to act. Rhodes, Jameson, Selous, Commandant Raaf, Major Sawyer, representing the imperial interests, and lacking only the lost Maj. Wilson, and dashing Capt. Borrow, to challenge the world to produce a more splendid group of nation builders.

But things change rapidly. On our concession is the hill on which as scout I built a huge beacon fire to warn the commander of the column that I had found the enemy in force. Now only a few months and I am opening up a reef under the shadow of this hill and some of the then enemy are now piling up the rock and such like service. The wild game is not quite used to the changes for this A.M. a huge gnu bull came up within 500 yds of our buildings and looked in amazement for some moments. He was a fine specimen, too proud and beautiful to shoot and I let him gallop away, his mane rising and falling with rhythmic motion as far as eye could see. His domain is hopelessly lost and some pot hunter will soon have his huge blue pelt drying in the sun.

Buluwayo is to be thrown open to the public in May and lots sold at auction. The upset price being fixed at £25, 35, and 45— size 50 × 100—and residence lots or erfs as called here of ½ acre same price. Tis said by some that choice will bring £100. So you see we will be in a miniature boom over here at once. I am going to Buluwayo Apr 4th and will be at sale.

The town located on our concession is to be immediately surveyed and I will donate what ground is needed for town. Stock raising and mining will of course be main industries up here for some time. I guess we could dispose of our concession including the scouts reef for at least £1000 each. But tis in a beautiful country and so far from fever if we do not have it inside 6 weeks the season is past. It is my firm belief that all this tableland will be fever free and if so tis a lovely country. The R.R. is now building at the rate of two miles per day towards Matabeleland, but I hope to see you with us before the R.R. gets here.

Concerning the ranch I am not looking for dividends from it. Maybe Roderick will be able to make ranching pay. His dad is absolutely a failure at it. And besides I want a little nest egg for him to draw him to America again as I want him to have his education under the Stars and Stripes, even if it is under republican and democratic rule, both of equal malodor. But there is a fount of energy in the American found in no other race under the sun. And the one great stumbling block to this country is the presence of the nigger whose labor is to be had for a pinch of salt per day. True he only does a pinch of salt's worth of work, but it enfeebles the white race just the same and servants are a curse to a strong race. Nevertheless I am already surrounding myself with them and we have now at our establishment 8 crude blacks. They are hewers of wood and drawers of water in a literal sense, and instead of having a Yankee wood pile each day's supply is toted in on a wooly head and instead of a well the water is hauled from the river ½ mile each day by a nig and so on and on until, though consciously, I am drifting into the ways of the country and when you see me again you will find me a lazy uninteresting piece of clay, sans ideas, ambition, or anything beyond the setting of the day's sun. It is remarkable how quickly one's ideas of the black change after being among them. When they get saucy and clear out or do some act of a worthless race you mentally reason it out about thus. He did not object to being my servant, and practically slave, for any love of country pride or independence. Far from it. It was simply to run off from your work to lounge around his own dirty kraal and force the women to slave for him without pay save sundry thrashings. So you say the lazy worthless wretch, he is fat and stout. I pay him what to him is a priceless luxury. He shall not desert me to beat even black women. I will gradually civilize the brute and incidentally he shall have my corn and get my wage. So you find yourself voting for the law that compels each black to work 3 months per year at a certain wage or pay a tax to the state, and your final views are diametrically opposite from those entertained when landing on these sunny shores. But every other idea almost received just as bad a shake up and one fully believes one's existence to be dual throughout and that our boyhood's fixed principles and solid truth is after all only one side of it, one facet of the jewel, and there is little reason to doubt but the same wonderful changes will continue after this short span of life is over.

A.M. The runners are ready to go to Buluwayo with the mail and I must close. . . .

Yours as ever,

Fred

———————

BBB to Rebecca Russell Burnham

Gwelo P.O. Matabeleland
Feb 25, 1894

Dear Mother,

Do you know what day this is? Ma does. I am sure I am thirty-two years old today and in five days more Fred and I have been married ten years. You know we used to talk of a tin wedding for that day. Never mind we will have as good a dinner as our larder will afford, talk over the events of the last ten years, talk about home and wish that you were all with us. But you are each as fond of adventure as we are, and am afraid would not be happy in our little camp until it gets larger. You could not belong to any clubs or lodges, attend any theatre, lectures, concerts or make *fashionable calls*. You know how I long to make calls but I suppose we will be able to make calls in Buluwayo next season. Several of my Victoria friends are going there and they are looking for quite a rush. Our calls in this country are of a little longer duration than in Pasadena. We all have tea and biscuits. I am so glad that I brought a tea set from London and it is such a pretty little set too. The only thing I lack is a biscuit jar. Have to use the bread and butter plate. Wish now that I had contrived some way in which to carry the one Mrs. Whitmore gave me. Speaking about dishes, I must tell you of my Matabele curios. Fred had a dozen or more leopard cat and silver jackal skins, all nicely dressed, a Matabele headdress, hood and cape all made of black ostrich feathers, all kinds of war implements and carved woodwork. When he left Buluwayo on horseback to come to Victoria he stored all these things with a Mr. C. in his wagon. Then Mr. C. went out west, stored all the goods left with him in a hut and when he returned everything had been stolen. So all I have now is a sugar spoon, some chains, which I shall use to loop back curtains with, a melted bead (We have a good many gold beads from the Simbabye Ruins.)[1] (I always forget how to spell that) The spoon and chains came from Lobengula's hut, an odd little wooden sugar bowl and a bread tray which I use all the time, three wooden jars and two immense trays over a yard not including the handles. Each made out of a single piece of wood and some of them quite elaborately carved. . . . The little one is expected the last of May or first of June. They put them into short clothes so soon in this country, at six weeks or two months. Does it not seem outrageous? So you see she[2] will want shoes and stockings at once then. So they will not want to be very large. If you make them at once they will just about get here in time. You can buy nothing here and she thinks they would be so pretty. Please do this for me. Ask Uncle for the money. I have already sent to him for books for Roderick. . . .

Monday morning Feb 26, 1894—Fred went over with Mr. Cumming to his wagons yesterday P.M. Brought me some books.

1. Zimbabwe Ruins.
2. Blanche is referring to her expected child. She hoped for, and had, a daughter.

Mr. Smith came back with him. He will stay here a few days until his partner Mr. McIntyre comes from Buluwayo. This Mr. Smith is an American. I should judge about forty-five years old. He has been in Africa before and is a practical miner. Howard got acquainted with him on the steamer coming to Cape Town. He has seen Howard since we have heard from him. Brought a letter of introduction from him. He seems to think a great deal of Howard, says that he is in with the right sort of men who like him and that he is bound to do well in Johannesburg. It seems good to see someone who has talked with him so recently. I would dearly love to see him and so would you. We said we would stay here five years before we make a visit. Over one year has passed and very quick too, although we have longed to see you many and many a time. Poor Mr. Smith has had the fever for the last few days and is lying down now. This morning before breakfast also, Mr. [Arthur] Dunn, who knew Fred in the campaign, rode over. He is smart and a good talker but I do not like his face. Mr. Cumming is coming again this P.M. Oh we have plenty of company. I have to superintend the cooking but that is all the work I have so I do not object in fact am glad to see company. If it happens to be someone Fred does not particularly care for they take them in over at the other tent. Mr. Ingram is my right hand man about planning meals. He is like a woman in that way. I like him and Mr. Bain too but Mr. Reid is awfully tiresome. I hate to send you this letter written on both sides of this thin paper. It will be so hard to read, but we only have a few sheets of this and some old blank books in camp. In honor of my birthday I put on my pretty pink dress trimmed with cream lace yesterday and wore my hair waved as I did when first married. Fred liked it so much and does not want me to cut it again. Roderick noticed it at once. He is so observant but said oh how pretty you look but you look older. Asked him if I should change it back, but he said no. I do not look older than Fred now. That last year or two in California told on him very much, but he is fleshier now than I ever saw him. . . .

We hear from pretty reliable sources that Lobengula is dead and we know that he was sick so think the report must be true. It is not thought that the Matabeles will rally around any other chief so the matter ought to be soon settled and I do hope it will be without any more fighting as there would had to have been had Lobengula lived and not surrendered. Fred had too many hair breadth escapes and it does not seem as though I could stand it to have him go through such dangers again. *I cannot* give him up. . . .

Your loving B.

━━━━━━━━━

FRB to Rebecca Russell Burnham

[Circa February 26, 1894]

Dear Mother,

B. and I have just had a fearful row. It will take me too long to read her letter. She won't tell me what she has written so how can I make my lies correspond with her letter, for I don't like this writing on both sides of closet paper anyway and can't read my own writing on it. We have a man in camp who brings a letter from Howard to me. He says he is doing well in Johannesburg and is to be assistant manager of a 100 stamp mill on the Primrose Mine. We are looking for a letter from him but mails are 3 weeks delayed by floods south of us. I suppose you have no good map of Africa. Neither have we but will have ere long and will send you one. Will mark on it the battle grounds and the place where the Gallant Wilson fell. Everything progressing as usual and prospects as bright as one could wish. *Strange for me is it not?* But you see this is another world and as different as Patagonia[1] from Korea. You can now wear the most unique bracelet in Pasadena. These beads were taken from the ancient ruins of Zimbabu—look up spelling in Dr. Z.'s work. Tis pronounced Zimbabe, accent on b. Cleopatra and Queen Sheba wore same kind when kins and even *she* would not have despised them for these are *pure* and without alloy. They do not match as they are found only one or two at a time by washing the debris of the ruins. Maybe each bead represents a separate string that hung on the voluptuous bosom of the tawny belles of long ago. Let some psychologist of Mahatma interpret their tale for ½ the world is listening.

Dip in weak solution of nitric acid then wash clean to brighten.

1. Mining camp in Arizona.

FRB to John Blick

> Burnhams
> (Scouts Reef) Gwelo River
> Matabeleland
> [Circa March, 1894]

My dear Johnny,

. . . We are hammering away on the Reef, have three shafts going. They look fine so far and show lots of free gold. Matabeleland is a great gold field, whether or no it will be my fortune to strike it rich or not remains to be seen, but of the value of the land concessions there is no doubt, and the future of this strange land is brilliant as one of its own glittering gems—not excepting its latest wonder worth £1,000,000. And I fully expect to see such young and active bucks as yourself and Razor fill useful niches in the world's mosaic and fill them in the land of the Southern Cross, but my boy the equipment required in this old century will require all that you can cram into your brain while it is yet plastic. Then once equipped and backed by indomitable will and persistency any path is open to you and you can feel yourself more than a fly on a bull's horn in building up and uniting this great country for one of these days a new flag will be born, the Southern Cross, the dear old colors Red, White and Blue, a united Africa, a just Africa where no man can eat another's bread. But it is a long time to wait and I am as anxious to see you over here as you are to come. I would like to show some of these slow going people what real live Yankees are like, for so far our nation is at a disadvantage and its representatives are mostly of the barroom type, miners, even the cowboys' breezy, daring ways. Why is it that we must represent our nation by such scum as drifts into these parts? But wait, we will yet have a great go at the big game. Right on this farm when we pitched camp were gnu, koodoo, ostrich and sable antelope. Lions have killed oxen within a few miles of this camp. Wild hounds and hyenas come right up to camp. My foot is on the hide as I write of a big spotted hyena and B. is sitting on a chair over which is thrown the skins of two tiger cats. There is in the river just below a family of hippopotamus. But of course all this game will be gone in very short time, but to the north is thousands

of square miles that no white man has yet trod and its magic holdings will probably be spared long enough for such as you, Judd,
Razor and other fry of your age. And mind you I am still gamy myself even if it is not as exciting as shooting greasers and Apaches
and Matabeles. Bye the Bye practice up a little on fancy shooting.
Tis considered a wonderful thing here. Try lifting a cork off the
water and hitting in the air. It can be done by 3 months practice 10
trials per day. . . .

Yours as ever,

Fred

———

BBB to Madge Blick Ford

Gwelo Matabeleland
March 11, 1894

My dear Madge and family,

. . . Mail came in at two P.M. and I did nothing but read letters
for the rest of that day. Fred had gone prospecting for a few days so I
read them all again to him. Mr. Dunn and Mr. Wallace sent us a big
roll of papers so it has seemed like living. . . . The letters were all
written in December. Some then were held over on the trip from
Johannesburg on account of the high rivers. One *down* coach was
overturned in the Murzingwane and Maj. Forbes' brother who had
led wounded across was drowned. The rivers have been very high
this season, still the rainy season not as I expected. It rained *sometimes* during every twenty-four hours of December and often a good
many sometimes. Then bright weather for about three weeks, then a
few showers, then several consecutive rainy days the last week of
January. Since then a number of hard showers but still a *good deal* of
sunshine. Beautiful weather now for almost three weeks. The thunder and lightening would not, I do not think, have even have frightened Kate. When we get good houses with glass windows the rain
will not annoy us, at least in the house. I suppose the roads will always be bad during the rainy season. We think the heavy rains are
over for this season. . . . Mother asks if we are really going to live on
a farm. No we were never intended for farmers. Buluwayo will be
Fred's headquarters and we will go on there within a month or so.
Fred wants to prospect during the winter and Roderick and I will

stay in Buluwayo. Everything looks well out here and work is progressing during this fine weather, but I do not want to stay here without Fred. This country is almost covered with old workings. Our boys are all well now and so are we. Mrs. Greenfield writes that almost everyone in Victoria is seedy [ill], as they express it, and a great many are down with the actual fever. Five of my old friends are in the hospital. We are so thankful that we are not there. No white people sick around here. Of course it might come yet but do not believe it will. The mornings and evenings are delightful. It is warm out in the sun during the middle of the day, but not hot. I think you would like the country Madge, and Jack and I know Helen[1] would for she would never have to wash a dish. I appreciate that very much. How would you like this Helen? I wanted to make a big peach cobbler for dinner so called Zonia and had all the ingredients placed on the end of the table together with the nice kneading board and rolling pin which Mr. Ingram has made for me. Had water brought into the tent and then I washed my hands, put on an apron and made the cobbler and called Zonia to take it to the kitchen and put in the bake pot which Longboy had all ready. I set the table but seldom clear it off. Have two boys who just get wood and water, cook, wash dishes and do the washing. Help is cheap in this country. Get boys for five or ten shillings per month cash or anklets that cost that much. Feed them on native meat and beef and salt. They like salt as our children do candy. Of course Zonia is ours and we gave a cow and calf for him for a year's work. Our driver is a colored boy and has £3 a month. Longboy, the leader has £10. When not off with the oxen one works in the mine and the other around the camp. The colonial boys all speak more or less English and are quicker to learn. They are Zulu stock. Some new boys came this week from the Mavenestadt and are good workers. They want ten shillings a month. The colonial boys want Boer meal, rice, Kaffir beans and meat and coffee to eat. We have four or five mail carriers here all the time and for two nights each week have seven or eight. So there are a good many boys to feed. We have a small beef killed every week. We seldom eat anything but the brains, tongue and tenderloin. . . .

Friday evening March 16—P.M. and brought us your Christmas letters and the Company letter from home written the day

---

1. Helen was Blanche's youngest sister.

after Christmas and how funny it sounds or reads rather to have you ask what we were doing on that day when I have written about it so long ago. And Homer says you are anxious about Fred on account of the ambushings of Maj. Wilson's party for you feel sure that he was with them. And did not I worry at that time, but ere this you have his letter telling of his marvelous escape through being sent for reinforcements. Thank God that the war is now over. I was rejoiced to hear that Loben was dead for if he had not been a patrol would have been sent after him next season and Fred would have wanted to go.

They have buried Maj. Wilson's party now, and my friend Mrs. Greenfield has had to give up all hope of Mr. G. being alive. She is going to stay up in this country and will very likely come to Buluwayo. I hope so for I like her so much better than the others there. Well we were all thinking of each other on Christmas Day and how we were scattered. Fred was coming to here, as I have already written, and arrived on New Years Day. I was so busy all next week and so devoted to Fred through New Years week that I have very hazy ideas of what I wrote at that time. I am afraid that it will be several years before we are all together again. I said within five years when I left you and over one has passed already. . . . Fred joins with R. and I in love to all of you.
B.

BBB to Phebe Blick[1]

40 miles from Buluwayo
April 5, 1894

Dear little mother,

. . . I am waiting for one of the boys to bring clean water so I can make scones for tomorrow's meals. . . . Started with an immense loaf but it gave out yesterday. Well this is another move for us in Africa. We left Mr. Ingram to superintend affairs at the Scouts Reef, Gwelo River on the first of April. Have been having beautiful weather but it rained on the 2nd and 3rd and made the

1. Portions of this letter are printed in Frederick Russell Burnham, *Taking Chances* (Los Angeles: Haynes Corporation Publishers, 1944), pp. 33–38.

roads very bad. Our bullocks are fat and saucy, our driver is no good and if it had not been for our fellow travellers' help we should had to have gone back after the Scotch cart and left part of our load. These wagons alone only weigh 4500 [lbs]. As it was we had to unload one night just at dark and in the rain, pull the wagon onto level ground and in the morning reload. We have about 3000 [lbs] on the wagon. But we crossed the Shangani yesterday at sunrise and will have smooth sailing now. To add to our misery that night Fred had the headache and I had the toothache. Another tooth which I had filled in Pretoria troubles me quite often and I shall undoubtedly have to lose it some day. Speaking of teeth Roderick has lost three lower front teeth and the first of his second set put in an appearance on April fool's day. He is having a vacation from studying now and is happy.

April 10th. Longboy came with the water then and I have not felt in the writing humor since then. We passed through the battle ground of the Shangani that day. Fred showed us just where he was camped outside of the laager that night, the position he fought from and the country they scouted over the next day and would have shown us the bones of a certain Matabele that he killed but the grass was too high and wet and he could show us more in a day or two, and so he did for we outspanned at noon in a regular Golgotha on the top of the Imbembesi Hill where the royal regiments attacked them at 1 P.M. and were so completely vanquished. They were surrounded by bush and kopjes at the Shangani but this hill stood out in almost open country. A very very poor place for the blacks to attack, as they found to their cost. But they were royal and thought themselves invincible. A great many of the bodies have been carried away but we saw enough. Fred showed us one particular one that he killed. This one was standing out in front of some of the others and calling Buya, buya (come on, come on) when Fred's bullet ended his cry. Roderick picked out a few of his teeth which we will send you. Perhaps John and Ray might like them. Our blacks would not touch the skeletons but Roderick had no fear. Stood on an ant heap by the side of the road and held a skull at arms' length in either hand. Then he piled three up on the heap and left them. The *brutes!* I have no pity or liking for them. No one has who lives among them. Too bad that they were not all killed. But enough of them. We are now in Buluwayo, their capital. Several restaurants in town but no hotel or houses to rent so we are camping in our wagon for a day or two. Mrs. Magear is only a few yards from us. Fred knows so many men here and is so full of business. Strange how well known he has become in such a short time. His deeds of daring in the campaign have fairly made him, and we are doing *well* in this country. He is a great favorite at headquarters. But you know how most people like him. And they seem anxious to see me for already we have received under our canvas awning Dr. Jameson (the Administrator) and Col. Rhodes (brother of Cecil Rhodes). They made a long call and had tea with us. Next morning Dr. Sauer,[2] who looks after the most of Cecil Rhodes' moneyed interests, and Capt. Bastard (a big man here) and in the P.M. The Honorable Gifford,[3] brother of Lord Gifford, Capt. Heyman, the magistrate, and Capt. Honey, the registrar. So you see we have received the bigwigs besides a number of smaller fry. It is to our interest to keep in with these men so I shall overcome my natural reluctance to society and turn over a new leaf. Now don't smile. I mean it, for I am determined that we shall do well in this Fred's chosen land, and when I make up my mind it is "sot." I could always talk to men easier than to women anyway.

April 11th. The public sale of stands was in March, but Dr. Jameson told Fred he could select a stand, which he did. It is a very nice corner one between 200 and 250 yards from the market square (center of the town). Price £30 but, if the town goes ahead as it certainly looks like, it will soon be worth a great deal more. Only 96 stands were sold at the sale but they brought in £4000. Only one or two went for the upset price £30. We got ours for that because it was a private sale. Stands are 100 × 140. One of the conditions on which the first 100 stands sold is that £200 improvement must be put on each stand before the next sale which comes off in August I believe. This was to keep speculators from buying whole blocks and to make the town look like a white man's town instead of a Kaffir location.[4] All houses must be brick with iron roofs. Materials are so expensive now that £200 does not build a very spacious house, but we will have three nice rooms with regular win-

---

2. Dr. Hans Sauer (1857–1939), like Jameson, was a former medical doctor.
3. Maurice Gifford, a close personal friend and business associate of Fred Burnham's.
4. The new Buluwayo was located a couple of miles from the site of Lobengula's capital.

dows and sash doors, coat of plaster and cloth ceiling, and oh yes a fireplace!

April 12. We still have the use of the Co. wagon and oxen and Fred was going to look after the building somewhat himself but today he engaged to peg 10 farms for Dr. Sauer at £10 each. He knows where vacant land is and will only be gone a week or at the most ten days so we have contracted the house and work will begin tomorrow. The hauling will be done with our team and boys. I say our team for we halfway expect to buy them. Lots of ways to make money with them if you have a good driver and we expect to have one next week. Three of the donkeys were lost during the campaign but we have sold the buckboard and the remaining three for £76 and the buckboard and six only cost £56. Fred had a salary during the three months at the mine, our living cost us nothing.

He has had a number of farms to peg so we have bought our lot and already have more than enough to build our house without touching the funds which uncle has sent. By the way the letter containing the draft for $500 has not put in an appearance yet, for last Sunday we received a letter from him[5] in which he said he hoped we had received the draft for 500 as well as the three for fifty each. Have written to the Standard Bank in Johannesburg about the draft for the first £10 and ought to hear soon. Expect the letter containing the draft for the £100 has been delayed and will soon turn up.

It seems as though there was really a chance for us to go ahead now. Competition is not so close now. After Fred returns from this trip he will go out to the Gwelo with Dr. Sauer to examine the reefs there, then he has more work for him. Fred is in with the right stamp of men now. They are liberal and let him do practically as he likes not like the Alvord Co. Things may shape themselves so that he will need John in a year or so. So study as hard as you can and you *may* be the first one to see us. We remembered both Kate's and Madge's birthdays.

April 13. . . . And I must get this letter ready to mail in the morning. We came out here to Mr. Cumming's farm on the 11th. It is five miles from town. You must know Mr. Cumming by this time. He was one of our party on the road to Victoria, a scout with Fred and a great friend all around. Well, he and Bob Bain, one of

5. Josiah Russell.

our American friends, have bought this farm and are running a dairy. They insisted on our coming out here to stay while our house is being built (a month). I was glad to come because there are only a few men sleeping in the new town. I would have had to live in a tent (and it is getting too cold for that). Fred will be away most of the month, and I am much better off here. We have a comfortable lined hut and are very cozy. Mr. Smith and his son, old friends of Mr. Cumming, are staying with him in a hut a few yards from mine, so I do not feel at all nervous at night. We have stored our goods in the tent and my cook sleeps there. Fred went away yesterday on horseback. The country is perfectly safe now so I have no apprehensions for his safety, but as you know I am not happy when he is away. But this is only a short trip and means a good deal.

There is a family of Hottentots here on Mr. Cumming's place. A father, mother, grown daughter and son and a number of pickanins. The father was in Salisbury at the time of the trouble and came in as a guide with the Salisbury column. The Matabele did not know it until the fight of the Shangani and then they were going to kill his family. They had to live in a sort of a cave for over a week, come out at night, catch fowls, try to cook them in this hole where the smoke half suffocated them. After the column entered Buluwayo of course they were safe. The women wear dresses and understand and speak English fairly well. They used to live in the Transvaal. Have a sewing machine, music box, flat irons, &c. The oldest girl is to be married next week. It seems quiet out here. We had so much company at the Gwelo during the last month and they always *happened* in at meal time. I remember counting the last five days. There were 15 came to the camp and 11 ate dinner with us. Then we had company during our three days outspan in Buluwayo, but do not expect any out here. Have only spoken to one woman for over three months now. Only Mrs. Colenbrander and three Dutch families in Buluwayo, but two English families came in day before yesterday. Expect a goodly number up this coming season. Roderick is sound asleep, our friends are also quiet. Can only hear the thrum, thrum of a Kaffir guitar and a few voices singing a monotonous song. Occasionally the dozen or more dogs rush out and bark at the moonlight. A rat is walking around over my ceiling. Mr. Dawson is going to give me a cat, but I will not take it until we move for fear if

I should move it we would have bad luck, and I am getting sleepy. Received your letter written Jan. 28 and Feb. 1 last Sunday as also one from Uncle. I think there must be one from Mother Burnham somewhere on the road up here. Uncle writes that she is in San Francisco with Etta, but suppose she will be home by the time this reaches you. Will write her next and send an article printed in the Colonial paper about Fred. Did you see the picture in the London Graphic of the capture of a Matabele by the American Scout Burnham, taken from Selous notes? It is a miserable thing but glad to see it nevertheless. He was interviewed yesterday by a man who is publishing a book about the Matabele War. Well I cannot say which it will be, whether we will go to you or you come to us, but our hearts and plans are always full of love for you all. Roderick was very much touched to think that Aunt Grace would only sing Marching Through Georgia for him. He says he likes to be here on the farm so much. He will never forget any of you. I could not do without him so shall not send him to Throop just yet. We were glad to hear that John was going there. Yes John it is a great thing to have influential friends. No the Boers do not talk German. It is all Dutch or poor English. Can you not drop German and devote more time to mathematics and chemistry? . . . Have not heard from Howard for a long time. He is so erratic. He wrote me every week while Fred was in the campaign because he thought I would be lonely but said he was only going to write once in a month or so now that Fred was with me, and he seems to be going to keep his promise, but we do not like it or think it fair. The wind is sighing among the trees and around the huts. It sounds gloomy and I am glad that I have friends so near. Oh some of the nigs are still awake. I can hear them. But I am sleepy so good night my dear ones with unlimited love to all from Fred, Roderick and your loving daughter and sister
Blanche Blick Burnham

BBB to Rebecca Russell Burnham

Buluwayo April 17, 1894

Dear mother,

I wrote a long letter home last week describing our trip in from the Gwelo, our settlement here and the commencement of our first real home in Africa. In that letter I enclosed one to you from Roderick thinking that you would be at home and I had to put double postage on anyway. It is too far to send letters to repeat anything so you must share your letters. Fred is very hopeful of his future and so am I when he is with me.

You know how dependent I always was upon him for happiness or contentment even when surrounded by both our families, and now you can judge how much more I am without any of you. I am *so* thankful that we have little Roderick. Fred thinks with me that we could not possibly have a better child. He is much better than when we left California. Yes he is growing tall and thin and his face grows more and more like Fred's. He is over entertaining our four neighbors now. I can hear them talking. Everyone thinks him so old fashioned and like him because he always minds so quickly and is so polite. They are talking over the experiences of the day and there is a great deal of laughing. They have been branding cattle and Roderick told me that he got so excited he did not know what he was doing. Childlike, he is so interested in everything, and so sympathetic. He always wants to hear the men talk over the campaign but several times after hearing about the Wilson disaster he has come to me and cried as though his little heart would break, so whenever that subject is broached now I send him out to play.

Zonia caught a little bird out at the camp for him and it was really wonderful to see how quickly it knew that he was the one who brought the flies and worms. He made a nice little nest in a box and nailed slats across it for a cage. Just about sundown I called him to come and give the bird his supper. Just as he stepped into the tent I heard a great twittering and squeaking and then *silence*. The bird had hopped out of the box and flew to meet him and he had hit it with his foot. It fluttered for a moment and then Pete took it away. Such a time as we had to comfort him. He would keep saying, O dear! O dear! To think that he knew me and was coming to me for food and I—killed it. O my! O my! Even last night when I was reading about a little chicken getting killed he thought of his bird and cried. He must have another when we get into the house.

April 18 Roderick wanted me to finish the Pixie book last night and then I was too sleepy to write.

. . . Now pray do not imagine that I am always dull and pity me, for indeed I am not and when I am, always try to overcome the feeling. I think Fred will be at home tomorrow, but only for a few days. It is all so quiet out here I would not live on a farm alone for anything, and I should certainly have to be alone a good portion of the time. Expect we shall be quite gay in Buluwayo. I do not think I was ever so anxious to get into a house of our own before. . . . By the way, all the family photographs were left in Forbestown with Howard. He promised to bring them to me. Do you know whether he has them with him? . . . No wallpaper in the country and I shall have the walls whitewashed with a cream or light brown color. What do you think of our African home? Will have a fireplace and a corner cupboard or two in the sitting room. The furnishings sound simple but no one has much up here so I will be as good as the rest. Time will change all that. We will have a railroad in a few years and all the comforts of life so will live in hopes.

Living is so expensive. Flour $17.50 per hundred pounds. Butter $1.00 a pound. Milk 25 cents a pint. Lard .62½ per pound. Fruit $1.00 and $1.25 a can. Vinegar from .75 to a $1.00 a bottle, and everything accordingly. So you see it costs considerable more to live than it does in California. This is certainly not a fever country and we are so thankful, for Fred would *not* have lived here if it had been and he thinks it is *the* coming country of the world. . . .

I hope that you did not have to worry long over the fate of Wilson's party. Those were terrible days for me, almost two weeks, and yet so great is my faith in Fred that I did not completely despair. He tells me now that if he had remained with Wilson when he saw things getting desperate he would have thought of us and made one of those quick dashes for life and escaped, and I believe he could have done it. Oh I cannot be too thankful that the war is over. The natives say now that if the white men had known of the bend in the river (and they were fighting back toward it all the time) they could have made a dash and reached it because they were shooting so straight and deadly that the Kaffirs never rushed them with the assegai. I wish some of them had tried. I may be selfish but I think with so many odds against them, each man should have looked out for himself, but I thank God that Fred was sent for reinforcements if he did have to ride through such a fire. Maj. Wilson evidently thought he had been killed for they begged the Matabeles to spare just one man as hostage until the war was over so that he could tell their friends. If they would do this, the men said they could come and kill *all* the rest and they would never fire a shot but the Matabele said, "No. We will kill them all."[1] But there I do not want to think any more about it. Oh joy! I hear Fred coming.

April 19th—Fred has been in town all day but I am looking or rather listening for him every minute. Have been very busy mending today. Have a nice supper all ready for him. It is such a treat to have all the fresh milk we want, and they gave us over a pound of fresh butter. All our butter up here is put up in tins but it is very good. Roderick was hungry and sleepy, so he has had his supper and is going to bed. He sends kisses and love to dear Grandma and Aunt Etta. What a long, long time it will be before this letter reaches you. Here he comes.

April 20—Have felt tired for some unknown reason today so have not written any. Have just had supper and Fred would like to write to you and Uncle but says he is too sleepy. Goes away again day after tomorrow to be gone two weeks. After that he will have more leisure and he will write. The last trip was a quick and hard one but he is perfectly well and happy. Says it is time for me to say good night. . . .
Your loving,
B.

———

BBB to Josiah Russell (fragment)

[Circa May, 1894]

Papers are so scarce here that we almost never get to see anything personal about the war. This one will say "Oh did you see such and such a thing about Burnham in the Graphic," or this and that in the Times, Telegraph or some Colonial paper. "No, where is it I would like to see it." Oh, so and so had the paper or else I sent it off and this is the way it goes. It is very provoking.

Fred leaves this evening with Dr. Sauer of the Rhodesia Company and will be gone three weeks at the least. Our house is progressing and will be about ready to move into by the time Fred

1. This story is unconfirmed.

gets back. It is a lonesome life out here. I shall be glad when we are settled in town if Fred has to be away so much. I ought to be getting used to it but I am not. The old Hottentot woman here on the ranch made some beer last week and the whole family drank for several days. They always dance on such occasions and sing. The old woman is so comical. Wish you could see her dancing, such queer motions and such a silly smile on her face. When the beer is all gone and she comes back to everyday life, she makes things lively because no one has been working. I think you would enjoy life here. We do as it is and how much more would we if our whole "family" were with us. But I must confess that it is not as pretty as Pasadena. So you still sing "Grace, tis a charming sound." Did she go to the church of the Angels with you? Are you not afraid of her pet Maggie? . . . [letter incomplete].

———

BBB to Blick family [fragment]

[Circa May 1894]

I get more homesick than I ever did before in my life. But just think dear people I have not seen or spoken to but one woman for *five* months and I only saw her for a few hours, and she was a Dutch bride of sixteen summers and could speak very little English. And bear in mind that during this five months since leaving Victoria Fred has been away ten days during the second month and five weeks since the second week in April. When he was away at home [U.S.], you know I was always at home or had Mother or Howard with me, some place to go and something to see but I must not complain. I am *more* than glad that I came to Africa for Fred's sake for although he would have liked the country anyway I know he would not have been contented or happy without me here, and I am *sure positive* I would have been miserable and a bore even to you with him so far away. These spells only take me once in a while and will be less frequent when settled in our new house and get acquainted with all the desirable people. Mr. Cumming and Bob are very good to us. . . . Mr. C. is an Afrikander and quite well educated. He is almost twenty eight and reminds us so much of Joe [Blick] in figure, build and actions. He is darker than Joe. Looks more like Judd, some Spanish blood. We all like him very much, especially Roderick. He talks so much to Roderick and is always giving him something. Gave him a leather belt with a little bridle for a clasp, but it had no purse on it as most of the men's have so I fastened his little pocketbook on with a thong and he is happy now. He has stopped making ships now and turned his attention to whips. Mr. C. has given him two boxes, those oval pasteboard boxes, of California crystallized fruit, but I have enjoyed the sweets more than he has especially the apricots. He takes him into town whenever he goes in the P.M. with the donkey trap. By the way, John wants to know the price of the buckboard and donkeys in Durban. Could not get a buckboard so bought the running gear of a "spider"[1] and had the rest made to order, $150. Six donkeys cost $130. Harness very simple. Fred let the donkeys run around Victoria and did not have time to hunt them up when he came back so we only found three to bring in here. We took the buckboard apart and packed it in on a big wagon, had a boy drive the three donkeys and (I am sure I have told you this) have sold them for $380. We may eventually get the other three, for a friend to Fred wrote him just the other day that he had redeemed a donkey out of the pound that he thinks is Ta-ra. He is keeping her until Fred tells him what to do with her.

. . . The missionaries are like little kings in this country, have beautiful homes and everything that heart could wish. . . . They never seem to make any real converts, but make money and spoil the nig so that most "missionaried nigs" get the big head and do not make good servants. My old Zulu, Longboy, is proving quite a treasure for a black servant. I was going to discharge him and get Tom again but hear that Tom is getting very smart and cheeky and I am afraid would take advantage of me for I *cannot* be severe with them. Now old Longboy (he must be almost or quite forty) is always good natured, never looks ugly when I ask him to do anything, does not know how to cook as much or be as neat as Tom, but I shall keep him as long as he will stay. He is a good washer. Has been tanning a lot of goat skins for me. But I will tell you about my house and its furnishings when I get into it which Mr. [Andrew] Main[2] assures me will be next or rather *this* week, before

1. Light carriage.
2. Andrew Main built the Burnham house.

the first of June I hope. He is to help me move and I would like to be settled before Fred comes back. They have given Roderick a little goat and he is making great plans for driving it. He can talk Kaffir a good deal now. There was a nice little nig living here on the place that he used to play with, but Mr. Cumming has sent all the Hottentots away. More families kept coming, they were always getting drunk on Kaffir beer and altogether were getting to be a nuisance so he ordered them all off last Friday. They were such thieves too, and all lived off from him [letter incomplete].

———

BBB to Blick family

> Buluwayo, Matabeleland
> May 11, 1894
> Fred's birthday

Dear folks at home,

I feel too disappointed tonight to write and this must be mailed in the morning so it will be about the shortest African letter you ever received. The mail came in yesterday but the office was so full Mr. Cumming would not wait for the mail. He went into town again today and did not come home until sundown. Felt like commencing a letter several times today but would not feeling sure he would bring me several letters from home and I hoped one from Howard. Judge of my feelings when he came home and said he had been to the office twice but it was so full each time he did not wait. These Afrikanders do not care for letters as we do. He will be in town all day tomorrow so *maybe* will get to the P.O. window. Very poor mail accommodations here, but will be better in the new town. So will just write, as the country woman says, to let you know that we are well and hope that you are the same.

No mail left Buluwayo last week on account of some change in the service. Fred came home last Saturday noon, almost a week before I expected him. Did not go into Buluwayo until Sunday A.M. so we had a good long talk. Dr. Sauer and Mr. Gifford did not go to Salisbury so they all came back together. Wednesday morning Pete Ingram and Fred went out to the Belingwa Mts. to locate miners for this Rhodesia Co. They have a Scotch cart, oxen, three boys, a white man to talk to the Matabeles and peg the claims. Pete and Fred have each a good horse. They almost give Fred "carte blanche" is that the way to spell it? Anyway you know what I mean, so they have gone well equipped you may be sure. Of course Fred made a name as the *scout* but he can do other things besides scouting and people are finding it out. This sounds like boasting but you know we would never talk so to any one but our own people and you want to know all about us I am sure. No need for _____ . There I stopped writing and have forgotten what I was going to say. This is Fred's birthday and I have made a big fruit cake and will keep it until he comes back which will be in about three weeks, leaving Mr. Ingram out in the mountains. Then he will ride back in two or three weeks to look over the claims. . . .

Your loving daughter and sister,

B.B.B.

BBB to John and Phebe Blick

Buluwayo, Matabeland
May 28, 1894

Dearest mother and father,

 . . . Oh, if I could only talk to you tonight instead of trying to write. I want to tell you something and do not know how to commence, but do not think that you can guess what it is so will have to tell. Do not be sorry for me because I am very glad or will be, if we have a little daughter about the seventh of next month. Shall not be so pleased if it is a son but will love him just the same. Roderick has been such a comfort to both of us. It does not seem such a risky thing as it did before he came. He has proved such a success and maybe God will be as good to us this time. Now you know why I have tried to be as cheerful as possible for I kept this fact *constantly* in mind during those trying months when Fred was away, determined if it lay in my power *not* to make our child a misery to herself as well as others by a bad disposition. How far I have succeeded time only can tell for I *had* to give up once in a while. Fred knew before he came into Matabeleland, but was so *sure* and *confident* that he would come out unharmed, that the war would be over by Christmas, and he would have me nicely settled in Buluwayo before the 7th of June, and was so eager and anxious for the war that I did not have the heart to oppose him much, but it was a dreary outlook for me at that time. But Fred was so good to get a letter to me at every opportunity, found a few pleasant friends. . . . I have had *perfect* health all the time. Fred is doing so well here. Our house will be finished tomorrow night and Fred will be home the last of this week so there is a great deal for which to be thankful. A little one will be something more for me to love and will give Roderick and I something to think about and keep us from getting homesick as we do whenever Fred is away. Yes, I really and truly think that it is a good thing. Should not have thought it so good if I had been at home with all of you around me to love and so many things to take up my time. Do I make you understand my feelings? It is so hard to write. Roderick shall not feel at all slighted. He is so wise and old fashioned and has such faith in me that I know I can make it all right with him and he will help us love and care for her. He will be almost eight years older. Oh why can't I get to you and *talk*. That is the one hard thing. Neither of my mothers can be with me but I am sure that *both* would be if possible, so I do not expect such perfect care as I had before, but do not be uneasy. Mrs. Nelson will undoubtedly be here as she left Victoria over three weeks ago, and is very fond of me even if she is jealous. She said she would come and stay with me, volunteered to come. I shall be very glad to see her for she has a good heart, if she *has* a quick temper. And now about doctors. There is one practicing here and two retired, Dr. Sauer and Dr. Jameson. Dr. S. told Fred that Dr. Levey was very good, but that if anything happened *he* would do all he could and now Dr. Jameson has returned and he has as big a reputation as anyone in S. Africa and I know he would come if necessary. So you need not worry for fear that I will not get proper attention. Fred will be with me and he will see that I am not neglected. Still I cannot help wishing that we made our entry into this world in a little easier fashion. I am so well and strong and grow stronger every year. Maybe a hale, hearty old lady yet with a big family, ten Fred says, but I am afraid we have commenced a little too late to reach that number. Well what are you all saying? I wish I could hear you. Have we not succeeded in keeping you pretty well stirred up since leaving the day after Christmas of 92, and is not this a surprise? Tell me what each one says about it, and don't you wish you could see the little girl. I have prayed, thought and talked little girl, until I shall be very much disappointed if it is not.

. . . Now, what shall we name her? That is the next important question. Please send a list of your favorite names and if I do not find one that suits our fancy, will call her (or him) "baby" until the names arrive. Is not *Dorothy* Grace's favorite name? But suppose that would be shortened into Dora and I do not like that.

We are so far away and it takes such a long time to get an answer, but we can see the dipper, but *not* the north star and when I look at it I am glad because you saw the *same* stars the day before. Can see the north star for some distance after crossing the equator but we are too far south for that.

Roderick's bird died last week and he is nursing a pail full of little minnows now. Just as he went to sleep tonight he said wouldn't he love to feel dear old grandpa's arms around him and how he *would hug*. He wanted me to come to bed but I must write of evenings now until I have written several farewell letters as an old hen with one chick. I am kissing you both good night.
Your loving daughter
B.B.B.

———

BBB to Madge Blick Ford [first four pages missing]
[Circa May, 1894]
The hut is lined with blue limbo [calico] and they [rats] run between that and the walls, over the floor, and squeal and gnaw. I do not get nervous but they make so much noise that they waken me a dozen times every night. Have never felt but two on the bed but in the hut where Mr. C. and Bob sleep there is no door and they simply play hide and seek or tag over them. Mr. Main was here last Sunday with a fearful looking nose. He tried to catch a rat running across his face. The rat escaped but his nose suffered. Cats are worth their weight in gold and very scarce, but Fred has a good friend who is going to give us a kitten as soon as we get into our new house. It is a *house* with tight walls, doors and windows so I think with the aid of a kitten I can keep them out. Poison by the wholesale but whenever one dies two come in its place. I have killed two here by hitting them with a stick when running over the ceiling. Such is life in a hut in Matabeleland but the ants do not bother us here at all, and the huts are new and the borers have not commenced to work. They are a

small hard backed insect that eats holes in all the native wood, sifting everything with a fine fine yellow dust. But strange to say they will not touch imported wood. There is not a stick of native timber in our house so the borers will not tumble the house down over our heads. Just for fun I will ask Mr. Main the cost of doors, windows, boards and iron the next time I see him. It is something awful I know on account of transport and the great demand.

Two of the boys begin hauling wood for me tomorrow and poles for the fence. Want to lay in a good supply before handing over the Company team. They told Fred to use it until we got everything settled so it has saved us a good many sovereigns. Shall have enough wood hauled to last a year or more $2.50 a load already cut here on Mr. C. farm or $5.00 if they deliver it. It is evening now and Longboy has brought the hot water for a bath for Roderick and so I must draw this epistle to a close. I am so glad that John and Kate are doing so well and am very proud of my university brother and sister and hope we will find work for them over here. Of course Grace you can set type or teach over here. We will soon have a printed newspaper. Pshaw, I can think of ever so many more things to say but must take this letter over to the hut so they can take it in early in the morning. Will send it down by coach which is faster than the present mail line so perhaps you will get it sooner than some of the others. . . .
With love, love, love
From all to all,
B.

You shall *each* and all have a letter soon if not sooner.

———

Telegram: FRB to Rebecca Russell Burnham

Buluwayo
31st of May, 1894
Dear Mother,

In order to keep up the sensational just inform your friends that you are Grandma now to a little African (Girl) wgt about 7 lbs.

Looks exactly like everybody in the family—June 3rd. BB is all right was sick only a few hours. I as usual was off.

I tell you we miss our large herd of relatives now.

This is news enough for this time.

Yours as ever,

Fred

B. was going to write a lot of letters but *moving* into our new house hurried up the stranger who doubtless wanted to get early experience at moving. We being such *novices*.

———

FRB to Josiah Russell

Buluwayo

June 5th 1984

Dear Uncle,

... The town is a buzz of saws and hammers and in a cloud of red dust, but good wells can be had at 35 ft and by next year we will have the streets sprinkled and soon well graveled. The B.S.A. company will furnish at cost fruit trees of all kinds and ornamental trees free. All the products of California will grow here. Climate about same, save that it rains about 30 inches per season, Dec. Jan. Feb. Mar. and April, about same season as California but they are warm rains and some thunder and lightening, no cyclones or wind storms. BB has sent description of our house &c. so you see it is not quite total barbarism here and it is all paid for and made by African money. I have not yet used a cent sent over to us. In fact finances are easier with me than they ever were before. Nevertheless I know these flush times cannot last long and shall make hay while the sun shines and get Grace and John to do same.

I advance them the money to come, $500 each, and as soon as they earn that amount they can send the money over for any others of our family that may have the African fever badly. I think Jack should come out here as a missionary. They all do well with the nigs and get good living no work and can make money on the outside. I have secured the holding open of a $100 per month job for Grace, special work on the paper here until her arrival. It is not so easy done either when at the B.S.A. offices are about 500 applications from England for jobs for every soft snap. ...

I feel that it is nearly useless to go into long details and pages

of yarns concerning war topics for we will all meet again and a long way this side of the river of shadows too. I read with interest your ideas of things after the events of war and leave others to shout any praises of the part they see fit. I am working for startling things yet to come and will succeed. . . .
FRB

———

BBB to Phebe Blick

Buluwayo, Matabeleland
July 2, 1894

Dear little mother,

I am going to commence this letter in time so as not to be hurried at the last minute as all my last letters have been. This is Monday evening and my letter will not have to go until Friday P.M. My two babies and Mrs. Nelson's little Annie are sound asleep. Mrs. Nelson is reading The Family Herald. I can hear the boys talking out at the fire where they are eating their "scoff." We have two big colonial boys sinking the well, and I have a raw Matabele for kitchen boy while old Longboy is off hunting for a wife. Have I written you about that? He was so good while I was sick. He walked miles after the doctor, medicines, hunting a washwoman, carrying clothes &c. Everything was in the old town then. Carried countless kegs of water, and the water is almost a mile away. All that without a grumble or single cross look, so we gave him some presents and among them, a black coat of Fred's. (More of this coat hereafter.) Well as soon as I was up and around the house again he told us that he wanted to go to the Matabele kraals and try to get him a wife and then he wanted to come back and work for us. (He had been with us for five months.) Said he did not want to work for any other boss, for Fred was a very good boss, not "cheeky" at all and always paid him, while I was a very good missus and never said "checha! checha!" (hurry! hurry!) or scolded, so he would like to work for us and bring his wife too if he could get one. But he was somewhat doubtful. Said maybe the Matabeles would say that he came in with the white men and killed all their brothers so they would not give him a wife. But a wife was very nice and he would like to have one. So Fred told him he could go and he got Charlie to work for us while he is gone. He came back after about ten days and wanted leave to stay a month. I am afraid he was a little tipsy and he will drink all his money up if not careful and then he cannot buy a wife. I hardly knew him. He had dressed himself up so gaily with a gaudy scarf around his hat, a bright plaid shirt, gray canvas trousers with red socks pulled up over them and big coarse shoes. He is very tall and thin so had his trousers drawn in around the waist until he looked as though he was wearing a bustle. Fred's coat hit him just above the belt and the sleeve just below the elbows, bracelets of brass, iron and leather, whiskers shaved until he looked a young gallant of 20 instead of an old slow poke of 40 as he really is. But he is a willing boy and never cheeky, but enough about blacks except that Roderick plays with them very little and I shall try my best to keep him the pure, modest little Roderick he always was and I do not think it will be a difficult task. But there are negroes everywhere and he is learning the language very fast. There are so many clicks with the tongue in the Zulu or Matabele language and he is very fond of using those words containing clicks. Fred is learning also but of course Roderick is the best because he is just the right age to pick up languages. I am afraid I shall never learn much. Will always try to have a boy that can talk a little English. Now I am going to read a little in *Nada the Lily*[1] and then baby will be awake soon and must be made ready for bed. So good night until tomorrow.

Wednesday evening. I was too tired and sleepy to write last night, so went to bed before half past seven. Baby does not cry in the night, but I have not got quite used to a baby yet and she gets restless about five until half past six and then it is time to get up. For the last two months before baby came I slept every morning until between eight and nine. The days are so short now and there are many little things to be done in the house yet. The sitting room is all finished except tacking up a few photographs and it looks really cozy. Have I ever described it? I am so forgetful.

. . . Our walls are smooth brown plaster (mud). Will have lime here sometime. But thank fortune I have board floors and day before yesterday I tacked mats all over them. The mats are six feet long about and vary in width from 1½ to 3 feet. About as service-

1. A novel by H. Rider Haggard.

able I imagine as our cheap matting but I cannot have bare floor and there is nothing else here. I have ten pretty goat hides scattered around and four of them are very pretty black ones, so the floors look nice. Windows draped with combination curtains, one half are muslin and the other a plum color and gold drapery cloth (cheap but pretty) which I brought from Naples, 15 yds double width and I am so fortunate in having it for there is nothing to be had here yet. My lounge is covered with it, back, seat, pillows and valance and finished off with a braid made from my old plum velvet sleeves, feather stitched with gold (yellow linen). Baby's bed, a box set up on legs, is lined with this same drapery and has a valance of it. I feel sorry for her when I think of all the pretty things Roderick had, but she is thriving wonderfully and does not seem to miss anything and looks very sweet under her drapery of coarse bobbinet.[2] Her basket is like our Indian baskets and is large and deep. My chair is covered with gray canvas feather stitched with blue and fancy-worked cushion, pillow and ottoman. Shelves and corner cupboard, curtains of drapery and top shelves covered with matting and matting dadoes. Is that the way you spell it? Books on the top of the shelves and dishes underneath. Corner cupboard is for my china and little pretty things on top. Over the fireplace we have a Matabele headdress, shield, assegai, battle-ax and a knobkerrie of rhinoceros horn. Italian portiere at the bedroom door and one for a table cover. Regular hat rack between the door and window. Two fancy fans and I will put up some photos. Camp chair by the front window, completely covered with a kaross[3] of rock rabbit skins. Have six cane-seated chairs. Now for the bedroom. Underneath our beds are boxes of canned goods &c. The washstand is a big tin lined box containing flour, potatoes, sugar, dried fruit &c. The bed is covered with pretty oil cloth, a strip of oil cloth tacked up for a splasher. Wardrobe, although made of boxes, is large and has five big shelves. The lower box is tin lined. Valances around the beds and curtains on the boxes. I made two pretty shoe bags. The bedroom is all arranged but the curtains are not made yet for the beds and cupboard. Sent to Johannesburg last week for a cook stove and we will have an addition built on before

2. Mesh cloth.
3. Kaross—native garment or rug of skins.

the rainy season comes. Some of this sounds as though I had written it before but I will not repeat it again. I am sure I wrote about Howard last week in my letter to Uncle.

Baby is so healthy and strong. I can fairly see her grow. Mrs. Nelson is like Etta was. She wants to take all the care of the baby, but unlike Roderick no one but mamma can take care of her at night. She is so good. Has never cried during her bath not even the first day. Sleeps all the morning, but very short naps after two P.M. until about 6:30 P.M. She smiles at us now and Mrs. Nelson says is really wonderfully smart for such a little baby and will certainly be like her father. Rather quick to tell isn't it? She is a great admirer of Fred but I am not jealous. She is a great help to me. Roderick is very fond of her. Fred has been gone a week now. . . .

Well, here it is Thursday evening and my letter must be mailed tomorrow. I forgot to tell you that I have an otter skin and five leopard cat skins. Shall have a kaross made when I collect a few more. How I wish we could see you tonight. I do not think that we would sleep much. I would like to show you our baby. Hurry up and send us some names or I will call her Nada (the Lily). Does it not seem strange for me to have a little girl. She is really pretty. Her eyes are such a dark blue but of course it is too soon to tell much about whether she will be a beauty or not. . . .

Is Grace coming or not, that is the question? Surely she will not fail me. There is no friend like one of your own family. Auntie is full of her praises. The travel and complete change will make a new woman of her. She *must* come. It will be lovely to have John but he will be away so much with or for Fred and—he is not a woman to talk with on such important subjects as babies and dresses. There is a photographer here, but only an amateur (I knew how to spell that word when I commenced writing it, but my memory failed before I reached the end). If I can get a good photo of baby when she is three months old, I will send you one. Some of the scouts had their photos taken before Fred and Pete went away. But they were taken out of doors and I am afraid they will not be very good. . . .

We thought of Grace on her birthday and wondered where you spent the Fourth and thought of the many jolly Fourths we have spent together. Fred was not at home. We will have to make some sort of a celebration next year for there are many Americans here and more coming. A very pleasant one, Mr. [Jefferson] Clark, expert for John Hays Hammond called on me the other day.

The town is building so fast, all bustle, movement and dust. I have not been away from the house yet. Mrs. Nelson has taken baby for several walks. I must go soon but I do not seem to care about it. Bob Bain is going to take me for a drive tomorrow. Came yesterday but the wind was blowing too hard. Mr. Glogg wanted me to go last Sunday, but I declined although it was a beautiful day and I did want to go but, although Mr. G. knows Fred very well and I have seen him often, he is too much of a talker and would tell the whole town. He told Fred that he would take me for a drive whenever I wanted to go, and Fred thanked him but left it for me to say no. Bob and Mr. Cumming you remember are our old friends and the dairy farmers where Rod and I lived in April and May. . . .
Your loving daughter B.

I may be too busy to write next week.

———

FRB to Josiah Russell

Buluwayo Aug 5th 1894

Dear Uncle,

Things are not so quiet and prosaic here as they might be from a war boom. We have progressed into a regular land boom and a town of iron, brick and mortar is going up as rapidly as ox teams can bring it, but we are 500 miles from end of R.R. and more, so when rains begin building must cease for a few months at least. Stands (lots) 100 × 140 on market square sold as high as £1000—$5000, pretty stiff. The town is like all Cal. towns during boom days, dust 6 inches deep, weather dry, sunny, and fine. I loaded up 5 stands pretty close in, sold one of my farms 6000 acres to do it. Don't know if I did right thing or not. Only thing I look at is I will be better able to unload stands than farms, for of course a setback must come here as elsewhere when a boom is on.

I see by paper that a lot of Americans are coming over here. But they must all know that so far there is no mill running and no rich placer mines to furnish money to the newcomer, that he must outfit himself and find his own reef before he can hope to win fortune. So far there has been a tremendous amount of pegging of claims and on very fair looking reefs generally and in about two years we will have an output of bullion. If a man wants to go into the cattle business, he can do so here on very small capital and will I think do well. Fruit growing would also [fare] well as all Africa imports California fruit and a can of peaches or pears cost 85 cts in Buluwayo.

All your statements of accounts at hand O.K. I sent my power of attorney some ages ago, I think about April 10th. Your drafts all turned up at last but I have not yet got the Johannesburg one, $109 cashed yet. *Red Tape* galore. Thank *God* my widow was not waiting for that money to buy bread. Publish this item for all Americans coming to Africa.

"All Americans proposing going to Africa take due notice that no drafts, checks, bills of credit or any paper whatever not even Bank of England notes which generally bring premium in most countries, escapes the discount shylocks in Africa. That robbery is rare and the best way to carry money is in English gold in a belt sewed round you."

The *Examiner* and clippings arrived and very glad to get them. Coxy[1] seems to be on every line but the unrest of the people is more and more prominent than ever before and must take definite shape one of these days. A rule or rather misrule of capitalists is no better than a monarch or a czar.

I see M. H. Sherman is about to get into hot water. He is one of the shrewdest scoundrels this country has ever produced. I have watched his career for 14 years now and he is not of the ordinary type at all. Were he in larger spheres of action he would have been a match for the great R.R. wrecker Jay Gould. His energy is like a volcano and he can bury the individual Moses H. Sherman absolutely to accomplish his ends. The U.S. is indeed in need of change when such men can [break] a savings bank (the peoples' in name). . . . It seems strange that Africa can be on prosperous times long with all the world in turmoil, and some fine morning we may wake up and find our lovely little boom has taken wings and gone. Well if it does, I shall not get unduly excited. We have here the liv-

---

1. Jacob S. Coxy led a march of the unemployed on Washington in the summer of 1894.

ing example of the black, who is a fatalist and watches the queer antics of the white man much as we would a squadron of mounted angels and Satan's choicest regiment of devils weave in and out in their constant warfare.

Food we can get here at any rate, clothing we don't need, shelter we all ready have, so if the boom must break let it break. It is only a trek or two into the wilderness where booms are [not] and never were known, and it is a strange thing how quick one forgets all about the tremendous issues of other lands and other days. The perspective changes so rapidly and sometimes I wonder if at the awakening after death we will in a few short hours have blotted from our new existence all of this. The same as a dream of the night (unless very very vivid) is lost by the time the odor of morning coffee strikes the nostrils. Certain it is the true proportion of events and things can never be reached in one short span of life.

[BBB writing] Fred was too busy to write any more so have I. He and Pete have just started for a two months trip into the fly country toward the Zambezi. Dread the long time and wish Grace was here. Will write to my mother next week.
B.

―――――――

BBB to Blick family

Buluwayo, Aug. 13, 1894

Dear little mother and darling old daddy,
. . . Fred wrote the news of his arrival in my last letter home. Well he stayed just exactly two weeks. Left again on the 10th for a trip north. Have taken donkeys to go into the fly country. The fly kill oxen and horses, and donkeys can only live for two or three months. Do not harm men except to be slightly annoying. They were very bad two years ago, but Fred hopes they may not be so bad this year. He thinks—Well, I do not know what he thinks for Dulcie[1] woke up just then and it is Tuesday evening now. She is asleep and Roderick is, as usual, drawing. It is the Stars and Stripes

―――――――

1. The Burnhams were slow to settle on names for their children. It took them years to decide on Roderick instead of Roy, and Blanche tried out several names for their daughter before choosing Nada.

this evening. Have I told you that we have received all the school books now? He is very pleased to use Aunt Kate's books. The arithmetic and geography are too far advanced for him yet a while. But I want him to have the Cal. books. He wants to know who those two girls in the lower cave on the Eagle Rock are. He was delighted with the photos and the letter from his dear chum. She [Grace] will be nearly here when this reaches you. I cannot tell you how anxious I am to see them. It is <u>so</u> lonely when Fred is away. There are a great many ladies in town but many of them are of the shady sort and I want to know who they are before I make their acquaintance. Mrs. Rorke[2] and Mrs. Holder have returned my calls but they are away on the other side of the town, too far for me to walk with baby, and Mrs. Rorke has boarders and Mrs. Holder a big family for which she does all the cooking and washing, so you see they do not have much spare time. Mrs. Campbell spends a day every week with me and Mrs. Nelson has been up to stay all night once since going home. Mrs. Hines (from Victoria) has spent two different days with me but none of them are Mrs. Greenfield. I had another letter from her last week. Mr. Hines has bought the stand cat-a-corner from us and will soon commence building. In the mean time they are staying two miles from here. She is very pleasant but is inclined to talk about her neighbors. When Grace comes I shall not care whether I have any "female" neighbors or not. We will always have plenty of gentlemen and even more when Grace is here, yes many more. So many coming and going when Fred is at home, but only three or four old standbys when he is away for you know I am not a flirting woman. Bob spent the day here today and went to the office, for the English mail was in. Not a single letter from Cal. Yesterday I had one from Howard. He talks of coming up soon. We will have the largest family of any of you then. Fred wrote Uncle about his investing in four more stands. One across the street from us. Two a block farther out on the other side of the market square and one out several blocks where we will eventually live for if the town goes ahead at all these others will be good business stands. Already there are shops in front of us at the side and

2. This is probably the Melina Rorke who, like many others, described Blanche Burnham as the most "practical person I had ever met." Melina Rorke, *The Story of Melina Rorke, R.R.C.* (New York: The Greystone Press, 1938). pp. 123–124.

back and the other side of our new stand. Fred bought stands for Pete and "Bill Nye" at £80 each and one for Mrs. Nelson at £40. I will send you the Buluwayo paper. During those few days Charter shares went from 27/ to 41/. Building is going on very fast and in the meantime canvas houses and huts. I went to look at our new stands with Fred the day that Mrs. Nelson was here. It is prettier on that side. Whichever way the town grows we will be O.K. Well I sincerely hope so for I was actually homesick this P.M. It is so monotonous for me. I have only been off the stand four times. No perambulator, baby is too heavy for me and I will not let a black carry her. Oh how I wish you could see her. She is so healthy and strong. Beautiful white skin but I am happy to say her new hair is dark brown instead of white as I thought it would be. But there is no doubt about her eyes being *blue* with such a big pupil. A square forehead like Roderick's and Judd's. Such dear little round ears and unlike Roderick's they set *so* close to her head. Such a jolly romping baby as she is with a big laugh and "ah goo" for every one. Wants to laugh and talk when she wakes up in the night. But she sleeps so little in the daytime. Nothing like Roderick did. I often think of you mother. How in the world did you manage to do all your work and bring up such a family? Perhaps I will learn to manage better when I have three or four more. . . .

Roderick's birthday is a week from tomorrow. Am going to give him a little party and will write about it afterward. He is out in the moonlight now cracking his whip. I must call him in and we must go to bed.

Fred thinks he can send word to me two or three times. I *do* hope he will not be gone two months. Pete Ingram is with him of course. Well good night dear ones with a thousand kisses which we wish we could deliver in person.

Friday morning. Miss Dorothy has taken it into her head to give up sleeping for the last three days. Wakes up at six A.M. and goes to bed at 8 P.M. Sleeps good at night but not more than two hours and a half during the whole day, so I am too tired to write in the evening. She is not sick or cross but wants you to pay attention to her. Mrs. Campbell is here today and is holding baby now. She wants to talk and jump all the time. She is so bright and sweet. Oh how I wish you could see her. Roderick and I have concluded that we must make a visit home in about two years so that we can see you all. What do you think of that. I wish we were going to start tomorrow but not without Fred. With a thousand kisses and un-limited love to you both and all the children from your loving daughter B. and grandson Roy and granddaughter Kathleen. B.B.B.

━━━━━

BBB to Blick family

Buluwayo, Matabeleland
Sept. 14, 1894

To my dear ones at home,

I do not know to whom I will address this letter but I think it is the Blicks turn. Madge objects to these general letters but what else am I to do. But I will forgive her for she did not know about our little Dorothy at that time. It is 10:55 A.M. and she has been asleep ten minutes for the first time since seven this morning. I have answered a business letter for Fred and will write to you now until she wakes up. Tom is washing the windows. (The flies are very numerous here.) Roderick is getting his arithmetic lesson. Has had the reading, spelling and writing. Well what do you think! Roderick and I, Dorothy stayed with Mrs. O'Conor, went to a dance last night. He wore his white suit and I my black silk with yellow flowers. Was afraid I could not get into the bodice but I managed. The skirt was always a little short but I am broader through the hips now so I let the hem down and put on a pretty black lace flounce. (Dorothy is awake now. She has been asleep just twenty-five minutes, which is ten minutes longer than she gener-ally sleeps. She is playing with the mosquito netting now.) While on the subject—of toilets—I will answer Madge's question as to whether I am tanned or not. I was very brown after our three and a half months trek to Victoria. Then I bleached out a little but was swarthy. Now they say my complexion is very good. I must take Dorothy now.

12:45. Baby is measuring the widths in her dress and while she is so occupied I will go on with my description. You ask am I get-ting older looking. Mrs. Hines told me yesterday that I looked younger than when in Victoria. I seem larger too, and although my white hairs are increasing they do not show in the waves as they did in the curls. Everyone likes my hair waved. Say it looks so quaint and unlike everyone else. In fact, not common, as Mrs. Whitmore used to say. Roderick looked like a little gentleman as he *is*. The ballroom was very nice and there must have been thirty or more ladies. No barmaids or shady ones there, but of course mostly married ones. Grace and I must learn to dance. Mr. and Mrs. Hines, friends from Victoria, are building just across the corner from us and while the house is being built Mrs. Hines spends most of the day with me as it is so hot in their tent. She is very pleasant and so nice to Roderick and baby. Much more of a companion for me than dear old Mrs. Nelson. Well Mrs. Hines says she can easily teach us to dance and as that is about the only kind of amusement here we must learn.

Sunday 4 P.M.. and I did not get this letter off last Friday. Could have sent these two pages but thought you would rather wait a week and have a longer letter. Last week passed so much more quickly for me on account of having Mrs. Hines here so much. Mr. Hines is away today and she stayed to luncheon with me. Beautiful bread and butter, lettuce and cress salad, and sliced oranges. Potted ham but neither of us tasted it. Roderick is spending the day with Mrs. Nelson. Mrs. Nelson never has anything to wear so I let her wear my cream skirt with a bodice of Miss Denham's. Mine was too small for her. Miss Denham was thrown out of the trap on the way to the dance and had her skirt all torn to pieces, so they sent over for one of mine and I sent the only one I thought she could wear, my gray one from Paris. They returned the skirts this morning. Mrs. Nelson had *washed* the cream skirt, not all over but about up to nine inches or a foot from the top. As a result it is all streaked and is about two inches shorter than the underskirt. I had no idea she would attempt to wash it. Would have known she would spoil it. Luckily it has a wide hem, but the chances are that it will be made over for baby. But the gray one, the only good walking skirt I have, well Miss Denham has spilled all sorts of refreshments over it, but fortunately did not attempt to clean it. Do not know whether I can get them all out or not and I have always been so careful with it. Well I have learned a lesson. I will never loan a dress again. The Nelsons are soon going out to their farm. Some of Mr. Cumming's relatives are enroute to Salisbury and Miss Cumming and Miss Bisadenen stopped over for a week. They were here for tea last Sunday evening. Mr. Cumming took us out there to spend the day last Monday. They were in for breakfast on Wednesday and I expect them here this evening to stay until Tuesday morning when they will take the coach for Salisbury. I do not care for them very much but I must show them some attentions for Mr. Cumming's sake. Mr. C. is building a nice house out on his farm. Mr. Main and Bob Bain have gone with their wagons for a month's trading trip. Fred told me to have Mr. Main build the addition for us if he did not ask more than £70 or £80 but he wants £100, so I shall wait until Fred comes back. Material and labor are both cheaper now and I do not think it ought to cost so much. Others are getting work done cheaper.

I have made some new friends, Mrs. and Miss O'Conor. A number of our friends were born and brought up in the same town with them and were always urging me to go see them and they are very nice indeed. Mrs. O'Conor is a nurse and a very nice motherly old body she is. They are only living four stands from me. The night of the dance I carried baby over there at 7:30 and called for her at 12. She had never opened her eyes during that time but Mrs. O'Conor wrapped her up so snugly for me to carry home that in unrolling her she commenced to cry but I soon talked her out of that and she cooed and kicked up her heels until I undressed, braided my hair and undressed her. Then she had a drink and went off to sleep until five in the morning. She is growing very pretty. Such dark blue eyes and very fair complexion. Her eyelashes are growing long and *dark* and she is by no means a towhead. Roderick takes more interest in her every day. Fred won't know her when he comes back. I am sure she will walk by the time she is nine months old, for she is always jumping. She is asleep now. I have put her down twice but wakens in a few minutes, so I am holding her on my lap. She will always take a pretty fair nap if I will do that.

This town is surging ahead very fast. Oh, if we only had a railroad from Johannesburg. That is so slow in this country. Oh, I had a letter from Fred last week but it was two weeks old. Sir Frederick Franklin, one of the mine inspectors, had visited their camp. They were then just on the edge of the fly and had made their camp to leave the oxen and cart with boys to look after them and were going to start with their donkeys the next day. Wanted to find something good so could not tell how long they would stay. That was Aug. 24 so

I shall still look for them within the two months. He left here Aug. 10, so the time is on the last half. Sir Frederick's wife was a New Yorker and he has been all over the states. He is very pleasant to talk with and staid over an hour. I had such a lot of callers that P.M., seven, and all between four and six. I am so thankful for my little tea set. I wonder if mother has sent me the tea cosey. Have only received one pair of canvas shoes and a little doily. No papers last week. They are generally a week behind the letters. I am sure I have told you that the schoolbooks had all arrived. I *was so* pleased to get letters from home last week. One from Madge, July 23. One from home, the same date. You cannot scold me for not writing when you let such a long time elapse. A letter from mother and one from Howard. He has concluded that he does not want the baby called by that name after all. He bids me tell all the Blicks and Burnhams that they always claimed Roderick, and he wants them to know that he has a mortgage on this little girl, that he spoke for her years ago, and that they are not to claim even one of her little fingers. Emphatic isn't he? . . .

We did not expect answers to our "surprise letter" quite so soon, and are now counting the days until Grace and John come. Your letters were all mailed July 31 or Aug. 1. They should start at least by the 13th if they come by the American Line as you suggest they will not stop over long in London and may be here within two or three weeks. Perhaps before Fred returns. Yes ma, I realize how hard it will be for you to part with them and how good you are to let them come. Yes, tell Uncle that we had the plan in our mind long ago but did not like to raise false hope by writing because we did not think of sending for them before next spring, but affairs have developed so rapidly with us during the last few months. We considered the plan well and think it a good one. I am so relieved to think that Grace is coming. I will take good care of her, father. I do not want her to get married unless she finds the right man in every respect. One like Fred for instance and I do not know of any such in this town. I will see that John does not learn any bad habits while with us. Without conceit I know of at least three young men who are much better men for knowing Fred and I so well. I only wish we had Howard nearer us. Oh, I can hardly wait for surely Grace and John will be here soon. It seems too good to be true, and did Grace have any doubts about coming? Poor mother. It does seem mean to take them from you, but you have all the others. We need them and it will do them good to see more of the world. . . . I must work very hard and get some sewing done before Grace and John come for I know we shall do nothing then but talk for some time. My tongue longs to commence. . . . And so Helen thought her new cousin would be black. That is too good. She has such beautiful, large, dark, blue eyes. It is evening now and she is asleep. Madge says she thought I would call her Nina or Essie. I would have loved to call her Nina for our little sister that I worshipped so but Fred says no, that Nina is a memory. This is not the same Nina and it would re-call past sorrows. That it is not as if Nina were living, but she died when a baby. In fact I think he considers it unlucky although he does not say so and I feel a little the same way myself. . . . Roderick and I have been calling her Dorothy for the last two or three weeks when I did not call her sweetheart or baby. People are so amused over her little black stockings. They never saw such a thing before. That is because she is a little American if she was born in Africa. . . .

Friday P.M. Fred came home yesterday morning and starts by coach next Monday for Johannesburg on business. Will most likely come back with John and Grace if they started on the 15. . . .
Love and kisses from all
B.

———

FRB to Josiah Russell

Buluwayo, Sept 22, 1894

Dear Uncle,
Have just returned from a trip to the Zambezi River, a vast wilderness it is and very interesting. Elephants walked round our camp almost every night and huge hippos often raised their queer heads out of the deep pools in the Inyati River and gazed in won-der at the new kind of savage now on their shores.

Night was often made musical by the lions and hyenas. The lions tackled our camp 3 times but we were unlucky in getting any of them although one was hard hit, and I followed his trail next day for several miles until lost in a rocky range of hills, the blood spoor dry-ing up entirely. We left our oxen and wagon and horses on the edge of the fly country and taking carriers and donkeys went toward the great river. Part of the country quite level but much of it is rough being made out of black slate ranges of about 300 ft. to 600 ft. high and covered with scrub, timber and occasionally large trees, but the travel is often helped out by the huge paths beaten out by the elephants and along all the streams by buffalo and hippo. Ingram and myself caught a hippo in a small pool in the Inyati River and lassoed him with a huge rope made of the bark of a particular kind of tree on which the elephant mainly feeds. We also had another rope made of waterbuck hides which on the first throw, after driving him from the pool with poles and rocks, we caught his lower jaw and soon had him snubbed to a tree solidly. We rode him just for the fun of the thing but he is a failure as a beast of burden or as saddle horse. We made every effort to drive him in to Buluwayo but it was useless and he tore up the earth like a cyclone and was as balky as a govt. mule and very vicious. . . . [letter incomplete].

———

BBB to Rebecca Russell Burnham

Buluwayo, Sept 30, 1894

Dear Mother,

When did I write last and what did I say? My mind is in a complete muddle with Fred just arriving in Johannesburg today and Grace and John leaving there for Buluwayo tomorrow. Fred will see them before they start. As you have doubtless heard they were too late to secure seats in last week's coach so had to remain there all last week. I had the letter of instruction all ready to mail when your letters saying they would start Aug. 14 and the telegram announcing their arrival in Johannesburg were received last Monday Sept. 23. They came so much sooner than I expected, . . . although Fred declares now that when he went north he told me they would arrive here about the 8th of Oct. and I must write to Johannesburg soon. So now when this telegram came saying, "No instructions. Much disappointed," Fred was so glad that he could say, "It's all B's fault. I told her to write." Well I will take all the blame and I am *so* sorry that I failed to have a letter there for them. I was just one week too late. In my mind I put myself in their place and can imagine how disappointed they were and vexed with me I know. They are due here next Saturday night. We are never certain at what hour the coach will arrive. So Pearl Ingram will wait at the coach office for them and I shall sit up here for them with the fatted calf just ready to bring in and put on the table. Oh, it is so hard to wait a week for them, and yet, since Fred had to go to Johannesburg, I wish they had been a week later and then they could have returned with him, but I am sure Grace will not want to wait another week in Johannesburg even for the pleasure of returning with Fred. He wired to John before starting and also to the coach office to reserve seats for them. Fred is with them today. The hard part of their journey is yet to come—the coach ride.

. . . Grace and John are young but it will be hard on them, but I will take good care of them, give them pillows to sit on &c. and the sight of little smiling baby will soon revive them. I am afraid she will never be named. Fred does not like Dorothy (glad of that). Roderick does not like Leah Nada (Fred's choice) and so it goes. I call her little happy most of the time for you *never* look at her but what she will smile even the minute her eyes are open in the morning. She grows prettier every day. . . .

Pearl Ingram is staying out on Mr. C's farm now but I see them every day. They were going to take us all out there today, but the wind was blowing too strong for baby. Roderick went with them. They will bring him back and come here for tea this evening. Last Sunday evening Fred invited Mr. Hammond, an old timer from Arizona (the Hammond of that San Francisco party), and Capt. Newman[1] to come here for tea. I had for tea salmon, lettuce salad with hard boiled eggs, blanc mange and boiled custard and cake. Mr. and Mrs. Hines came over after supper and we had a very pleasant time. . . .

Yours lovingly,
Blanche

━━━━━━━━━

Grace Blick to Blick family

Buluwayo, Matabeleland
South Africa
Oct. 14, 1894

My Dear People,

This is only Monday and the coach don't go until Friday, but if I expect to get much of a letter written I shall have to begin now

---

1. Norris Newman, editor of the Buluwayo *Chronicle*.

and write every chance I get. Baby takes nearly all our time and then B. has a good deal of company coming in at any time, and as there is no place to go and write but this one room I'm afraid your letters won't be very good. It's very warm this morning and so dusty and windy. John and Fred and . . .

Thursday A.M.—Pete came in at this time yesterday and I didn't have time to say that Fred had a lot of nigs and is putting in a foundation for the two rooms that are to be built on these two rooms and he and John are bossing the job. They did a good deal to it yesterday, and this morning John is working, and Fred has gone to see a man. Oh dear, the baby is crying and I must take her. You will only get notes from me I am afraid mother. There seems so much to do when there is a baby.

Afternoon—Well, I am at it again curled up in my easy position on the lounge. I mean Roy's bed in the bedroom. Capt. White, one of the big men of this country and the son of a lord, is talking to Fred in the other room.[1] Fred is off again day after tomorrow and John will be boss of the men. He will get a carpenter to help him. . . . I am not going to work for several weeks. Fred doesn't want me to work for the man he first got me the position of. He isn't good and the man on the other and better paper is all right. You know there are three papers here and it's easy to get a place, because the men get drunk and leave all of a sudden. Oh dear, the men are in the other room and are talking such interesting stuff. I'll have to go out. It seems that John and Pete are going out on a pegging trip of a few weeks and leave tomorrow. Fred goes in a few days too. They all go for Capt. White. John is perfectly happy. He likes Pete and then he is going someplace. They take good provisions and a nig to do the hard work and mean to have a good time. B. and I will be alone with the children and we mean to have a good time too. We were planning some of the tea parties we mean to give when they are gone. Mr. Cumming and Mr. Bain will be here yet. Mr. B. is the other one of B's friends. He returned yesterday from a trading trip and was here all day. He is as nice as the other two and the baby's most devoted admirer. Such a rolling about as she got all day. Fred pays very little attention to her. He thinks she is very nice and wonderfully bright but seems

---

1. Captain Charles White, who served as a scout during the Matabele War.

afraid to hold her, while those three men all take as much care of her as we do. She kisses you now and puts out her hand to come to you and that wonderful smile of hers is really too fascinating. No one can resist her and the result is she is badly spoiled and some-one has to have her all the time. Roy is like his father. He never kisses her or holds her but says she is a fine baby. He is a fine boy and Fred thinks there is no one like him.

Wednesday 10 A.M. Work all finished and baby asleep. John and Fred piling up rocks. Roy gone to school. There is a private one just opened here and B. is getting her sewing ready. She is making Roy some waists. She keeps him dressed nicely. . . . The pillows you sent she needed very much. In fact J. and I would have been pillowless without them. I sleep on the lounge and J. sleeps on the floor. By the time they come back from their trip we will have plenty of room. Of course there are no good beds in this place. A wire mattress only costs $30 and we sleep on anything. Oh I can tell you this is no paradise. I shall never spend all my life here by any means. B. and I are coming home in two years with the children, and Roy is to remain in Pasadena and go to Throop. If Fred can't come when we do, B. is to stay a year and if I don't come back with her Fred will come over after her. John may come too. Of course in two years it may be a far different place but now it is very new, windy and not really disagreeable but still not *very* pleasant. One could find far worse places to live in though, and if we can make any money we will be all right for it isn't at all dull or lonesome. So many men come here and everything is full of busi-ness. Buildings going up all around us and new people coming.

. . . I haven't been downtown yet. We are going when the baby wakes up. Will take her to a nice old Irish woman and leave her there. I miss John and Pete ever so much. Pete was here all the time only nights and we all like him so much. They left last evening and I wish I could have had a picture of them. Both of the boys were on neat little numbers with their guns and blankets, big hats on and John had gotten some light cord britches and looked very nice. Behind them were three big Matabeles loaded with the provisions. They had sacks of stuff on their heads and on their backs and looked too funny for anything. They hadn't many clothes to wear and so hadn't much to carry in that line. They will do the work. This morning there were five women within the yard flirting with

Longboy who is working for Fred now. One of them had a baby on her back and the others piles of wood. I went to the door with baby and they all came up to see her. They jabbered and grinned and it sounded to me as if they wanted to trade babies. All I could understand was "morch-a-tel-pickanin," pretty baby. I smiled back at them but hung to the pickanin. She looked whiter and lovelier than ever with her lovely blue eyes, but she wasn't afraid to smile at them. I never saw such an angel [letter incomplete].

———

John Blick to John and Phebe Blick

> The City of Killing [Buluwayo]
> South Africa
> Oct. 16th, 1894

Dear Papa and Mamma,

Chub will have to do all the writing for I have lost the knack, anyway I don't have time. I have been bossing nine big nigs out in the back yard for the last three days. They don't know a word of English except Yah boss. I am learning Zulu fast. I don't blame the whites for wanting to kill the nigs. They are as helpless as babies. I wanted three to dig a ditch to lay a foundation for my hut. I wanted it square so I told them to dig it round. I see they have got it square as a die. I have two down in the well drilling for blasting. Water is the drawback here. This P.M. Pete and I are to go on a short prospecting trip for the Rhodesia Co. We have to find and stake 100 claims. We will not be gone more than three weeks but as soon as I get back I am to go out on the Gwelo for five weeks. Fred will go out with me, but I will be alone out there for he has to go away off in another direction for another syndicate. I don't think I'll have much time to lay around and play tennis.

Dinner is almost ready, the roly-poly is a failure, so I hear B. telling Grace. Pete has gone to sleep on the lounge and is a dandy fellow. We will have lots of sport. Nigs do all the work. We will have to do a good deal of walking.

A fellow just came to Fred, one he and Pete saw working a tunnel last May. He had done a hundred and 20 feet of work, fulfilled his contract and when he got into town without a bean the boss told him to wait until his partner returned from England.

This old man is an American. Fred came in and changed his clothes and is going down to kill the boss if he don't pay up. Fred is one of the most *popular* men in Matabeleland. . . .
Your dutiful son,
John

———

FRB to Josiah Russell

> North Western Hotel
> Johannesburg
> South African Republic
> Oct. 94

Dear Uncle,

The press of business leaves little or no time to write especially a long letter or a very good one. Events are jogging along quite smoothly though rapidly. This town is now a city nearly as large as Los Angeles, and it is very finely laid out and is a much better looking town than when I first saw it. I am today just pulling the leg, as the slang of the country expresses it, of the manager of a large paper to get him to send to Buluwayo a really trained editor, one who is used to frontier work. They have a good plant in Buluwayo but need a better man. I think I will succeed and if I do in a few months you will receive a paper quite representative of the country and of the hopes and aims of its people. I want to find a good dentist but cannot do it. There is only one genuine American dentist here. There is one great quack doctor here and he is coining money, but I think he is a fraud.

I have been looking after Howard some since I came. His position is fine here and he has the credit of being the first assayer on the field and is chief chemist to one of the largest mines and stands a chance of a future raise, but I must absolve him from blame as life here is extremely peculiar, and he had to assume a great deal more than he really knew, and then to keep up had to buy expensive books and apparatus and work night and day. He is now comfortably fixed and has his outfit nearly paid for but he has been in bad health and doctors run in $100 on him and the druggist ½ as much more (they are all thieves), but if his health holds out he can attain a big reputation here. As to my own finances they are of course tied up in the new country. If the country proves good I must win. I see there is a great interest in everything African in the U.S., but this field is already stocked with the shrewdest class of adventurers on earth, men who have been all over the world and for the average American to come over here thinking to live by superior wit or knowledge he will get left.

The only class of emigrants that have really interested me just lately are the missionaries (the new). I must tell you more about them. The Wessels family were Dutch and sold some diamond mines for an immense sum of money, but they were religious people and really want to use it for good. They have seen all their lives the useless waste among the missionaries supported from home and know the absurd position they occupy in African public opinion. So he (Wessels Jr.) conceived that a true spirit of missionary work should be carried on by self-supporting people who would never call on others for a $. Believing, in spite of the fact that only one Matabele convert had been made in 30 yrs, that they could be reached &c. took a tour all over the country and when he selected a suitable position applied to the Chartered Co. for a grant. Dr. Jameson told him they had given largely in Mashonaland and elsewhere and it amounted to nothing, but after having the scheme fully explained to him and knowing the judgement and skill of Wessels he agreed to give them a show in Matabeleland and about ½ doz are now started on active operations. Wessels' plan is this— to get people who are used to frontier life—to get families, people that have enough knowledge of the ways of the world that they have already accumulated a small amount of money or at least never had to be a burden on any community—to get people who think enough of their religion that will put it before gold hunting and lastly that the religion shall be protestant (Seven Day Adventist is what Wessels is himself). They must be willing to teach the nigger to work by personal example as well as pray. The further details of his plan was to have the families settled in a small village adjoining a large common. This common will be allotted to the Kaffirs. They will be constantly in touch with the villagers. Each villager is to be absolutely independent. He owns his land, buys and sells and makes his living the same as if he moved onto a farm in Iowa or Kansas among a Christian community. He contends that free land, good local markets and plenty of work will make a great success. I agree with him except as to the nigger, but as long as he is on the common and not in the parlor playing on the piano I don't care much. Wessels next started and travelled round the world to see if there were any of these zealous self-sacrificing people and he found them in the U.S. Farmers in Ill., Iowa, Kansas, Michigan &c. who wanted to sell out, bring their families, bear their own expenses and after all end their days not in ease but in toil. It seems strange that the spirit of the crusades still exists but it certainly does and he showed me lots of letters to prove it. Now after the wire edge of instantly converting the nigs has worn off a little, these people coming here expecting to die of African fever and be martyrs to the elevation of the sunburnt race will find themselves in a good climate, rich soil, with probably more comforts around them than in any other country they could have come to.

So I am aiding Wessels in every way I can to bring such people over and shall see that they do not get into the fever district. I sent you some clippings showing our material progress. There is invested on this field (the Rand) £63,000,000 in mines alone returning about £5,000,000 per annum.

Tell Mrs. Talmadge I am as ardent a nationalist[1] as ever and hope to see this country run on those lines one of these days, as soon as we can cut loose from the imperial leading strings, but the golden milk of the mother country is hard to refuse, however we will get weaned ere long.

Adios,

Fred

John Blick to John and Phebe Blick

Buluwayo, South Africa
Oct. 30th, 1894

Dear Mother and Father &c.,

Chubb is taking care of the kid so I must write if I want it to go on the next coach. Fred has about a dozen boxes filled with nails, rivets, screws, bits, chisels, shot, cartridges &c. I have been working all morning trying to get them into shape but haven't suc-

---

1. Burnham is referring to Edward Bellamy's Nationalist movement.

ceeded very well. Will get some nigs to help me. Fred has more stuff piled around him than ever before. He has three or four saddles, seven rifles, two shot guns, 3 or 4 big six shooters, leather bags, sacks &c by the doz. He has a good set of tools but they aren't fit for a nig to use. So darn dull, rusty and smashed up. B. is over to Hines across the street baking a cake. Mrs. Hines has a stove. B. has one stove on the road up, will be here in about a month. Grace has laid the kid down to make dinner so I must take it. It's squalling like a good one. Dinner over and kid is asleep. . . .

Roderick has just returned from school. He only goes a half day and doesn't get out until one. I don't know whether he learns much or not. You remember how thick and heavy he used to be. He has made a change and is growing long and gangling. Fred is proud of him. He thinks now he will be big. I tell you Fred is pretty hot stuff out here. He is known all over the country. I was told yesterday that he was one of the smartest men in Matabeleland. If the country goes in, Fred will be strictly in it and so will I for I am to go right in with him and will be lots of help as soon as I get onto the ropes.

I haven't chawed, drunk, or cussed or gambled yet. That's more than the majority can say. Roderick is telling Longboy in Kaffir to bring in an iron. He talks Kaffir like a trooper. I wish I could talk as much. Mrs. Hines' big naked nigger just brought the cakes over. They are a complete fizzle. . . . Worth here about $1.75. Of course they laid it onto poor Mrs. Hines' stove and fire. Porky, Chubb had a hand in it so of course you know where the main fault lay. Gosh they are jawing. We are all going out to Mr. Cumming's ranch tomorrow and B. was going to finish the spread. Chubb is ironing the kid's dresses on this table and it has rickety legs as you can see by the writing.

There is a little carpenter shop just across the road. There are seven men busy at work all the time working windows, frames, tables, &c. They are just coining the money. This town is a freak of nature for an 8 month old town, 600 miles from a R.R.

Our boxes will be here in five more weeks if everything turns out all O.K. F. will be here in three or four more days.

Yesterday and today have been as nice as any in Pasadena.

Blanche is making Grace a black skirt out of some sort of black stuff. I wish I had of brought more light shirts, at least a dozen. The

kind you got me for $.75 will cost $2 here. Handkerchiefs and socks are scarce also. I read a good American novel last night until after one. I thought of you all eating your supper as I went to sleep. I heard a big racket by the side of my house and thought someone was trying to get in. I paraded all around in my shirt tail with a big gun and finally ferreted out an old white rooster who was so old that he had fallen off the wagon onto some roof iron. I put my gun up and went and crawled in bed and covered my head up and went to sleep. Chubb jars the table so I can't write.
Adios yours,
John

Maw, Blanche makes me build shelves all the time and don't want me to rest like you used to do. Its contrary to my bringing up. I won't stand it.
J.

———

Grace Blick to Blick family

Buluwayo
Nov. 7, 1894

My Dear Dad and Mam and Kitten and Judd,
I have been having lots of fun this afternoon bossing a little nig while he washed the oil cloth on the floor. You can get a good deal of work out of them if you stand right over them and give them a good kick once in a while. They like you all the better if you abuse them, but I can't bear to treat them as they call it here or "shambok." I sat upon the lounge with my feet in under me and the kid in my lap and yelled Kaffir at him. The words I use are rather limited but I can make signs. You should be here to train them Kate. I didn't make him go in under the lounge or under the shelves and the next time he will leave them again. His name is File. He is taking Longboy's place while poor Longboy is getting over a little fever he had.
Monday is a quiet day here. Nov. 4, the day the army entered Buluwayo. They call it Occupation Day and they had all kinds of spirits for drink. We drank and had a very good time. I wore my new gray dress and B. her Paris serge. We felt quite elegant. Mr. Cumming came for us with a white mule. You may think that is a

scrubby turn out but if you were here you would be thankful to ride in anything. Nearly everyone else had to walk. You know carts and such things are very scarce here and horses more so. So we drove up to the grounds in state. There was a tent put up for the ladies and some chairs. We were there for the first race, 100 yds, because Bob [Bain], one of the "particulars," was to run. He has been quite sick and he lost that race but won the quarter mile, and he was handicapped ever so much but came in way ahead. He is a lovely runner and they say the fastest in Africa. Anyway he beat some of the Johannesburg champions and you know the English are great for spirits and races. He won the cup and I am to have the first drink out of it. We haven't decided whether it shall be champagne or condensed milk. Mr. C. says we can have champagne if we like, but as its champagne and $8.00 a bottle I prefer milk. These men are too free for anything with money. Pete paid $7.50 for a plate at the big dinner for John the other evening. I think J. will tell you about that. This is a gay old town. We don't go out much but we hear all the news from those mine men who are here every day and they tell us everything we want to know. Bob was quite bad after the races and we kept him here all night and all the next day and dosed him on stuff. He seems all right now and has gone back to the farm. Pete went off this morning on business for Capt. White, to be gone several days. We miss him for he is here most of the time. As soon as he gets back he is going to give a dinner for B. and I on the farm and it is to be as good as one of mother's dinners. He is a fine cook they say, but I've only heard *him* tell about it. We are not to know a thing he is to get, and Mr. C. has to take care of the baby while B. enjoys it as many hours as she takes. She eats as slim as ever. You get so tired of the stuff you eat here. Not a potato since we came and no fruit and vegetables. Only meat, tea and bread. Once in a while we make a pudding out of canned jam or cook some rice and raisins. You people are in clover and if I were you I'd remain there. I don't want to see you out here with nothing to eat and the wind and dust so fearful. It may be far different in a few years but now, well it might be pleasanter. When B. and I come home in 2 years we will know whether we want you to come out or not.

Nov. 9th—day after the races. Well we went to the races in all our glory. I went with Bob, and B. with Mr. Cumming. It only cost them $7.00 apiece before the afternoon was over. You know things are cheap here. Seats in the grandstand $2.50 and drinks .25 apiece. We had one drink and a lot of candy after we came home. I would be shy of the girls if I were a man out here. John is in no danger. They are *very* scarce. The men all flirt with the married women. Don't for an instant think B. does though.

Fred came home last night after a nine week trip, in fine spirits and today he has taken several new contracts. All the men seem to think he is so smart and they run after him all the time. He has the biggest men in the country asking his advice about things. He is very much liked here and is as full of business as ever. He is just the same dear old Fred though, always thinking of someone besides himself. It's late and I must retire. We missed a fine drive tonight with the "particular." The old wind is blowing a gale. We were going to the king's old kraal.
Love to all bye, bye,
Your loving
Chubb or Grace

Nov. 13—Your letter failed to go last week as the coach changed time and I knew nothing about it until it was gone. So I'll tell what has happened since for have had a nice ride with Mr. Cumming down to the king's old kraal. Of course the huts are all in ashes but we saw the ashes. His [the King's] house was in the center, his impis quite near and all around were the huts of his servants and soldiers. We saw the place where Fred and Pete camped outside the town and all the other points of interest. His [Cumming's] farm is three miles from this Buluwayo and was his old house. Cecil Rhodes is building a mansion. The foundation is all done and when the house is finished it will be the first in Matabeleland. We came home by moonlight and had a very nice drive. Last night I went to the swellest dinner I ever attended. Mr. Carey, a very nice young man from Los Angeles and manager of the finest hotel here, gave us a dinner. Mr. Cumming was the only one who wasn't an American and he has been among them so much he is nearly one. There were eight men and B and myself. We wore our finest dresses and had a gay time. And Judd, I tasted champagne for the first time. Awfully good isn't it? I was gay after I had finished a glass or two. Mr. Carey did things up swell.

Champagne is only about $8.00 a bottle (I only tasted it mama), and no one drank much. I do think it's good though and if it hadn't been for the principle of the thing I'd have finished my glass. I had Mr. Cumming for a partner and he never tasted his. He gets gay after a few drinks and I think he was afraid to start last night. Mr. Carey gave me the menu as a souvenir of the evening. He drew the American flag on it. I'll send it to you and you put it among my other valuables, Kitten, I want to save it. We ate from 8 till 11 and had a very pleasant time. Pete carried the baby over and the waiters fixed her a bed on chairs and she slept all the time. All of the men wanted her to wake up for she is such fun. After we came home she entertained us for an hour. You never saw a cuter youngster. The boys were quite sure she had *too* much, the way she acted. We are anxious for Pete's dinner to come off. All of us and Dr. Hammond are going. In a few days we are going for a drive to Hope Finnkani, a missionary station fifteen minutes from here. I like riding much better than I used to. I am so perfectly well. Fred isn't going to let me work at all. He says as long as he is making as much money as he is now I am not going to work. B. needs me for company and he and John are going to pay my debt. I am sure I don't object to the arrangement in the least. The press hasn't come for the paper I was to work on and the other paper only pays women $20 a week and men $25 and $30, and Fred said it wasn't high tone enough for me. You see they are very swell here and as there are no women work but barmaids, they are rather shy about having me set out. I have a fine time and have not been at all homesick yet. There are so many coming in all the time and the baby is enough for one woman's whole time. I find my hands quite full with her. Fred is the busiest man in town and one of the happiest. He has great plans for all of us. Father and mother are to come here in two years and Homer and all of us are to live in huts across the river and have one big dining room. I am sure his plans will all come true. Mrs. Burnham and Auntie are to come and such a fine home as we will have. He sold his farm for fifteen hundred pounds yesterday. Pete has half of the farm and so of course half of the 1500 pounds. I think he will be a good catch as far as money goes if he wasn't so ugly and has such a queer disposition. If he hates anyone, he is something awful. He has a good deal of property here too and lots in this town are valuable. You will be sure to see Africa papa. Everyone predicts that I'll never go away. If I was willing to bet, I could make a lot of money. Last night one of the men bet 100 pounds I'd be here ten years from now. Don't you fret though. I am going home unless you come out. B. and I have lots of fun planning the trip. It doesn't seem possible that we are so far away. I think of you as just over the hill and indeed the trip is so nice I am glad it is far. You will have such a good rest. I must retire. I am quite tired. Chum and I took a long walk today. Oh yes, a young man, a miner, gave me an owl like Quimbo Sunday. My first hit here and not a monkey.

G.B.

John Blick to Phebe Blick

Buluwayo, South Africa
Nov. 18th, 1894

Dear Mother,

This letter is all for you and you must read it for yourself. If you only knew what labor it's costing me, you surely would. This is a lovely day, but pretty hot. You are 54 years old today, and you can bet we all are thinking of you and of Father on the 15th. Just think of it. Fred is going to England. (Grace tried to read this and couldn't so of course you can't.) Well as I was going to say F. goes to London on business or intends to. Of course things are liable to turn up anytime and keep him from going. If he does, he will only be two weeks away from you but will be so busy he can't come over. England seems a long way off from you but only a short way home from us.

I have my cart nearly all packed for my trip. Such stuff as I have got. All sorts of prepared meats, extracts &c canned fruits, tinned fish, jam, tomatoes, lime juice, banana chutney, raspberry vinegar, bacon @ 60c per lb &c. Well my grocery bill for three months amounts to $250. That doesn't bother me any. I get $100 per month and board. The average miner here lives for about $15 or $20 a month and consequently gets the fever or something else. Fred believes in eating good stuff (scoff) and then you won't get sick. That's the way Fred and Pete always do and they never get sick. The way some of the men live here is awful, but little better than the nigs.

I start from here Tuesday with ten oxen and it will take us seven days to go seventy miles. The oxen are poor and can only travel about ten miles a day. I have a driver and a leader and also old Longboy to do my cooking and washing and be general camp boy. I will also have ten boys to work in mines. I also have a white man to boss who understands mining and drill sharpening. The first thing I will do will be to fix up a good camp. Have some nigs build me a good hut or two for the rainy season. It is to be close to a police station, 100 yds or so, which is to be located there in a few weeks. A policeman is going down to comm[andeer] me some boys and see that the[y] furnish me one oxen a week for meat for the boys and make them furnish me in milk. You see Capt. White is the fellow Fred is doing the contract for and he is commander of the police, so I will get everything I want. Some of the boys are too proud to work and have to be made to.

I am to sink seven shafts all in the radius of 2 miles from my main central camp. I will have to chase around and boss the boys up timber shafts, sharpen the drills and picks and look after scoff, dynamite &c., boss the whole thing. Fred will never come near it. I will have to send in a report to Pollick, the manager of the White Syndicate, every month. I'll be kept pretty blame busy from sunup till sundown but will try and find time to write a little after I get things started. There is good grass down there, so will let the oxen fat up for a week and send them back for another load of stuff. Can't take it all down this load. Bebe has been teaching me how to make sourdough bread, blancmange, dumplings &c. She had the *recipes* all written out in a little book for me. Mamma, you won't know me in about three months. My whiskers will be about a foot long and I'll be the color of *chocolate*. How is Fan and the buckskin colt and the guavas in the back yard. I would actually give $15 for all the oranges, or apples, or guavas I could eat. I could eat onions, boiled cabbage or anything. I'll not say anything about grapes. A fellow gets hungry for fruit. I don't mind it myself. Grace and B. and Roderick are getting anxious to get some. How many chickens have you got now? Does Judd stay at home anymore than usual? How is old Mag?[1] I would rather see her than any girl in Pasadena except one. Gosh I am getting anxious to see her. I haven't seen a

1. The Blick dog.

girl since I left Johannesburg. I looked at a pretty barmaid about a week ago, and B. fairly jumped on my neck and swore that if I did it again she would skin me alive, so I haven't dared to do it again.

I have been busy the last week building shelves, tables, and bedsteads for B. After I finish one job she won't let me sit down and read like you used to but makes me do something. She says that I will find out that I am not with my mamma now.

Just saw a nig go by all dressed up for Sunday. He had the shirt of a ring streaked and striped bathing suit on. He had his head up as though he defied the earth. Here comes one of our boys with a fikey of water on his head from the river, weighing about 100 lbs. They carry everything on their head. The baby is laying on Pete's lap and he is leaning over to let her grab his mustache. He says she had got sense enough to see and appreciate it, nobody else can. She is laughing for all she is worth. Don't let Judd see the last of this about the kid.

Goodbye. Chubb wants to set the table.

With love,

Your little Johnny

Grace Blick to Phebe Blick

Buluwayo, Africa
Nov. 18, 1894

My Dearest Mama,

And you are 54 today. I wonder what you are doing and if all the folks are not there and having a good dinner. We had a beef-steak pie, a bread pudding and last and best of all some tea made of the tea I brought from home. We have only a little of it left and we save it for such occasions as this. We get only the very poorest of black tea here and Fred and B. dislike it so much. When F. goes to London in a few weeks he says he will bring back some green tea if nothing else and some good coffee. Only the poorest of all kinds of food is sent to Buluwayo and you have to eat it or go without. I am not getting thin on it and can eat an awful lot. You probably had a delicious dinner and lots of fruit. We had jam. No company but Mr. Ingram for a wonder, and he is one of the family. He is dressed up swell today and looks quite, no I won't say handsome for he couldn't do that, but he looks nice. A dress-up suit here is some soft white silk shirt, white pants, tan shoes and a belt, a cap or big hat. I think the white suits are very pretty and they look so fresh and cool. John is going to have some of them. He is telling you about his trip. Fred is so good to him and wants him to have everything just as nice as if it was his own. He is quite a father to us, orders me about and lays down the rules as to what I shall wear. He insists on my having flannel underwear and that I shall wear it all the time. You get so warm here and then cool off so suddenly that you have the rheumatism. He is even busy today, if it is Sunday, and has a man here talking business. He, Pete and Mr. Hammond go to London in a few weeks to float mining property. If they succeed, they will each have a neat little sum of money. We may go to Durban to spend the four months they are away if we can rent this place for a good price. They say Durban is beautiful and B. and Roy long for fruit to eat. All kinds grow there and very fine. We will know in a week or so if we are going and will go as far as Johannesburg on the coach with them. B. is anxious to go with them for she knows Pete will take all the care of the baby and six days are quite long shut up in a coach and going fast. . . .

Thursday Nov. 22—Several days have tripped along since I wrote last and this dull rainy night while B. and I are alone I will write some more. John went yesterday. Fred the day before and Pete and Mr. Cumming today. John went off well equipped and quite gay and contented. We have been awfully busy this week. Pete had a lot of business in connection with this London trip and I have been his secretary. Dr. Hammond has been here every day to boss the business and two days and one night. Mr. Cumming was here quite sick and we took care of him. All the copying is done and the men have all gone off to peg claims to float in London. We are quite sure of our Durban trip. . . .

Dear old Longboy has gone to be John's servant and a good one he will be. He is as faithful as a man can be and will take good care of John and not leave him. We hated to part with him but thought John was the one to have him. We miss his "Yah Misses" very much. The one we have now is a perfect fool. . . . Dad's letters are always treats and I devour them first of all. He need have no fear of my marrying an Englishman. I don't know any here very well. We stick to our own people and feel quite at home. The Afrikanders are very much like our people and we like them nearly as well. . . . I must go to bed and to sleep. I am afraid of the thunder which roars dreadfully and often Kate.

Bye, bye

Love to all,

Your loving Grace

———

BBB to Blick family

Nov. 22, 1894

Dear ones at home,

. . . These shafts that John is going to sink are on Mr. Nelson's farm, and John's main camp will be within a few hundred yards of their huts. I think I wrote you about their going down there some two months ago. Mr. Nelson is going to work with John. I am glad that he is so near Mrs. Nelson. She will be good to him for my sake but then I know she will like him. What a dear good boy he is. He was so good to do odd carpenter jobs for me. I did have to keep him at first [at] it pretty steadily for three or four days to get things finished and now I wish I had a book shelf in the dining room. We are all alone now. Fred, John and Roderick and our "three particulars." It seems very quiet after all the business meetings we had last week. All the papers for the flotation of the company in London were drawn up here. Our sitting room looked like a lawyers office for three days. Pete and old Doc Hammond have gone today to look at the last purchased property and Mr. Cumming went in another direction to peg some more claims for them. Fred went Monday evening with Mr. Orpen to show some farm pegs and peg 35 more. He expects to be back in about ten days. Will ride almost constantly. Everything seems about settled for the London trip. Fred, Pete and Dr. Hammond go. Their expenses are paid. They will be gone several months. I cannot tell you how glad I am that you let me have Grace for a while. Think of how lonesome I would be. Tonight the rain is falling gently and the muttering thunder has a weird lonesome sound. I would not be sitting up writing to you if Grace was not here. . . .

Love B.B.B.

John Blick to Kate Blick

35 miles from Buluwayo
Nov 24, 1894

Dear Pork,

It's too much trouble to reach for ink so I will write with lead pencil. I am occupying your favorite position now, lying down. You are a little brick to write to a fellow. I guess I will have to come to the conclusion that you are better than all the other girls put together. Your letters are fine and have but one fault, and that is that, the end comes too soon. I have just finished my dinner of canned green peas, raspberry and current jam and bread and tea, but I could still eat some of your cooking. Learn to be a dandy cook as when Lyda and all the girls go back on me you can keep house for me in my old age.

. . . I am lying flat on my back writing with both hands in the air. They get tired and I have to rest every little bit. I am afraid this pencil will be a little dim by the time you get it. This makes the third day that I have been all alone without a thing to do but eat and sleep and I still have four or five more. Our pen gave out so I had to send on the cart with a little scoff and picks and shovels. Mr. Nelson will start the boys to work and have my hut built and send the cart back. I also sent to Buluwayo for more fresh oxen. I am getting lonesome without a thing to do. Longone does all the cooking and I just lay around and hunt and sleep. I wish I knew whether you read Kay's letters or not. I hate to write the same thing twice.

Three hours later—I just awoke and found papers laying all around. I shut my eyes in trying to think of something to write and went to sleep. Longone has taken the gun to go kill some meat. He says, "Hamba bolla enyome." I will teach you a lot of Kaffir when I come home. It's awfully hard but I am getting on to it. I must get me a Kaffir grammar. Are you taking Greek this year? I hope Longone kills a buck. We finished our last one up last night. Does Judd kill anymore? I wish he was here. He would make things stink with game. I have plenty of milk; Kaffirs bring it to me. I give them a handful of sugar or a cup of coffee for a quart or more. They bring it in carved wooden jugs of various shapes. They carry everything on their heads. Their skulls are at least an inch thick.

You would think they were solid all the way through from the things they do sometimes. The women are far filthier than the men and the men are filthy enough. We killed a buck the other day and they took the insides, cleaned them out with their fingers, and cooked some in the coals and boiled the rest. It was enough to turn a fellows stomach. I wish you were here to cook my supper. I could give you anything you wanted to cook with. One thing that I have is lots of stuff to eat. I think I will make me some custard for supper or have some mock turtle soup or potted turkey. You can get everything here but vegetables. I would love to have some fried potatoes. I have a lot of California canned peaches and Libby's and Armour's beef. You see U.S.A. on lots of things out here. . . .

Two days later. I must finish this for I want to send it back to Buluwayo by the policeman who is liable to pass anytime. There are three or four nigs squatted around me now watching me write. It's lots of fun to hear them talk. I spent all day yesterday in trying to pronounce one word. They are very expressive in their speech. They try to imitate everything. . . .

I saw a lot of women catching ants yesterday, a big white ant with wings. They were going to eat them. How would you like to plop your lip over some nice juicy ant jaws. I would rather eat angle worms. Two rats got in a fight on my bed the other night. One big fellow got caught in Blanche's hair when she was out in the Gwelo. How would you like to have one up your leg about the size of a ground squirrel. Do you think it would make you squirm? I can fairly see you trying to kick the plaster off the ceiling. I am lying flat on my back under a tree about 50 ft from camp. Longone is washing the dishes.

Tell me all about mother and father and give them my love.

John

Grace Blick to Blick family

Buluwayo, South Africa
Nov. 29, 1894

My Dear People,

You will get only a note this week as I've had no time to write. We are so busy sewing and getting ready for our trip. Roy and I have just been out for a walk. The first time I have been out for two weeks or more and then had to go after dark. Buluwayo is no heaven I can tell you, and I am more glad than I can tell that we are going to leave it. We may never come back. Who thought three weeks ago that we would be going to such a nice place as Durban. By the time you get this we will be nicely settled in our new stopping place and I hope I shall care more for it than I do for this. If it wasn't for Pete, Bob and Cumming we would surely die. They come to see us every day and as we like them we don't mind how often they come. Fred and John are both gone now and we are all by ourselves. If baby didn't take all my time, I should be lonesome. As it is, I don't have time to think about it. Three very nice ladies called this afternoon. One I came up in the coach with. I like her more than anyone I have met here. She is very pleasant, pretty and stylish. We have to make some calls before we leave. The magistrate's wife is a person of great importance in Africa, and you are to feel highly honored if she calls on you. It makes no difference if her reputation is shady as this lady's is. We have not called yet and I think it quite doubtful if we ever do. Who cares if she is the magistrate's wife? If she wasn't, no one would look at her. There are ever so many ladies in town now, and a great many coming all the time. . . . B. is reading this morning and Roy is out by the campfire talking to Jack, our new boy who washes my dishes over again. Baby is asleep and Pete has just gone. Fred we are listening for every minute. We might as well be in Durban (God's country) as here for all we see of Fred. I have been here two months now and Fred has been home just two weeks. Isn't that fine for B.? I wonder that she hasn't quite died of lonesomeness. I know I should have in her place. They don't know how long they will be in London. Maybe several months. We are going to have a Xmas dinner before we leave for we have been talking of one for weeks and if it does come off before it doesn't matter. I wonder if this was Thanksgiving day at home. . . .

Your loving,

Grace

John Blick to Phebe Blick

Filabusi
Dec 10th 1894

Dear Maw,

I am suffering with one h— of a tooth ache and I am not in much of a mood to write. She is one of those kind that's about 3 in. longer than the others and I have to keep my jaw reared open about a foot to keep from touching it. I hit her three times while eating dinner today and came very near swearing every time. I wouldn't mind lying on the lounge and have you and Porkey heat rags and bags of salt for it. But I have to go out in the rain and labor. I have her tied up in a big handkerchief so as not to take cold in it. I expect all this is good for me. I know Father will say so. I will be good and tough when I return and in good time for the wood pile, hedge &c. Little things like those now would seem nothing to me. I would show up that wood pile and grub out all the stumps in the arroyo and never kick once. A fellow can look back and see what a soft snap he had before he had whiskers. If this letter sounds homesick, you know the reason why. Anyway I am my mamma's own baby boy.

Well, I must crawl out of my hut and get the boys to work and will write some more later. I don't know yet how I will spend my Xmas dinner. I think I will get darn few presents but would like to give a lot. Make Porkey write a lot more. She is beginning fine. I'll bet you have something to do with it although I give her all the credit. Goodby, my tooth feels better and the sun is out. I think that has a good deal to do with it.

Dec. 11th—My tooth is better but my jaw is beginning to swell. I hope it doesn't get like the one I had there in Pasadena. This is one that was too far gone to fill. Parker thought a long time as to whether he would pull it or not. I wish he had, but he said it might go a year or two. It is just a little more than half a tooth and is no good anyway. I will make a stab at this again a little later. It may take me a week to write this but I'll get her finished somehow.

Longone has gone after water (manza) to make tea for my dinner. I am going to have bread and butter, tea, kippered herrings and loquat jam. That wouldn't be bad with you with a little celery or something, but here it gets stale. Everything is put up in cans, even the butter is put up in pound tins. It is made in Denmark.

Anyone would know that it was made a long way off. It is better than none.

My hut is about 12 ft. in diameter, walls about six feet high with the center of the roof about 8 ft. (Circular drawing) and is made with poles so, about the size of your wrist and are fastened together with bark. The circles are made of timber sticks. The walls are made by setting poles in the ground close together with several bands around like barrel hoops. Two women plastered it inside and out with mud mixed with manure. Of course they did it with their hands. Kate they don't go at it daintily like you girls in the clay modeling class. They are smeared from head to foot. One had a little kid and she would take a piece of grass and make a clean place for the kid to get something to eat. It was a cute little girl and made me think a lot of Bess.[1] I think it was smarter than Bess though. I wouldn't of touched it for a dollar. Its clothes consisted of two strings of beads around its neck and one around each ankle. The tea is ready and I wish you were to share it with me. When I come back to Pasadena I'll build you a little hut down under one of the oak trees. They are fine and cool to sleep in and you can fix them up nice where you have things to hang on the walls.

If things have turned out all right in Buluwayo, all my relations are nearly out of Matabeleland and I will have to keep the family reputation up. . . .

When I go back I will go up the east coast of Africa and through Southern Europe like F. and B. It is just as cheap and you can see so much more. Then I will have gone completely around Africa. I would like to go clear through it. When I reach Pasadena I will have seen a good deal and will have lots to talk about. . . .

Thursday—No rain yet but it still looks like it. Mrs. Nelson sent me over a fine big piece of corned beef. She is very nice to me. I ate dinner there the other day. We had a section of a big catfish, one about 4½ feet long. There are monsters in the river close by. I am going fishing before long. They call the catfish here "barbel." It is very little different from our catfish, and is full a good eating. Oh yes, my tooth is all O.K. now and I feel in fine health. Will finish one shaft this week. Then I will have to make a temporary camp about 4 miles from here where there are three to sink. I look

1. A child in the Pasadena neighborhood.

for the cart out in about four days and I think there will sure be some mail for me . . . [letter incomplete].

———

BBB to FRB

Cape Town
Dec. 16, 1894

My darling,

Such a beautiful morning and the loveliest anthem being sung in the cathedral just across the street. I am thoroughly enjoying myself, sitting here in the window and writing to my sweetheart to the sound of the beautiful music. Things have happened so rapidly in the last month. I have not been as well as usual, and my mind has not been able to grasp it all at once. I seemed in a sort of daze after leaving the steamer that day and it did not seem as though I had half said goodbye to you. You have gone away so many, many times during the last eight months for absence of from ten days to six weeks that some way I did not realize this time how far you were going and for how long until last night when it came over me all at once. "May God keep watch between me and thee when far apart from one another" is my constant prayer. You went away so hopeful of success, and my darling you left us in such a beautiful place. I am so glad that we did not go to Durban, first because we should have missed that delightful never to be forgotten journey from Johannesburg to Cape Town and secondly because Cape Town is just as lovely if not lovelier than Durban, and the climate is simply perfect, exactly like Southern California. The rains are over, while it must be very sultry and hot in Durban. We are out all day long and do not feel the heat at all, although we hear complaints about the heat. In the evening you *must* wear a wrap as we used to do in Cal. But now you must want to know about our plans for the season. We went the next day to see Mr. Hammond's friend. He was very kind and said he would advertise in the papers for us, receive the replies and make selections of the good locations for us, but that we could not expect to get anything before Monday or Tuesday. The housekeeper, really a lady, told us the same. There were very few advertisements in the papers, and that room of ours was very uncomfortable. So we told the landlady that we would stay at least a week if we could have a different room. So we are in a nice large room with a big window facing the cathedral. Everything is peaches and cream in hopes that we may stay longer. If we do not get everything we want, it is our own fault, for we can have anything that is in season simply for the asking and without extra charge. So we have strawberries for breakfast, fruit every meal and a dish of strawberries sent up just before we go to bed. The housekeeper or one of the girls is always waiting around to take Nada while we eat our meals. Two of the girls have said they would leave this place in a minute to be her nurse. She will stay with any of them and is always so happy. But we do not intend to have a nurse at all. This is a very free and independent place, and while you see most nurses still you see mothers taking care of their children also, and that is the right and natural thing to do. The nurses here are all girls and they are too knowing to have around all the time. We bought an *American* perambulator the day after we got here, very springy and open for 37/6. More reasonable almost than at home. There are the most beautiful stores here when once you get inside of them. Ready-made clothing of all descriptions and just as reasonable as at home and some things are cheaper. There are no such pretty ready-made dresses in Los Angeles. Everyone on the streets seems so bright and happy and you see so many people out. You may be sure of finding us here when you come back. Have not the slightest wish to go to quiet Durban. Open air concerts once a week in the Gardens. Promenade concerts in another place in the Gardens very often. Perfectly select and proper for ladies to attend alone, price 1 shilling.

I am so sorry that you did not have more time so that you could have seen a little of the gardens. The International was in the Gardens. It is a name applied to that part of the town going up the slope of the mountain. It is full of trees and is the select part of the town. And the most beautiful part of it all is the Avenue lined on each side with over-reaching oaks. Botanical Gardens on one side and a park on the other, with beautiful houses all along. Just a mass of shade. No driving is allowed just around there. Oh it is beautiful. We were wild to live somewhere near there as soon as we saw it, and fortune has not deserted us yet for I answered an advertisement in the Times for a furnished room in the Gardens and went to see it yesterday.

We will move in next Wednesday. We have an upstairs room, an *immense* one with a vine covered roofed in veranda. An immense oak sweeping the roof of the house. Not furnished for light house-keeping but we can buy a kerosene stove and do just as we like. We have the use of the bathroom but it is downstairs. The girl will fetch and carry all the water. We do the rest of the work ourselves. The balcony faces the west and we have a beautiful view of the round mountain, the lions head, not table mountain. We cannot see the ocean on account of the trees. I saw Mr. Windsor yesterday and he said we could not have a better location. He had had no answers to the advertisement and said he would withdraw it. He is very pleasant and wants us to know Mrs. Windsor. We pay £3 per month and if we use gas 10s extra. That is not bad for such a place. The furniture is sufficient but plain, which is much better for us with the children. Will describe the room and its dimensions in my next letter. There are two entrances to the place, one through a brown door in a big stone wall on the Avenue and the other from the street at the top of the Avenue. It is in the old Hope Mill estate. . . .

Sunday evening—Well we all slept for about an hour then dressed and took a cab out to Sea Point. Were gone two hours. Cab hire is cheap enough only 5/. Drove all along the beach and got out and sat on the rocks for a few minutes. Just the kind of a beach I love. Miles of rocky beach with the waves dashing and booming over them. I had to fairly tear Grace and Roderick away and Nada seemed loath to depart also. She took the waves seriously at first and then with glee. We are going down to spend the day soon and then I am going to put her little feet in the water. We can go out on the tram, a much nearer but not as pretty a way as we went. Grace says that she never wants to leave us as long as we stay in Cape Town and is sure that father and mother would never sigh for Pasadena again. They could safely sell their home there, beautiful as it is. The beautiful glistening ocean, the towering mountains behind us and a beautiful soft blue range to the right of us. Trees, fruit and flowers. Durban is not in it my dear. Do not invest your spare cash in Durban but buy us a home in Cape Town. See more life here in one day than in a month in Durban. Thank you dear for bringing us to Cape Town. You must make arrangements so that we can stay here at least a week or two when you come back. Something on every night—almost. A regular panorama passing our window all the time. Not simply white people and Chinamen as we see in Pasadena but all nationalities here, and some wear such picturesque dresses. Mother would love to live here. But like in most seaside places there are *fleas*. They bother me considerably but maybe they will not be so bad in a private house.

I have wondered so many times whether you were seasick and oh I hope you were not. Your room was so close to the bar I am afraid you will find it very noisy. Where are you tonight and what are you doing? I hope that you are writing to me. How is Pete enjoying himself and how is Dr. Hammond satisfied? Remember us to him. Sorry we did not see Mr. Glass to bid him goodbye. He was so pleasant. Love to you from all of us and a share to Pete. Your loving
B.

———

FRB to Josiah Russell

On board the *Norham Castle*
Enroute from Cape Town to London
Dec. 18, 1894

Dear Uncle,

It has been some time since I wrote you. Events have crowded themselves upon me so rapidly that I have not had an hour unoccupied. The last from me was about the time of the sale of stands (lots) in Buluwayo. Since then I have been away on several expeditions. One to the Zambezi River, one down south, one or two east beside a flying trip by coach of 1000 miles, and just now I have finished the locating of 100000 morgen or 200000 acres of land for the DeBeers diamond syndicate, and have pumped up a scheme to go to London on. Probably you have seen in the London Cable news of certain rich finds I have made in the old mines of the ancients in Matabeleland.

I have only one thing more to do to free up the cup of romantic adventure here and that is find the hidden treasure of King Lobengula, diamonds, gold and ivory. I have the thread of its unravelling in hand, but I fear its unwinding will be vast and intricate.

I have brought all the family save John to Cape Town to have a change and rest. Grace is with B. to sort of help her do nothing.

G. is well and weighs 130 so Africa seems to suit her. John is also well. I left him up in the mountains running a mining camp.

Expenses are heavy. It cost me 800 to land us in Cape Town, but Blanche will rent a furnished cottage and cut down expenses. Howard is in very poor health and will have to resign his position of 200 per month. I saw him for a short time only at Johannesburg. He will have to come down to Cape Town and stay with Blanche and recuperate.

The baby is I believe the strongest I ever saw. Roderick was a sturdy child, but she is stronger.

Great beds of coal have been discovered north of Buluwayo which insures the building of the Cape Town R.R. up to the Zambezi River. And already the Charter Company have acquired from the government the control of a vast territory north of the River, and next season a large number of pioneers are to cross the river. Dr. Jameson will probably take charge in person.

This northern movement coupled with the great mining activity of the country will make Buluwayo the great starting point for all the vast continent lying south of the lakes. The telegraph wires are pushing on quietly and the connection between Cape Town and Cairo is as sure to be made as the crossing of the Rocky Mountains were to the Americans. I am going to London on a mining and irrigation scheme. I've 120 square miles of land in a block through which runs a river and it is on what is believed to be a healthy plateau but on this subject I should like to see another season pass to positively declare.

Blanche will have a picnic in Cape Town as they arrive just in time to revel in all its fruits. It is like Southern California in this respect, in fact the Pearl River is a repetition of San Gabriel Valley in climate and productions. Walled in by mountains, the strong trade winds do not reach them. One can easily imagine oneself in California even the Yellow Hottentot closely corresponds to the Mexican and the Indian coolie to our John Chinaman.

I am really now having an easy time and living on the fat of the land even if it is on the salt water. I eat and sleep and then sit, move and sleep again. Ingram is with me and is gaining in flesh every day. So am I.

We were both pretty thin from constant riding and campaigning, but I expect I shall be very glad to again tread the soil of Africa with its fevers and niggers, Dutch, English, and worthless Americans and its drawbacks of every kind.

It is the arena of action and nation building and is the only spot left over which hangs mystery and romance and unknown possibilities.

It seems hard to come so far on the homeward journey and not see you all, but I doubt very much if I can possibly spare the time to come over. B. and I talked it over. I would have brought her along with me but she does not like ocean travel, and did not want to go home alone so we decided to wait another season, and if I am successful next year we might meet the older members of the family in London and do the European trip together.

I am in great haste to catch Mr. Rhodes before he leaves England as the success of my projects depend largely on his approval. Still I am not hopelessly committed to this scheme and shall not lose a wink of sleep if it fails. I already have plenty to do in Buluwayo. But if it should succeed, I will be in a position to aid the progress of settlement in this country in a rapid manner. A certain Mr. Morris, once I believe state senator for California, has been over here and reported favorably on a fruit colony scheme, on nearly the same lines as Chaffee brothers of California and Australia. I believe it would be a grand success, for here we have a large population for good local market, as well as being in touch with English markets on equal or better terms than California.

We touch Madeira Island tomorrow, next London and soon I will be in the whirl of business. Mud, fog, coal dust and a sea of humanity. Such vivid contrasts to the wild and lonely jungles that it seems stupefying and when sitting in the lovely salon of this ship dressed in the regulation dark suit and assuming all the little dainties of etiquette I can I often wonder if the swallow tails around me cover such savages as Mr. Ingram and self. I enjoy it though but would not for long. 16 days is ample. Ingram says 10. Still modern travel on southern seas is a poem of quiet ease and creature comforts, press the button and if you can't even reach out to do that tip a steward and he will press it incessantly for anything you like. The sea is nearly always like a mill pond, save the throbbing of the engines one would think the ship rested on ground.

Later—nearing the end of our voyage. I am already getting restless and pace miles on the deck every day. Everybody sleeps, eats, sleeps. My fellow passengers are upper middle English who travel for pastime or on some extremely mild business, smooth sleek people, but how can they enjoy this thing for months?

A few days ago I was eating and sleeping but I was tired and very thin. Now I am rested I must do something so climb ropes, walk deck, pitch quoits, and play games. We have one live English Lord on board. He is about 22 years old and quite a nice young man in every way.

Still later. I intended to write more. We have been in a gale for 24 hours. We land at Plymouth instead of London and I will close and mail this.

Adios,

Fred

BBB to FRB

Lydbrook House, Hope Mill
Dec. 26, 1894

Dearest Fred,

Well it is the day after Christmas and mail day also. Just think we were together for seven Christmas days and not for the last four. Still yesterday was a far happier day to me than last Christmas. I shall never, never forget that day. You are far away now but I do not have to think that maybe a Matabele is throwing his assegai into you. We spoke of you so many, many times yesterday. Grace thought you were at Madeira or near there. Were you thinking of us? Nada commenced moving over the floor yesterday, not creeping but sitting up and hitching along. Roderick was sitting a little distance from her playing with his new game "The Chartered Forces in Matabeleland." (Two Maxim guns, six white men, horseback, and 12 Matabele. Little iron figures.) Nada saw her father and Uncle Pearl amongst them and made a brave and successful effort to reach them. She kept Roderick changing his position for half an hour or more. She would eat any kind of fruit, but seems to prefer bananas, and the old lady says they will not hurt her so she eats at *least* half a one every day. She has been so very good since we moved into our own room. Sits on the floor or in her perambulator about three fourths of the time. She is beginning to play now. We told Roderick that Christmas was his day and we would do whatever he liked. Of course he elected to go to Sea Point. We had a lovely time but wished for you and wondered what you were doing. Roderick needed a new suit so I bought him a navy blue sailor suit with long pants, a new hat, a rifle that shoots caps and a stick and the Matabele campaign. He was a very happy boy. He bought with his money a frame for father's and mother's pictures for Aunt Grace and a frame for his photo and yours for me. He also bought "Marcella" by Mrs. Humphrey Ward author of "Robert Ellsmere" you remember. Everyone was reading it when Grace came from home. So we have you and father and mother looking at us in our everyday life. We bought confectioners sugar and made the most delicious candy that we have ever made. We enjoy our meals so much here. We have just what we want, fruit and vegetables and very reasonable too. I am keeping account. We like our room *so* much. Will write you a long letter next week. I wrote 20 pages to Mother Burnham for this mail. I have written Howard twice and sent him the draft the day after you left. Will write again today. Have not heard from him at all. What does he mean? Long, long letter next mail. I sent you a long one the last time.

Love from all the family to our darling.

Ever your loving,

B.

BBB to FRB

> Lydbrook House, Hope Mill
> Cape Town
> Dec. 30, 1894

My darling,

This is the third letter without one from you but your letter from Madeira is on its way to me now and maybe you are giving a few moments of this Sunday to me also. It will seem so good when each mail brings a dear letter from you. You are in London now. I am thinking that you will not be able to get your suits made at once on account of the holiday time. I know how eager and anxious you are to get to work.

. . . Roderick gets his lessons every day and plays with a little girl that lives downstairs. . . . Grace bids me tell you that she is read-ing a good book on socialism today. It is Marcella, the one Roderick gave me for Christmas. I have finished it and it is very good.

. . . Would it not be lovely to carry out our old plans and have our people all settled in a homestead a mile or two out of town with an acre or two of ground. Horses do not cost much in this country and there are some beautiful ones. What do you say my dear, if you are successful, let us sell our property over there and invest our old age stake here where we can look after it ourselves and rent it to fa-ther and mother and your mother. They can take care of it for us while we are away and if they sell there will leave little money any-way. Our property there does not bring in any income anyway. Did you know there are 70,000 people in Cape Town? We will take a look around when you return. The houses here are all so plain and substantial. I am sure they cannot be very expensive. They all seem to be of rough brick, plastered over and slate roofs. Most of them are square and some are built with a court like father built for Mr. Shoemaker, but I like a deeper court like the old Spanish adobes.

You know we must have an air castle to talk about so Grace and I have built the house for the tribe and furnished it plainly but comfortably even to making the beds and cooking the first meal. . . . Wouldn't it be fun, and then I could go with you more. Write me as much of your plans and schemes, dear, as you can find time, for I am beginning to realize more and more how very little we have been together during the last year and so little time for the long confidential talks that we used to have. I think I am gaining flesh. I certainly feel well and my throat is *so much* better. It was very bad just before leaving Buluwayo. Roderick has not com-plained once and Grace says she almost wishes that Africa was not quite so healthy for it keeps her altering her dresses all the time. She is very happy and contented and writes glowing letters home. She has gone for a walk now with Roderick. I wanted to go too but the wind is too strong to be pleasant. So here I am writing and Nada is sitting on the floor with her lap full of the kind of acorns that we used to play with when we were children. Not many fruit trees right here around us but so many many shade trees, mostly oaks, elms, ash and big tall spreading blue gums. Houses fairly hid-den in the green. Perhaps I will have a letter from Howard tomor-row and then I will write more.

Monday evening. Midnight and the bells are ringing out the old year and in a few minutes will be calling in the new year and may it be a happy one to us all. I have just looked in the big journal for your resolve on New Years day 1893. "No resolves made. Tolerably well satisfied with last year and will simply continue in all the dear old vices." Is that what you are or will be saying tomorrow? I do not think we will *ever* have a happier New Year than we had last year. I can close my eyes and see you and Pete riding out to us under that big tree.

Good night sweet heart

B.

Part III
1895
Empire Builders

Cecil Rhodes and Dr. Leander Starr Jameson, whom Fred Burnham characterized as "two great men who...held in their hands the destinies of Africa." From *Scouting on Two Continents*.

BBB to Rebecca Russell Burnham

Cape Town, Africa
Lydbrook House, Gardens
Jan 21, 1895

My dear mother,

This has certainly been a red letter day for us. We were lazy this morning and did not get up until almost nine o'clock and just after breakfast while we were considering whether we would sew or go for a walk the post man brought me a letter from our agent in Buluwayo and such a good long one from John. He is doing splendidly on that contract. Fred will be more than delighted with him. . . .

Oh yes, John passed the wagon containing our boxes just one day out of Buluwayo so they would get there before he left and he could see that they were properly sorted. I am so sorry that we could not *have* had the pleasure of opening them before we left. It would have been such a treat to me, but the things will keep. I wrote you about the dreaded stage trip turning out to be more of a pleasure trip than a hardship. I should not give it a second thought if it was not for Baby. She will be harder to take care of than when we came down and some way there is no one quite like mother when she is tired. Children do not say mamma in this country. I know you could stand the stage ride but if Fred is successful with a few of his schemes I think we will have a home for you and my father and mother here in Cape Town. We will never stay steadily in Buluwayo. Fred will be away so much of the time. We do not know what our future life will be but I feel almost confident of seeing you within a year. Baby will not be too old by that time. I will not promise to have another one for you. I could not improve on this one. But it is a strange thing for me to say, who never knew what to do with a little baby. I hate to see her getting older. I would love to keep her just as she is. I seem to know how to be a mother better than I did with dear old Roderick. Why is it do you suppose? Is it because I was alone so much? I practically had her alone and then I believe nursing her makes a difference. Anyway I love her most devotedly. Roderick is just as nice as ever and we do not know how we would get along without our little man and doesn't Baby admire him. We took them out to Sea Point a week ago yesterday and all got nicely sunburned, but enjoyed ourselves very much, especially Roderick. He took his bathing suit along with him. It is not a nice beach right here for bathing. It is too rocky. No bath houses except one or two shanties of one room for an hotel. But we saw at different times during the day boys and girls undressing among the rocks. I suppose they thought they were sheltered from public gaze by the rocks but I imagine others saw them besides ourselves, and yet it would be a terrible thing to have bath houses and both sexes go in bathing together as we do. Well, I should not want anyone to see me in one of the suits that they wear here. When we all get over here together we will go to some of the nice sandy beaches for the summer and scandalize the natives, but we will show them how to bath and at the same time look nice.

I am sure it costs much less to dress prettily over here than it does in Pasadena. Grace has grown so very plump that none of her dresses will allow her to get into them, so we have had to make her a new outfit. . . .

Fred is very much pleased with his reception in London. He had only been there four days and had met his old friend The Hon. Maurice Gifford and his brother Lord Gifford, the Secretary of the B.S.A. Co. Had two invitations to dinners and was going the next day by invitation to see Miss Thompson, Major Wilson's fiancee.[1] Rhodes and Jameson were in Constantinople but were to be back about the 10th to attend a meeting of the Chartered Co. He says everyone makes a great fuss over what he and Pearl Ingram did during the campaign. They had fine dress suits made and are doing the thing up in style. They already had one scheme nicely started and Fred was going to a business meeting that P.M. Their letters were very cheerful. Our seventeen letters have been so much excitement for us that we are too tired to sit up any longer. It is only half past nine. I have written seventeen pages and Grace has written eighteen, so I think we will say good night.

Tuesday evening—We have been looking over some Graphics, Sketches and Pall Mall Budgets which Mrs. Bartley loaned us and it is now getting late, and I must not neglect dear Fred. He writes me that he sent you some views from Madeira and I sent you two photos of your little granddaughter last week. The

---

1. Major Allan Wilson, who was killed on the Shangani, December 4, 1893.

artist only caught the last end of that smile. I only had three of those finished, one for you, for father and the other for myself. Her face was turned to the dark and it does not look so well but she looks so cute in that little chair. Isn't she a graceful little thing. She just dropped into that position herself in the big chair. She is a very self-possessed young lady and never seems embarrassed. She is so sweet tempered and dearly loves a romp. The higher you toss her and the more you kiss and hug her the better she likes it. This morning while she was sitting on the bed in her nightgown, Roderick, Grace and I each held out our hands to her. Grace was standing up and thought Baby would surely come to her. She looked at all of us and then put her little hands down on the bed and started for Roderick. Don't you think that she is pretty. The photo is very good but of course it does not show her pure fair complexion, dark blue eyes with a laugh in them most of the time and her lovely golden brown fluffy hair. I wanted to send you a lock but it is too short. It is coming in very thick and fast. It pleased me very much to think that you would like to have her called after me. Fred suggested Bebe once. I almost wish now that I had named her during the first two days when I had her all alone for the more people I ask for names the more confused I become. It will be hard to ever call her anything but Baby. . . .
Lovingly,
B.

John Blick to James Blick

Filabusi
Jan 22nd, 1895

Dear Papa,

This I believe is the first letter that I have written to you but of course you read the others. It's well to stand in with paternal head for I may want to borrow a few hundred to get home on or something like that.

I just have a few minutes to write while my boy is frying some fish and making some tea. I have just returned from two shafts about five miles away. Ten miles is a long walk in the hot sun. My work is pretty well scattered just at present. I would have been early enough but I have taken on 75 ft more work. These two shafts five miles away are in darn hard ground. One is down about 42 ft and the other about the same. One is to be 40 ft and the other 30 ft. Just as soon as they are finished I will be all in good shape. The other 75 ft is only about one mile. I expect to finish down here by the end of Feb. Then I go about 30 miles from town and sink a 30 ft shaft that finishes this contract. I think by that time Fred will be back. I will probably have more work for White. I have done 200 ft in the last two months. Just as soon as my dinner is finished I am going about 1½ miles from here and sharpen a lot of picks and drills.

A fellow was down to inspect my work yesterday. I worked him just like a full grown man. The shaft he went down in I was afraid was going to fall in on him but he said it was all right.

I can't make anyone believe I am only 19. I haven't had a soul say that I was under 22. A fellow swore the other day that I would never see 25. They are beginning to make me feel old.

When I have kids of my own to sit on my knee I can tell them like you used to that I had a full beard at 19. I had it cut off while in town so only have a mustache. It isn't quite as large as yours but larger than any Joe ever had on his lip.

Here it is near the end of January and we have had but a few showers. December and January are the two rainy months. People don't know what to make of it. The grass is all gone or nearly so. The small streams are all dry and the Kaffir's corn is only about six inches high. There will be lots of starvation next year if it doesn't rain pretty soon. It must rain so the grass can grow or transport cannot come up from down below. It looks something like rain today. We may get some pretty soon. It's better for me when it doesn't rain. Meal &c. will be awfully high next year. Kaffir meal is $6.50 a hundred. My 12 boys eat 200 wt. a week. Their bill amounts to something. Flour is $23.25 a hundred. Wages are high so it doesn't seem bad. Well I think my scoff is ready so I'll chaw off. I think I can send this in town sometime next week. So long till later.

Jan 25th. Johnny has got quite a severe bellyache so I thought I would lay by this forenoon and trust my boys to work all right. The work is too scattered. Monday I will take all my boys over to the two shafts that are 5 miles away, have six work in the daytime and six work at night. Three at a hole. I will sleep betwixt and between.

My boy just came and told me that a dog was going past with some meat in his mouth. I took the gun and the first shot at about 150 yds hit him in the ribs and made him sick. He ran a little ways and stopped and I walked up about ten feet from him and shot him in the head. I have killed more dogs than anything else in Africa. Every staat has about 100 dogs and all of them are the biggest thieves on earth. We always shoot them when we get them away from the staat.

I haven't heard a word from home for going on three months. Grace has likely received some. I expect a letter from her in about three days and she will send any letters from home that she has received. I must write a letter to a fellow in town asking for some money. I hope you have plenty of contracting to do. Write and tell me what you are doing and what you have been doing.

I am getting anxious to see you all. Also B. and G. and Fred. I haven't got a single relation within 2000 miles. I think its a shame. Anyway I am all right. I look for Fred about the end of March. I'll be darn glad when he gets back Pop. I'll be worse than ever about helping myself and heavens knows I was bad enough. I even have a boy to untie my shoes and I call my cook 50 yds to come pour out my tea when the pot is sitting by my side. He pours it out puts sugar and milk in it and stirs it up. Does everything in fact but drink it. Well I must go over and see what my boys are doing. They may go below where I want to make a drive or incline etc. My belly feels very peculiar and it's now about eleven. I think I'll wait till it begins to grow cool. It's only 1½ miles away. I ate too many sardines and new bread last night. I think that's what's the matter. . . .

Your loving son,
John

━━━━━━━━

BBB to FRB

Lydbrook House, Gardens
Cape Town, Jan 27, 1895

My darling,

. . . Oh, what would I not give to see you today. It is almost seven weeks since we said goodbye. It is almost six o'clock now and the day though short has been so lonesome. I did not sleep well last night and Grace says it must be because she took your letters out from under my pillow. I will see that they are put back there tonight.

Tuesday evening and the wind is blowing a gale. It blew yesterday also. (Oh dear! See what a blot I have put on my letter but we will play it is a kiss like the children do and then it cannot be too big.) We did not go for a walk yesterday but Grace went downtown in the morning. Mrs. Lowinger and Victor spent last evening with us. We are going with them Thursday evening to a benefit concert for her son who is going to Buluwayo. They are suffering from drought in Buluwayo and are threatened with scarcity of food because transport cannot get there. No letter from John this week. I expected one for he said he would write before going back to the mine. No letters came from home either and this morning I felt quite happy thinking that the steamer would come in with your letter. Just after luncheon Mrs. Caldecott brought in the paper and we found that the Norham Castle is not expected until Thursday morning. The barometer dropped immediately. I was blue and I am afraid I was *cross* so Grace insisted on my going for a walk with Mrs. Caldecott. We walked for almost two hours and the wind blew us about in great shape. It freshened me up wonderfully. Came home, ate a hearty supper and here I am writing to you. I hope that you have some copies of your interview, for the African and Westminster Gazette are daily papers and we could not get them here. The meeting of the Chartered Co. seems to have been a very enthusiastic one. How very fortunate that you should be there just at the time to be able to take advantage of the boom. Nothing will surprise me that you may do. But if I am to go with you wherever you go will it be advisable to bring the folk over here because they will not be happy away from the other children if we are not with them all the time. Grace does not get homesick at all. She is an astonishment to herself as well as to me. Fate must have something good in store for her here in Africa. Oh, I want to talk to you. You have been away long enough my dear so do hurry up and come home but it is needless to tell you to do that for I know you are trying your very best. But, the letters are so old when they come and we have no idea of what you are doing *now* this very moment. Be sure and bring your "dude clothes" home with you. If diamonds as "large as doorknobs" and "pearls as large as goose eggs" are rolling about in the London streets please bring us some. Grace says bring her a pearl!

Roderick is still out at Camps Bay. I wish they would bring him back. We miss him so much. Nada grows to look more like you every day. Such a lovely dimpled chin and her dear little white hands and feet are small patterns of yours. I am *so glad* that we have her to love. She is a regular little tom boy already. The lady down below (a grass widow) is singing "Come oh come my love to me" in a most effective manner for I hear his footstep on the walk. She sings the same song every evening and it *always* brings him. Wish I could sing it as effectively.

Good night my darling,

Your loving B.

Grace says I must fill up this blank if I say nothing but "Come, oh come my love to me" so here goes. Come, oh come my love to me. Come, oh come my love to me. Come, oh come my love to me. Come, oh come my love to me. [Blanche has written the phrase bigger and bigger each successive time to fill up the page.] Oh dear, Grace says I have made a mistake. I never could keep a tune. It is come my love, oh come to me. Good heavens she says I have not got it right yet. It is, "Come my love, Oh come my love home."

FRB to James Blick

The First Avenue Hotel
High Holborn
London, Feb. 16th, 1895

Dear Father,

I did not sail 16th as expected but go on the Dunnottar Castle 22nd Feb. Ingram and myself are expecting to sell some of our stock in one of the companies and have been talking over business investments. Cape Town seems to strike us both. We have such large interests up north it might be well to throw an anchor out just to steady the drift of our financial craft. Should we be successful we will both buy a stand (lot) in Cape Town and I will build a house at once—and Ingram in a few months—of about £50 each. It depends on cost of land. I think we can get stands for about £200 to £300 in good quarter of town. They rent for about 20% per annum, but I should want it to live in part of the time when not in Buluwayo. I shall also build in Buluwayo one house. Would you care to come out and superintend the job? I don't want you to touch a tool if you come. I merely mention this as things move rather quickly with me and if they should jump that way I would be pleased. I have a letter from John (indirectly). He has done well so far and I am pleased. He made £152 net in five weeks. I hope to hear of him when I get to Cape. He of course will not make the same on the last part of the contract as it will get harder but he will probably clear John's and Grace's expenses to Africa at one stroke. Not bad for a schoolboy is it? I shall have him with me when I go north. Write me at Buluwayo as it will reach me [portion of letter missing]. I believe there should be £500 net in it per annum[1] and chances of bigger contracts later on but I cannot stop to attend to it. Of course it may be decided to give it to city as there may be some feeling about my getting too much from the Chartered Co. already. Can't say. I am looking for the boys to follow me to Cape in about two weeks.

Later.

Adios,

Fred

—————

John Blick to Phebe and James Blick

> Buluwayo March 26th, 1895
> Just got letter from
> you haven't read it yet.

My Dear Mamma and Pappa,

By Jove its been a duce of a long time since I have written to you but you must not think that I think any the less of you because I don't write more often. . . . I actually don't believe you would know me. I am so awfully fat. Kate can't be more so. Just think, I weigh 154 lbs and when I left Pasadena I only weighed 134. That's

---

1. Here FRB is apparently writing of his attempt to get a street sprinkling contract.

pretty good isn't it and I never felt better in my life. I don't even have headaches like I used to at home. I don't think I am all fat for I have been growing a good deal. My clothes fit me like the paper on the wall.

Just think I was for 4 months without a vegetable and the three days that I have been in Buluwayo I haven't eaten scarcely anything else. Don't you worry about me being sick mother or about me having my morals corrupted. It's true you get a good deal of bad company out here but it makes me better instead of worse. I'll tell you when I take my first drink and have my first smoke. I am afraid my hair will be gray by that time. I had the wrong kind of bringing up you know.

It was all right for Grace and Blanche to go down below. I couldn't of been with them more than a week anyway.

I just came in town to get some provisions and see if the folks had arrived. They haven't showed up yet and there was no mail from them. . . .

You have heard a good deal more of Fred's doings than I have. I have only had one letter from him and two from Blanche and Grace. In their last letter they expected Fred and Pete on every boat. I am only 40 miles from town now and as Art Cumming has loaned me a mule I will come in next week. I have but one mine shaft to complete. Then I am coming in town. Of course Fred will have plenty for me to do. If he hasn't, I can get work from Dr. Hammond who is to manage the Syndicate that they have just floated. I hope you are in no need of money. I will try and send you 50 to $100 just as soon as Fred arrives. He owes me $400 the 18th, when this month or the 20th of Apr. I will have earned $500. That isn't bad is it? If I can only keep it up all the time. But that's where the difficulty comes in. You see Grace isn't earning overly much. The gold is so unsatisfactory in this country that its hard telling whether the country is going ahead or not. If it does, its a good place for young fellows but otherwise no good. There are any amount of fellows out here without work now. The houses are *all*, bar a few of paper, of brick with iron roofs so a carpenter doesn't have much work except job work, $7.50 per day.

What do you think of a sack of spuds selling for $215. Not bad is it. It was the only sack in Matabeleland. They were sold by auction 5 at a time. All vegetables except potatoes are *very* cheap.

Gosh I could go a good big dish of fried spuds just at present or an orange or an apple.

I opened one of the trunks the other day and am now chawing on dried peaches off of our own place. *Gosh* they are good and so are the apricots that Rayzor and I swiped at Hewitts. Blanche told me to eat everything good I could find in the trunk. I looked for that bottle of crystallized fruit but I'll be darned if I could find it. They are going to bring me something good to eat when they come up. I hope Fred will bring me something good from London. I want a good watch and a good razor. You say that Judd has written to me. I haven't received it yet but tell him I will answer it as soon as I do. It has gone down to Cape Town and will probably be up on this mail. They send all your letters up as soon as they get them. I scarcely know what to write about until I hear from Fred.

Well its 2½ miles into town and if I don't wiggle the post office will be closed. . . .

Love to all.

I am your fat sassy and loving son,

John Blick

———

FRB to James Blick

Buluwayo
[Circa April 6, 1895]

Dear Father,

You will receive by this mail a letter with check for £150. Forward this through the bank and ask for N.Y. draft of exchange, which will cost you about 3/6 (85 cts). The bank here demands 2½ percent on London and more for N.Y.

Well, your infant has done fairly well so far in Africa. Cleared $2000 on his first contract in four months. He has paid me £200 for himself and Grace and sends you £150, gives Grace £10 and has balance for pocket money. I am looking anxiously for Judd and Homer every day. Grace has not made any money yet but has gone hopelessly in love with a young man here and is as spooney as anybody. Who would have thought it of the sedate Grace? She swore on arrival that she would not fall in love with anybody here &c. &c. Would wait until B. picked out a man for her. But this is a strange country and all things happen on different lines than at home.

John will be able to make up your losses this year and you can rest easy. Each of the other boys must send in £100 each to pay for their raisings. I am about to get a big contract on canal here. Shall take it for you. There ought to be $5000 net in it. Will try and have it in shape for you when I return from the north. . . .

Yours as ever,

Fred

John Blick to Phebe and James Blick

Buluwayo
April 7th 1895

My Dear Old Daddie and Mammie,

. . . I was in Buluwayo just six months yesterday and have paid Fred the $1000 that Grace and I owed him and enclose a check to you for $750 and have about $150 pocket money. Not bad for a kid not out of his teens is it?

I think that $250 will straighten out all your little debts and leave you $500 for the bank. Now don't you think for a minute that I give you this reluctantly or want to keep it for myself. I am still young. I might give you $750,000 and then not feel that I had done more for you than you have done for me. I hope this will find you in better spirits and in good health.

You can imagine how I feel about going north. I am simply wild to go. Pete and I with another Yank start day after tomorrow. Fred will overtake us in about two months. Just think, I will not know till then whether Judd and Homer have come or not. We have everything that money can buy for this expedition, rubber blankets, boats, hammocks, the finest guns made &c., so you needn't worry any about us.

This expedition is the talk of all Africa and England. If it is a success, Fred and Pete will become notorious if not so already. Imagine Johnny shooting elephants &c. We are going to find gold north of the Zambezi if we have to go to the Great Desert, so don't know when we will get back. We will think ourselves lucky if we get back for next Xmas dinner.

This is really the forerunner of a larger expedition which Fred will take up later. We are going into the very heart of Africa, the black interior which is absolutely unknown as no white man has ever seen it.

There is really no danger attached to it, we are so well equipped. When I get back I will be no little spring chicken will I? I can hold my head up and wear spurs and a goatee then with good reasons. I feel luck[y] as well might Judd and Homer, to be allowed to go along. Fred has had at least 100 applicants to go, but has refused them all. He hasn't selected but one man besides our family. It's hard to find the right men. . . .

Mother, you will have to console yourself with Mag for a few years yet. Old Chubb will be back next year. She and Pete are as soft as ever Joe and Daisy dare be. Pete is a darn good fellow and will make you a good son-in-law and me a good bro-in-law. I can't think of anything to write but will be able to when I return. So goodby for a spell from
Your loving son,
John

FRB to James Blick

Buluwayo
April 10th, 1895

Dear Father,

This day I have closed a concession north of the Zambezi River of 100 square miles (⅓ is mine). For this grant James Doré of London has to expend £10,000—½ inside one year—in Matabeleland. It is his purpose to take out a canal from the Insezi river 45 miles from Buluwayo and start a colony. It is likely I will get this canal contract. If not, I will be able to give the management of the ranch to you anyway, which will be far better than Pasadena contracting. By the time you can arrive here I will be back from the north and have plenty for you to do without your taking hold of a hammer or plans either. John and the other boys I shall work the vinegar out of. As the money for your expenses out is now in Uncle Josiah's hands and only needs your signature, you had better come out at once, and if you don't, I fear you will lose

Grace as she is wearing diamonds and a lovely opal and diamond ring and I did not buy it either. But my private opinion is that it is all right even if the final ring is worn.

Now if things go right I will meet the Grandmas in London. B. will be with me. We will have Roderick come over from Germany[1] and Uncle Josh come along as far as London anyway, and then come out to Buluwayo. Homer and Judd will be able to make their salt I guess if John can do as well as his start. And then if all of you like the country we could pass the hat and collect money enough to bring out the balance of our tribe or disliking the country as many as chose could return to Pasadena. I doubt if you will be one of them. Come out and get a rifle on your shoulder among the big game and grow young again while your children grow to be men. John has written to Ray Conger and to all his best sunday girls and gone north today. I overtake them at the Zambezi River.

Yours as ever,

Fred
See No. 2 by B.

———

BBB to Blick family [fragment]

[Circa April 1895]

He [John] looked like a picture as he rode away this morning. We are looking for Homer and Judd. Have received the letter after Homer received the cable. Would you like to come father and make a £1000? Fred and I might meet the mothers in London. This is just one of our little air castles but *some* of them are often realized.

Well, supper is over. It was a very quiet little supper without John and Pearl. We had a good old fashioned talk and Nada amused us for half an hour after supper. She has a wonderful little way of weaving herself into ones affections. She has taken her father's heart by storm. He picks her up and pets and plays with her like a father should. She is so friendly with everyone, even the ne-

1. The Burnhams sent Roderick to Europe for schooling. He was briefly in Germany and France but soon returned to the United States.

groes. She will smile at them and touch their big black hands with her little white ones. Ponto wheels her about a great deal in the little carriage which we brought up by coach from Johannesburg or Cape Town I mean. She is getting so many little cute ways. Oh I must tell you about the boxes. Mr. Cumming was taking care of them out at the farm and brought them in to us the day after we came into the house. (Mr. [Couright's] lease was not up for two months but they gave it up and let us come into the house. It was full of ants and fleas and we are still fighting them.) We have had a mess of corn and also one of the apricots and we thought of home and the dear little mother as we ate each mouthful. The crystallized fruit we also enjoyed. Thank you so much for my pretty lawn dress. It is just as pretty as can be. Baby's stockings are fine. Tell Helen that the necktie is very pretty and I will send it to Roderick. . . .

Friday morning—We did nothing but talk about you all day yesterday and as a result had Grace write you again last night. I think she has told everything. It is so hard to write and explain all the little things. Fred thinks that father is *very* anxious to see Africa and he would like to have him do so. I would love to see mother but if Fred finds any mineral north of the river we will start for London in Oct. he thinks. Grace and Pete will either go to Cape Town or London at about the same time so you would only have the boys and perhaps not all of them at the same time. We will always be wandering but we could see you part of the time every year if you were in Africa. We will *never* live in Pasadena and I do not know when Fred will find time to visit there.

Hard lines isn't it little mother. What a pity that we should all think so much of each other. How I would love to talk to you. Would you rather have two or three thousand dollars at interest and live in Pasadena with so many of us over here and only the chance of an occasional visit from some of us or come to Africa? Wynberg, three or four miles from Cape Town is simply lovely, *far* prettier than Pasadena, and if we are successful we can have a home there not a new one but an old place with fruit and flowers. You would not sell your place unless you chose this as your adopted country. I would dearly love to see you but I think it would be best for father to come first if he wants to come. I am sure Homer and Judd will like Africa for a time anyway. Fred will never leave it, except on trips. But maybe Homer is not coming. I know Linnie would hate to let him come. We are wondering whether she is with you or it would have been nice for her to have gone home for a visit. If Homer likes it, will she be willing to come? I am going to see Roderick next Christmas if there is any money in the bank. Oh I miss him so much. Grace and I will be *so lonely* when the boys are all gone. I cannot bear to think about it. I commenced to wean baby last night. Grace took her into her room to sleep. She did not cry much. . . .

With oceans of love,

Your loving daughter,

B.

FRB to Rebecca Russell Burnham

April 11th 1895

Dear Mother,

Things are progressing so far favorably. I have made another deal of some advantage to me. Howard has also done well and I have sent him to Germany with Roderick to put him at school. Now the scheme is if I survive the northern trip I shall come over to London this coming winter and want you to meet B. and I there, also Uncle J. If I am again successful in London, you are to come out with us and we will buy a place in Cape Town. I want Mr. Blick to come out first and take a big contract here and if he likes it he can send for Mrs. Blick and she can come out with you and we will all buy a place in Cape Town suburbs, very lovely pine groves and ocean drives and towering cliffs and mountains. Plenty of black and Maylay servants at $5.00 per month. At Cape Town you will see us once in a while as we flit back and forth in and out of Africa. B. and I will probably keep up our travels till we die. Ingram, Grace's proposed husband and my friend, is like myself a rambler and a money maker. Cape Town is the Pasadena of Africa and Durban its Riverside. None of us will ever do business or live in America again, that is certain. South Africa with all its faults is my adopted country and in welding it into a United South Africa I will have the privilege of striking a blow. We will yet roost under the shadow of the Pyramids and have picnics at the Victoria Falls. I am off in a few days with a big expedition far to the north, laying a stepping stone in the stride of the northern march of the race. There is little doubt that most of our tribe will finally wind up in this country. Buluwayo is growing rapidly and in a few years will be a big town.

I must fill out a big order tonight and cannot do justice to a letter to you and yet this is the last for a long time from me, but as everything is moving along on the lines mentioned in my previous letters it is not so much matter. B. will send you a photo of Roderick who is now a fine looking boy and will have a fine education first in Germany and afterwards in the U.S.
Goodbye with love,
Fred

———

BBB to Rebecca Russell Burnham

April 11, 1895

Dear mother,

Those gentlemen who had rented our house gave it up to us very willingly I thought. I know the reason why now. It is literally alive with fleas. Other people are bothered with them also. They must be in the soil. I have tried to get rid of them with flea powder, salt, copperas, and they only grew fatter. Now I am going to cover the floors with paraffin tomorrow. Fleas, ants and bed bugs bid fair to made our lives miserable. . . . Pray for Fred to be successful. Never saw anyone so busy in all my life. His gloves were all too large but he had brought him a supply from London. I have told Roderick about his presents and shall keep them for him. Had some photos taken of him the day before we left C.T. The proofs arrived last mail and I send an order for some today, so you will soon see what a beautiful bonny boy he is. I cannot tell you how I miss him but you know for you had to give up Howard when he was about Roderick's age. They are going to write every week. The first letter he just wrote Dear father and mother. Howard wrote the letter and he signed your boy Roderick. Howard was so pleased to have him. I know he will be good to him and I am sure that he will make him study. He took him for a sail every day for the week before he left Cape Town. They sailed about April 1st. Mrs.

Schroeder wrote me that he would not say that he missed us but she heard him crying once in the middle of the night. She went to him and he said, "Oh if I could only have my mother for five minutes." It nearly breaks my heart whenever I think of it. I *must* see him by next Christmas. Thank fortune Nada is a girl and will not have to be sent away to school so soon. I commenced to wean her last night. She did not act very badly but no telling what she will do tonight for she has no two moods alike. . . . I have a lot of little business affairs to attend to this A.M. as Fred's business is so busy. Will have more time to write after he is gone. But we will be so lonesome. I dread the next four months. Grace is going to marry Pearl Ingram. They are very happy or were before they had to separate. Grace bids fair to lead just such a roving life as I have but she says "I will go wherever Pearl says."
From your loving daughter,
B

BBB to Phebe and James Blick

Monday
Buluwayo April 22, 1895

Dearest father and mother,

Mr. Orpen dined with us yesterday. He leaves tomorrow morning for Cape Town to attend parliament. He is a very influential member, an old friend of Mr. Rhodes and always stays at his place during parliament. His son and his son's wife are coming today to spend a few days with us. Fred knows them very well and they seem to think so much of him. He had to go down to see about some farms for Mr. Doré. Will be back on the night of the 24th. We are all anxiety for Friday to come and bring Judd. We want to hear whether he thinks you two would come to Africa. But we will write this and send down to Cape by Mr. Orpen and another will follow by regular mail. . . .

As usual I will have to move alone, but I would rather because I do not want to be moving when Judd is here. We must clickety clack what little time we have with him. Our new place is very pretty. Three trees in front of the house and a dozen or more at the back of the house. Fine view of the town and in an elegant neighborhood. Too many neighbors and shops around us *here*. We shall not sell our other four stands just yet. Fred is so sorry that he did not send for both of you when he sent for Judd and Homer. He had to let the water contract go last week because he had no one to put in charge and he *has* to go north at once and could not stay to see it through. It would have taken a month. If you were here, you could also have been manager for Doré at at least £30 per month. And so things are turning up every week or so and no telling what will be on tap when you get here. As long as the Chartered Co. exists there is no danger of our starving. You cannot understand what a pull Fred has here and how he is sought after by other companies too. Says he lost a thousand pounds ($5000) by not being able to take this street sprinkling contract. You *must* get here to look after Doré's business for him. He is so anxious for you to have the trip, says you have had so little enjoyment in life that you deserve some pleasure now. . . . [unsigned]

Grace Blick to Rebecca Russell Burnham

Buluwayo, Africa
May 12, 1895

My Dear Mrs. Burnham,

I think B and I would give almost anything to be talking to you today instead of writing. When you answer this we will be doing something so entirely different that you all seem so far away. We are not having much fun now as we are alone once more. Fred and Judd are a good many miles away and we have had one letter from there already sent back by a runner and then from Pearl's part of the expedition. By the time this reaches you they will all be turned homeward again and by the time you answer they will be here, but in the meantime, oh dear.

We feel most awfully deserted for Mr. Cumming is at the Bulingwe [Mine] and Bob is in Johannesburg. We have two men friends but they are English. Mr. Lowinger from Cape Town, who was an opera singer and has a beautiful baritone voice but who is in a surveyor's office now, comes over several times a week and sings for me or reads to me which he enjoys as much as we do. "Faust" and "Carmen" are his great pets and he sings by the hour. His wife was a friend of ours at the Cape. He adores Nada because she makes him think of his baby Ohna. Mr. Miller is here a great deal and we like him very much. He is engaged to one of Mr. Cumming's sisters.

I am thinking Bob will be soon engaged, and poor Mr. Cumming will have to leave. He won't be able to stand so many engaged couples around. His six sisters are very pretty and full of fun. Some of the married flirts around here will have to step down. There are seven or eight of the latter in Buluwayo who have a fine time riding, driving, playing tennis and dancing with the young men. Everyone talks about them but they don't care. One of the most dashing young married women skipped for England a few weeks ago with one of the handsome young men who had some money. We met them at Tuli and she told us she was going home for a few months. When we got here we heard the whole of the tale. She was worse than any of the others I think. But anyway there are two circles here already. The fast one and the "upper ten" and these giddy young creatures are going to be snubbed, although the same men are in both circles, fortunate fellows. Some of the ladies here are very nice. We call on about ten and really like them. I suppose there are a lot more but we don't happen to hear about them and as B has to call first she waits until she knows who they are and then calls. We are over the river now and as all of those we know are friends we will have them about all in one day as we are so far away.

. . . Mr. [Jefferson] Clark the big mining engineer American has the place next to us, and Mrs. Greenfield, who is to be married in June, is to live on the other side of us, and Mrs. Fletcher and Mrs. Harrison, the Company's surveyor's wife and sister, on the stand back of us. In a few months this will be a gay place. I am very glad that you people are prepared for the news of my engagement and that you have no objections to Pearl (his mother named him Pearl, but some unkind young friends of his changed his name to Pete). I think Ingram a lovely name don't you? Quite equal to Burnham if it hasn't quite as many letters in it. You would like him I know. All the ladies do. He is so quick to wait on them and never forgets little things. When you come over and we all live in Cape Town we will have some sporty times. You would enjoy life at the Cape. It's simply glorious there. The sea is what I always wished the California sea to be. And the drives are delightful. Oh, I do hope they will find something splendid where they are going and then we will all be able to do something. Pearl wants to go to America to see his people and I don't *mind* going in the least. But if they don't find much, Cape Town will be as far as we will get. Pray for this expedition will you! . . .

With love,

Grace

BBB to Rebecca Russell Burnham

May 12, 1895
Sunday P.M.

Dear Mother,

. . . Did I ever tell you that Fred spent several days at Rider Haggard's and he gave him his photo, a great large one and several of his novels. Fred liked him very much. His cousin and his wife came to Cape on the same steamer with Fred and he took me to call on them and just before Fred went north, R. Haggard's brother and cousin took supper with us. We can get up quite dainty meals now. Have had Fred's parliamentary friend, Mr. Orpen, a number of times, as well as his son and his wife. They just about worship Fred and he *begged* Fred's photo to give Cecil Rhodes. . . . He is the dearest old gentleman, Mr. Orpen I mean.

Lots of love,

B.

BBB to Rebecca Russell Burnham

Bulawayo,[1] Matabeleland
June 11, 1895

Dear Mother,

. . . Let us talk about dear old Fred. Grace says that she never knew that he was half so good until she came to Africa. She thinks

---

1. Bulawayo—the spelling was changed in 1895 to distinguish the new white capital from Lobengula's *kraal*.

with me now that he is almost perfect. I say *perfect*. I had such a good letter from him today. It was almost twenty days old. He expected to meet the others at Panda-ma-Tenka in three or four days. They were going very slowly cutting a road through brush and very heavy sand. Very warm weather and they could only trek morning and evening. Oxen are *so* slow. Still he was very cheerful. He had sent Judd and Jack Stewart on ahead to be getting pack saddles ready with Pearl and John. He could not or rather dared not leave the wagons for something would have been sure to have gone wrong and delayed them. He had received letters from Pearl and John. They had pegged off some splendid coal ground at the mouth of the Juay River and were back at Panda waiting for Fred. Pearl had gone on up to the falls (60 miles) with a Mr. Baggley but was coming back to meet Fred. Everything was progressing finely, the donkeys and mules were in good condition. I know everything is all right on this side of the Zambezi and Fred thinks that it will be on the other side. We can only hope and pray. They were all well. Fred said for me to tell you where he was and send you his love. He sent us all the letter would hold and would have sent more but the "nigger" could not carry any more.

I expect you wonder how we get letters from them. They take a couple of boys or more from the different big kraals and then send them back. For instance Pearl had two boys from Imgunyanai that he took to Panda-ma-Tenka with him and then sent back to meet Fred with letters. Fred gave them his letters, and they came back to their own kraal and the chief sent the letters on by two other boys to Gambos where Taylor the native commissioner is, and he sent two other boys to Bulawayo. They carry the letters all enclosed in a big envelope addressed to Mrs. F. R. Burnham, Bulawayo. They generally go into the business part of the town and then begin to accost people saying, "Upey" (Where). Well almost everyone knows all about this expedition and the boy is soon sent to Mr. Moffat's office and he brings the letters over to me. He has brought me three but this one was taken to Capt. Spreckley's office and as he was coming over this way he brought it to me. Mr. Moffat, the secretary, told me that he had several letters for Fred from Lord Gifford (Fred's great friend), and that he was on his way here and will be here in a week or so with the latest news and instructions, and that he would send special runners straight to

Panda, so we will be sure of getting letters to Fred at least that once. . . .

With love and kisses from Nada,

Your loving daughter,

B.

———

FRB to BBB [fragment]

[Circa June, 1895]

. . . The coal veins in this country are enormous, 20 ft thick and it burns beautiful—tis a Bituminous coal. John is still sick but not serious, but as he was never sick before he makes a great deal of fuss and I guess wished he was with Mamma sometimes. I am sending back some boys with the two white men who are to bring us up limbo to pay off carriers. There are hundreds of hippo just below the drift. We are going to kill one to make fat to grease up our pack ropes. Bill Nye is better but not yet strong. It relieves a lot of heavy work to know that we will have a peaceful entry into the country. I must make up my coal maps tomorrow. Pete's mule is best saddle animal he says in Matabeleland and we are both going to leave good animals there to ride home on.

The meat is again palela in camp and hunters are out after it. So far everything is lovely and inside 20 days from now we will be rushing another runner back with the news of our finds—if any. Tell Grace there is a young lady missionary up here and I think Pete's stopping on the river is dangerous. I must write long letter to Moffatt. Pete wants me to send the enclosed note to Howard as he says he will fully *understand*. . . .

June 6th—Yesterday was a red letter day. I had an audience with the King, met the missionary and his family and made all arrangements for the crossing of the river. I must first describe the river. Imagine yourself on the Mississippi at Stoney Point on a lovely day in September. The forest trees slightly tinged with red and yellow and the banks waving with the tall rushes 12 to 15 ft high, the rounded bluffs timber-clad look much like Clinton but not so rough as Lyon's and the islands correspond to Little Rock and Beaver. The sun shines bright and a gentle breeze from the east just ripples the blue waters. The river at Kazungulla is about

600 yds wide, the narrowest place in many miles. Just above the crossing, the Chobe comes in and on the tongue of land between the two is the beginning of the German possessions and a clump of tall palms wave their plumes in every breeze and nod to the black waters of the Chobe or the white of the Zambezi. It seems too bad that such a fine looking valley should be ruined by fever which creeps on one unawares and in spite of all precautions. But at this time of year tis not dangerous. The missionary living here have been 9 years in this valley. Many have died but deluded souls they still hold on and even have children. But they look sallow, wan and their span of life must be short. If it could be arranged that they could get out of the valley every rainy season, it would be all right.

It all seems strange and queer here. The tall naked savages, some colored with red pigment, darting across in their frail canoes hollowed out of logs and bringing over my goods, swimming my donkeys, mules and a lot of cattle, guns, powder and war material which at present seems luckily I shall not need. The strange horns and hides the natives bring me to trade, beautiful woven baskets, and strange carved wooden dishes, made of teak wood and ebony, carved crocodiles and alligators on the cover of the bowls, at night the snort of the hippos and alligators, the cry of strange waddling birds, different bloom on the flowers, different leaves on the trees makes the trip well worth the pains to one who can really see.

Later—All my boys were left on the other side and a big canoe sent after them has been held up by a strong wind blowing up river, so six of our white men and the boys can have the pleasure of watching us eat our meal on this side. They must wait for the night and maybe two days to cross. They must live on climate and scenery.

Later—All came over in the evening and tonight we go on a great hippo hunt. There are numbers on an island just below our camp. The moon is now full all night and the river by night is a marvel of beauty. The beating of tom toms and the low soft music of the Kaffir piano, the gleam of fires through the reed huts and circles of naked savages make an impression not easily forgotten and on such a day as this I find my rewards for the long and dreary treks without water and endless thorn of the western route. I listened to the account of the missionaries with keen interest. Mrs. Jalla says in 9 years she has only seen one white woman except some missionaries. When I leave here I will be treading on new ground and what it may hold in store tis hard to say [letter incomplete].

BBB to Rebecca Russell Burnham

Bulawayo, Matabeleland
July 23, 1895

Dear Mother,

. . . I am hoping and praying that Fred's northern trip may be successful so that we can get away from here for a few months. It is dreadfully dreary although there are getting to be some nice people here now. You make calls and receive calls. That is all the society there is. Three weeks ago from Sunday to Sunday we had thirty-five callers. Gentlemen call here as much as the ladies do. That was an exceptional week, but we always have someone everyday if only Mr. Cumming, and he is just like our brother. Bob Bain is going to marry one of Mr. Cumming's sisters and Mr. Miller, the man who built our house, is going to marry another one of them. There are six sisters and seven boys. We went out to the farm last Sunday to see them and some of them have been here two or three times this week. We went in to the church bazaar last evening and left Baby with Mrs. Newman. Have I ever told you about Capt and Mrs. Newman. (There, Baby woke up just then. Does she not take a long nap?) I have fed her with some crackers and broth and she is playing with Zic, the puppy. Capt. Newman gave the pup to Grace. They are our neighbors over here. He was an officer in the Imperial Army, but is a newspaper man now. He is an old scamp but always treats us very well and he has the dearest wife. She is older than he is. Was a widow with some money and several children. . . . It is three weeks now since I had a letter from Fred. I shall look for one in a week or ten days and hope I shall not be disappointed. He sent me a description of the river which I must copy and send to you. They crossed 65 miles above the falls so did not see them. Kaluba, the son of the Barotse King, has a kraal there and also a mission station. He is very civilized and wears tailormade clothes, stiff white shirts, and collars and a derby hat. He does not speak English, the missionary interprets for him. Pete went there first. The chief was very friendly and gave Pete one of their strange carved wooden bowls, with an alligator carved on the top of the lid and these words burned out on the inside, "Presented to P. Ingram by Kaluba the Barotse fighting chief—date. Success to you and your party." The bowl is about twenty inches long and six or eight deep. I have a number of wooden bowls but nothing so fine as that. Kaluba sent messengers to Luinka, the king, to get permission for them to prospect through his country. The missionaries were confident that he would give them protection. This family of Italians have lived there nine years. They have two children living. There is a young lady of 40 staying with Mrs. Jalla.[1] They treated our boys very nicely and had a special service for them in the chapel. This place is a fearful fever hole during parts of the year. The river is 600 yards wide at this Kazungulla. The natives took them across in canoes. It was a pretty long job to get everything over, but it was all done safely. Everyone seemed in good spirits. They were just entering into the really new country, had pegged off forty miles of coal, twenty ft. thick, good bituminous coal. How I hope that they may find gold. Fred sent back two white men, and fourteen Barotses with an induna, small chief. I kept the blacks over here and fed them up well so they would think well of the "little man's" country. That is what they call Fred. The induna wanted to see Dr. Jameson to get a representative of the Chartered Co. sent to their capitol. But Dr. Jameson has not yet returned so the induna had to return. They carried over mail and limbo (calico) to pay off the carriers that [FRB] is now using. A number of people came over from town to see these Barotse. They seemed to be pleased at first, but I do not think they liked being gazed at along toward the last. They were here four days. They thought Baby was the most wonderful thing they had ever seen. She would touch their hands with her little white fingers but jump back and laugh when they would go to take her. It pleased Ponto so much. He is such a good boy to the baby. I must try and get the Baby's photo taken sitting in her cart with Ponto by her side and Zic jumping up after her feet.

He is a very interesting boy. I must get someone to ask him his history some day and then I will tell you. Most boys have a dozen so called brothers, but Ponto has none and seems to feel

1. The wife of the missionary Adolphe Jalla of the Paris Evangelical Missionary Society.

himself too good to associate with others so I am spared the trouble you have with most of them who are always wanting to go and see their brothers. Once in a great while he goes to see our old Pete who is now working for Mrs. Newman. I like Ponto. He is one of the rare boys whom you can treat kindly and he does not take advantage of your kindness. He plays most wonderfully sweet music on a hollow gourd fastened on to a bow and sings a variety of songs, especially for an hour or so after dark. He has built him such a pretty little hut of closely woven branches out under a cluster of trees. It looks very pretty. I have given him old clothes and blankets and he is very contented and has no desire to leave me. We have to send over to town so many times during the week for groceries, meat, bread, washing, &c that he does not have time to breathe some days especially if we have callers and he has to wheel baby so I am going to get a boy eight or ten years old next week. (5 shillings per month.) I only have to pay Ponto 10 shillings. I believe he is about 15 or 16. Feed them on meat and coarse corn meal or a kind of red meal. These boys are not so cheeky as the ones that speak English. They are too smart. Ponto is learning to understand very well. Old Longboy came over a couple of weeks ago. He is going to rest until the boss comes back. . . .
Yours lovingly,
B.

———

FRB to Rebecca Russell Burnham

Bulawayo
Aug 18, 1895

My dear mother,

The Northern trip is ended and I had promised to write you something of the long journey and happenings. But I will be so busy now that I fear you will not get it until I meet you in London, which I hope ere long to do, and Uncle Josiah also, and I will spin you yarns until you will be sick of the name of Africa. However tonight I will just tell you a little of the last end of our Northern cruise.

Judd is back with me and Ingram. I crossed the Zambezi River at the Victoria Falls. You can get full descriptions of them from such able writers that I will not try to explain in detail all its peculiar wonders. It has a beauty all its own. The broad blue river widens out for its great leap and numerous small rocky islands, on which tall palms are waving, break the monotony of a single sheet of water. The rock is black basalt all round the Falls for many miles and the contrasts of color between forest, reeds, rocks, and yellow grass is very vivid. The long purple ridge marking the borders of the valley makes a picturesque setting for one of nature's wonders. The river plunges into a black chasm a little less than 400 ft at one fall and then its two mile sheet of water is compressed between its narrow walls only a few hundred yards apart. If I was asked what impressed me the most of all the various sights, the awful roar, the circling clouds of spray and mist, the dancing rainbows, or gurgling whirlpools, I should say above all the sense of energy and irresistible force grows upon one. It gives one a faint gleam into what the building of a mountain range, the sinking of a continent, or the crash of a planet might be. Days might be spent here and pass as hours, by moonlight gaze on its banks of clouds like northern fields of snow, or in the somber darkness of the night sit on some projecting rock and hear such sound come out of this gash in mother earth as though it were a mortal wound and this the surging out of her heart's blood. Ones own utter nothingness is brought home as no prayer book passage can bring it and one feels the same strange calm as when death is just upon you.

From the falls to Bulawayo is about 200 miles. Ingram and myself wanted to find a more direct route than via Panda-ma-Tenka road to the west or up the river Guay which bears far away to the east. We knew at this time of year it would be a dry trip but hoped to find some (pools). Ingram and Judd left the Falls four days ahead of me, not knowing that I was on my way down country from the north. I had 12 carriers with me and not far from the Falls picked up two bushmen who are supposed to be the best guides and trackers in Africa. They knew the water holes for a short distance and then were of no use to me at all. I had saved a mule for the dry belt but it, being stung by the fly, perished of thirst after the second day and I had only ridden 3 hours. At the last known pool I called up all the blacks and told them to fill their calabashes and that we would strike southeast. We traveled that night but reached a great sand belt covered with thorn bushes and waited till daylight hoping to get round it, but it seemed limitless, and it came out hot and a dry wind blew from the east. At noon I examined the water supply and found the fools had drank all. A nig can no more save water and food than some spendthrift's money. Though death hang over him he will not practice self denial in the slightest form. Had I been able to watch or carry each calabash of water and rationed it out all would have been well. We tore through the thorns' great fish hooked willowy creepers and stiff unyielding spikes. It tore the flesh of the naked savages and before night my clothes were in strings. The men began to suffer and although they slept they tossed and moaned. Next day we struggled hard. The thorn belt seemed even worse and only once in a while could we get an old elephant or giraffe spoor that went a little way in our direction. The soft sand seemed to grab you by the feet and hold you down and the smart of innumerable scratches and punctures began to tell on all. I knew that water *must* be found next day or some would die. We struggled hard to reach a ridge we saw to the southeast hoping it might be the edge of a valley in which might be a pool, but night found us encircled in dense thorns and deep sand. I had miscalculated on this thorn belt for if the country had been as most of it is north of the Zambezi River we would have been able to push clear to the Guay if every pool had been dry. I knew that in spite of our greatest efforts the Guay was miles away and unless we forced our way at night we must all perish. I had saved a sack of water for myself but the first night out a great horned spike tore a gash in the side of it and the water dropped in the sand in an instant and I saved and used less than a tea cupful of water, so after all I was on [the] same footing as the blacks. I called up all the blacks and told them they must not stop but must push on at night. We had thrown away everything of weight and nearly all our food. I kept my rifle and ammunition to kill game if we ever reached the river. That night's march is hard to describe. Imagine yourself naked, walking through a thicket where every leaf is a thorn, and so dark there is no possible way of avoiding them. I took the lead using my gun as a fender and having good leather leggings and shoes was secure from the knee. I also tore up my saddle blanket in strips and wound round me. My greatest fear was lest some hook would tear out an eye. We progressed very *slowly* and one could actually hear the thorns scratch on the skins of the blacks who moaned and crept and pulled along after me, but the nights are cool and the men did not go crazy. But day light showed a sunken eyed dejected lot of men who were covered with dried blood oozing from an infinite number of small wounds [that] made their whole appearance wretched in the extreme. We rested for a time and the sun came up. Three vultures hovered over us and Fusi, a man who had fought under Loben and been one of the great impis sent by that King to fight the Barotse in the Zambezi valley, came up along side of me and pointed to them, said they would soon eat us as they had feasted on Loben's impis who perished on retreat in thousands in this same country, small pox having broken out among them, and in some of our camps we could still see their bones.

But we must push on; here two bushmen lay down to die but I got them on their feet and we moved on, still thorns but not quite so dense. To tell you how hard I looked for the ridges along the river is impossible. The sun began to burn, my lips to swell and my mouth and throat dry. I put my finger on my tongue to see if it was really dry. It was, and then I knew another 24 hrs would end all. At about 10 or 11 o'clock that day I got flighty in the head and the men scattered a good deal. I scratched a message on my gun in the A.M. but clung to it and in the afternoon when it got cooler I was all right again but took the opportunity of writing on the barrel to B.B. and you a lot of items that I have since rubbed off as tis all over now and everything lovely. But just about dark that day I came to damp sand in a small water course and the wretched wrecks that staggered along with me clawed it out in handfuls and sat round the hole waiting for the water to run in and swallowing water and sand together. I got a calabash of mud and water and went on the back track and saved all but one man. Some were mad and all terribly torn and exhausted.

From this water we reached a large kraal on the River and I left all my men there to recuperate, and I pushed on to Bulawayo doing 45 miles the last day in. I am a little thin at this writing but otherwise in splendid health. You know I recover quickly from any hardship. I am having a fine rest up now at Bulawayo. King Macomber[1] is far north of the Zambezi, so is John Blick. Judd

1. A. Kingsley (King) Macomber, one of many Californians arriving in Rhodesia, was the son of Dr. Harry Macomber of Pasadena.

Blick came down with Ingram and crossed same dry belt I did and lost a man and some mules of thirst and were three days without water. But the country King and John are in is a well watered and fine country.

We passed through several tribes and saw much country never before visited by the white man. People who work iron and people who work copper. People who live like wild beasts and use poisoned arrows. People who wear a horn on the head several feet high, carry a bundle of slender assegais, fight you at night and go perfectly naked. Selous gives good account of them. We were at the place they killed his men and turned him back a few years ago. At one kraal the Induna came down to see me and told me he was very sick (he had a stiff neck). I told him I was somewhat of a doctor myself and would try a cure, but in his younger days he had been an elephant hunter for Westbeech[2] and Mr. W. had doctored him with salts, so he told me if it was not Boss Westbeech's medicine he would take it. I told him no. I would simply look at him through a big eye and my medicine was strong enough. It would burn him. About 20 of his head men gathered round to see the charm. My eye consisted of the lens from a good telescope I had and getting the sun at about 2 P.M. had no difficulty in getting a focus on the Induna's neck. He bobbed round some at first but on being told it might kill him he clenched his knees with his hands and while his face went through many contortions I burned C.C. on the back of his neck (That is the B.S.A. brand), so if the government ever lose him they will know him when found. I then told him that by the time the mark on his neck was well the stiffness would be gone and that if not I would have to look at him hard. Thus just then I focused on the chief's blanket and being a powerful lens it almost instantly burned a hole and set it on fire to the profound astonishment of all and the convincing of the Induna that a white man's eyes were strong. I will tell you much of the strange customs, music and habits of these tribes when I see you.

Our company have done well this year financially and all

2. George Westbeech was a trader who first visited the area in 1871 and became an advisor to the Lozi in their relation with the Europeans. He had a station at Panda-ma-Tenka where he was courted by whites who wished to do business with the natives. He lost the favor of Chief Lewanika in the mid-1880s and was replaced by Francois Coillard, a French Protestant missionary.

things African seem prosperous. But it is a peculiar country and not all can live in it. In fact I think it is harder and harder for our race to colonize as time progresses because the modern colonist either wants to fly to the wilds and ere the novelty and romance is worn off make a fortune and return home or else wants to take with him all the press the button conveniences, and soft spoon vitals of civilization. Nice raised young men burning with ambition and desirous of hand to hand encounters with lions and tigers go all to pieces and fly home to mother when actually brought hand to hand with hard labor. I have answered only a few of the letters sent me from lack of time and the queer questions asked.

We have built a new house across the creek and out of town. It is more pleasant but now I think we will have Mr. B. build us a better one. I expect the whole northern expedition back again from the Zambezi by Nov. 1st.

With much love,

Fred

James Blick to Blick family

Bulawayo, Rhodesia, S. Africa
Aug 31, 95

My Dear Folks at Home,

This 31st day of August 1895 we are all well and in good spirits. Bulawayo is a much more boomed town than ever Pasadena was. Think a public government sale of lots was had on the 29 and 30th at which 400 lots were sold at a grand total of £175000 = $875000. One was knocked off for the sum of £3000 = $14640.00. No improvements on it. Next to £2500, $2400. The 1st days sale of 177 lots for £86420 an average of nearly £500 or $2440. The day before the sales Fred was offered a big advance on the cost of his and Pete's lots, about 200 percent on cost, so he sold every lot they had expecting to buy at the coming sales but everything went so high that they did not buy, so he is out of house and home. Has the use of this house for two months at $39.00 per month, after which he will have to pay about $50 or 55 per month. Expects to be with me on (Insezi) the farms of the Doré about 50 miles from here. John, Homer and I will take all of B's household goods with us, so when B. sets up housekeeping again she will have to get an entire new outfit again. Fred and B will spend the winter in London with Roderick, Howard, Uncle Josiah, and Mrs. Burnham. Roderick is now going to school in London. Howard and his wife are there. Grace and Pete expect to spend the winter in Cape Town. Judd, if he is not laid up with the fever, will contract same as John did or may work by the month for the Northern Exploration Company. Is at work for them now at £20 per month and scoff. Now this of course is not to be told outside of the family (Sabe). John is at work now for the Company. Gets the same as does King. With the wages they each get a block of the stock. Judd may go next week about 150 miles north of this to peg some claims on a reef of bankette (a reef of granite all cemented in a solid rock), many of them carrying immense quantities of gold. Will be gone 6 weeks to two months. He smokes as much as ever. John will not get down till the last of September unless he should get the fever, in which case he may come sooner. Pete had a severe attack of it. It is a severe attack of fever and ague (chills and fever). The gall seems to scatter all through the system and they become as yellow as saffron. We were rather disappointed at not getting a letter from home Friday, until Mr. Russell's letter was opened by F and contained a postal from Kate to Uncle, also one from Mrs. Talmage. Then I thought of course [of] your being at the Island.[1] I am glad you went and had a good time. So I willingly wait till next week. In order that your letters make connections with the ocean steamers it must be mailed on Monday and not later than Tuesday overland. As the ocean mail leaves every Wed at 11 o'clock A.M., so by mailing one week in advance it will be OK. It takes 42 days to make the trip. B. had a bed bought for me ½ bed cost $25.00 besides the blankets, about $7.40 a pair so you see it cost something to get even a bed. It is iron with a woven wire bottom very nice and easy bed. I keep it as long as I stay here. I do not expect to stay longer than 1½ or two years at the outside and maybe not that long. At present B. and Roderick and baby expect to come back with me. However something may turn up in that time so we can't build up any hopes on this. I will write every week while I am close to an office. I think a Police Station is very close to Mr. Doré's claim. Will

---

1. Santa Catalina Island, where Burnham and the Blicks owned property.

have 40 miles of fence to build, prepare 100 acres for irrigation, build storage reservoirs, a house, stables and kraals for the negroes. So you see it will be a job of opening up a farm on a large scale. Will have 20 or more black boys. F. will go and have it surveyed and level stakes set for grading &c. The soil in this country is a dark red, looks exactly like Spanish Brown. The whole country looks as if it had passed through a terrible fire. All the rocks have been subjected to an immense heat. Grass seems to be a kind of bunch grass and nine tenths of the brush are thorn of the different kinds. One called by the Dutch (wanghapish) "wait a little." Thorns turn both ways and if you get into them and your clothes were caught you had to "wait a little" to get loose. The lady that came up with us happened to pass under one of them without her hat on and the wind blew a branch so it caught in her hair and she had to wait a little. It took two men to get her out and I took her child out of her arms. Cut the limbs off and then untangled them. I don't think I could be persuaded under any circumstances to send for my family dearly as I love them to come to this part of God's footstool. Cape Town or Durban are places that a person of refinement might live if he could put up with English society. In Natal, coffee, tea, and many kindred things are grown, but give me the San Gabriel Valley to live and die in. So I am on a visit only to this country and per chance, if luck favors me, get some of what all of humanity are striving for in this world, and then be compelled to leave it. So if life and health are spared me I will be with you in a few months, say 18 or 22 at the farthest. B. and Grace are in good health. G. is not near as fleshy as I expected to find her. B. looks fully as young as she did when she left us in Pasadena. I think she looks some fleshier in the face and I think heavier.

This is a beautiful sabbath morn. Wind from the southeast. I am all upset as far as the points of the compass are concerned, until I take a thought that the sun is north of me. At noon my shadow falls to the south instead of north. "Baby," it seems she has no name yet, is fat and healthy, is very fair, a perfect blond with blue eyes like her father's is now, so she walks every place and gets up on her feet when she falls, but oh dear, this red dirt is a holy terror on her clothes. She looks as though she had been in a pot of red paint and more especially if she gets wet which is not an unusual thing. So the care of a baby is no fool of a job in this land of naked negroes.

It is now about sundown. Grace and Pete are spooning in the bedroom and B. is entertaining Company. Homer has just come in and B. has introduced him. I am in the dining room and do not care to go in as you know my aversion to strange society and especially that of people who are out more into society, a desire of curiosity to see and be seen. It seems she is a widow of the war, was married last Monday and if I mistake not this is the 2nd time since her marriage she has called on B.[2] Judd I believe has gone out to Mr. Cumming's farm, 4 or 5 girls out there. I think it is about 50 miles from here to Mr. Doré's place. They pronounce the name Dora. The contract will be closed this week. I can't say how it will be about getting my mail. May have to send for it. Can't say till later on. I hope I can get it on the arrival of the English mail (Fridays).

Monday morn the wind is blowing like in Iowa or Kansas. Commenced in the night and it makes a terrible noise over this iron house. The entire outside of this house is iron, the center room is ceiled on the inside with ½ in boards, two of the others are lined with cloth. B. and F., when they build again, will build brick and iron roof, no shingles in town, all roofs corrugated iron. Pete is going down to where John was last winter to peg some claims. Judd and a prospector will go up on the Gwelo River to peg a large no. of claims and if Fred succeeds in floating them, for which the prospect are bright, Judd will get close on to £300 for his summer's work. John will make a big slice and Judd thinks John will want to go home. I can't say as I have not seen him yet. . . .

The sales of lots for the two days sale was £149000, $725000. I think the profits are as crazy as they were in Pasadena. Most of the lots were bought for syndicates in London. You see how easy fools and their money part but I think a large gambling scheme lays behind this. The Charter Co. stock is held by the men who form these syndicates and so sell their own lots to themselves at a high price and thus compel outside parties to pay such high prices for lots on which to build. They are now going to build a large theater, on a lot which they paid £3000 for. Is to be a stock concern all of which is now taken. I think F and P took $500 each. Fred made about £1000 in selling his lots. I will now close hoping this will find you all well with much love to all.

2. Mrs. Greenfield, now Mrs. Cowan.

I remain your loving husband and father,
J. S. Blick

———————

BBB to Phebe and Kate Blick

Bulawayo, Matabeleland
Sep 1, 1895

Dear little mother and Kate,

You can see by the above that I do not keep very accurate account of time since I have my family around me. We did not expect any of them until Sep 1st. You cannot know how nice it was to have them all come ahead of time and spare us the anxious waiting and looking. Still John is away but Fred says he will be back before Oct. 1st. He has everything to make him comfortable and will bring the whole outfit back by the regular road, so Johnny is all right little mamsy.

We spend some very happy hours talking over old times. Pete and Grace went out to the farm last evening, and Homer and Fred went back to their old Kansas City days and Clinton escapades. But you were not here, but we remembered and talked about you. You and Kate were awfully good to let father come to us, and Fred is so happy and interested with father and Homer and planning for their contract. John will be with them. Judd wants to do something else. Talks of going on a short trip for the N.T.E. next week.[1] He coughs very seldom now. While we would have loved to have seen you, I am sure that you were wise in not coming. It is a good place in which to make money but it is not a homelike country, and the people are not our people. Fred and I, as we thought when we wrote asking you to come, are going to England in a couple of months. Pete and Grace expect to go as far as Cape Town with us and be married there. I think we will surely see you when father goes home next year. It seems a long time to look forward to but not so long when we look back. It does not seem so very long since the last Christmas we spent together. We will hope to be together again a year from this Christmas and with plenty of money for

1. N.T.E.—Northern Territories Exploration, the syndicate on whose behalf Burnham led his expedition north of the Zambezi.

your old age stake. Your home is too lovely a one to give up. To part with such a home as this does not hurt one at all. Fred has sold all of our property in Bulawayo but will reinvest. A big boom and stirring times here. We will not build until we come back from England so will move what furniture we have down to father's ranch . . . [no closing].

———————

James S. Blick to Blick family

> Bulawayo, Rhodesia
> South Africa
> Sep 8th 1895

My Dear Folks at Home,

The mail came in Friday. I had not read it yet so I can't say whether I am one of the lucky ones or not. This is the 2nd mail since we arrived two weeks ago, Aug. 24. Am now very busy getting ready to go to work tomorrow and John will be with me when John gets back from his Zambezi trip which will be the last of this month on 30th. . . .

We are getting ready to start down to Mr. Doré's place. . . . Will start tomorrow Sunday about 8 or 9 o'clock. Fred and B. will go with me in a two-wheeled cart called a cape cart with seat and top to accommodate 4 persons. Always takes a driver to drive the mules, 6 of them, and have always been handled by darkies. Will not allow a white man to handle them. B. and F. are going to London, England this winter as I presume you know before this as F. sent money to his mother and Roy and Uncle Josiah to meet them in London. Grace and Pete will go with them as far as Cape Town and be married, stay during the rainy season or summer of this country. We are going to build a house and stable before the rainy season sets in. Homer will start Monday with the material to put up our buildings. B. and Grace want to come down and stay 3 or 4 weeks with us while F. and Pete are looking after some mining proposition. Judd is going north to prospect which if he is successful in finding good paying mines will make about 4 or £5000 in three or four months. Then again he may only make £20 and his board. He is sent out by a company and if he finds a reef with gold in it he will get £1000 for the discovery and £125 for every block of

10 claims that he pegs. The reward is £250 but he has a miner by the name of Lewis. John may make quite a speck if he finds gold on his trip. He is now on his way down and will get here about the last of this month. There is quite a batch of mail here for him.

Sunday morning—am 1st one up. Had the darky make the fire. Tried to get H. up. I've been up quite a while. Took up Baby, held her while she ate a cookie or two. I have set her in my bed while I write. She growled or gooed about it but when she found that I meant to keep her there she succumbed and is eating her cracker. Fred and B are up now. H is making a move to get up. We had to tie up a lot of jackasses to keep them from eating up our scoff that we have for the next 3 months. Our feed for Selous and boys with a few tools cost us about $500.00, so it costs to live here if we do get a good price for our work. . . .

J. S. Blick

James S. Blick to Phebe and Kate Blick

Bulawayo, Rhodesia, South Africa
Sep 18th, 1895

My Dear Mamsy and Katie,

Be assured you are not out of my mind many hours of the day or working hours of the night. Fred and B could not be any better to me than they are. Pete and G. are very kind. I don't think we will be parted many months or years. Something will turn up by which we will be united *or we will turn it up*, you understand. Now let us live in hope as if we have to die in despair. Today B. and G., the baby and I rode out to Mr. Cumming's farm or milch ranch. Mr. Cumming's father, mother, with 5 or 6 sisters, are there. We dined there and had a very pleasant time. Mr. and Mrs. Cumming Sr. are very pleasant Afrikanders (i.e.) African born. They make you feel at home, are real jovial, as are the daughters. I don't know as I can blame B. and G. for liking to go out there. I notice Judd leans out that way. He says Mr. Cumming Sr. said to him one day when the girls were all present, *now there they are take your choice*, and the baby they fairly worship her, and you bet she improves all her opportunities and has a gay time. They have there young ostriches running in the yard. They will follow her about the yard and she calls them birdies. . . . I can't say as I can notice much change in my eczema as yet. However hope it may benefit me. If it don't, I am having a royal good time anyway, if nothing else. Am in a way to make some good money and not have to work very hard either. We expect John now every day with his full fledged whiskers. Judd and Homer say they are going to raise a full beard. Won't they look blooming? . . .

Sep 19th. Grace has just gone with Mr. B. Bain and Miss Cumming, the one Bain expects to marry, have gone over to the races. Will be back here for their lime at 2 P.M. B., the baby and I will go over and look on. F. has gone to Gwelo to attend a law suit as a witness for a mining company. Will be back first of next week. . . . I have not received the paper you sent me with King's letter in. Think it may be in next time as the mails are so large they cannot haul it all on one load of the coach. When we came up there was 2700# of mail and they took one ton (2000#) and left the 700# which of course was all papers and the agent told me that it was increasing every week. His contract required him to haul 2000# mail for the sum of £100 per week and for every # over that amount he received (1/6) one shilling six pence per #. That leaves Mafeking every Wednesday morning. The regular line running in conjunction with the English mail steamers leaves Mafeking every Sunday morn at 5 A.M. and if on schedule time must arrive in Bulawayo at 2:30 P.M. the following Friday and for every hour they are behind that time they forfeit £10 per hour so you see it is not all sunshine for the contractor and for each passenger they charge £22.10 about $110. There were 8 on the coach = $880.00 for passengers alone and 1 ton mail $960 = $1840 per trip. I will endeavor to give you some of the prices. Flour per 100 $10.65. Kaffir meal £2 = $10 which is Egyptian corn ground. Potatoes# 12c. Butter# 37½. Eggs per doz .75c. Can peaches .66 cts. Can jam all kinds per can 37 cts. So if a man has a big appetite it costs him something to appease it. Carpenter wages 30 shillings per day. Masons 35 shillings. Raw Kaffirs 10s a month. As to white labor I can't say, as they do not work unless it is mining. I think they get £25 a month and scoff. John and Judd receive from the Co. they are at work for £20 a month and scoff and £250 if they discover a large paying reef and peg a block of 10 claims. Judd is on a special trip. If he finds a good reef he gets £1000 and £125 for every

block of 10 claims, so if he is successful he will have £1125 = $5558.75. *This of course is not for the public. . . .*
Your Papa and Hubbie,
J. S. Blick

———

James S. Blick to Blick family

Canterbank Farm, Rhodesia
Sep 27th 95

Sunday 2:10 P.M.—My Dear Folks,
We arrived at this place at above date all in good shape. John will be with us by tomorrow evening. Will come on horseback if he can find his horse. If not, he will be later than the above date. We will start the work in the morn and rush it to completion. Will put up the stable and storeroom first and then the house. While we are at work on stable will have the stone put in for house &c. I am writing this while sitting in a Matabele hut which we will occupy until the house is ready. It is round, 12 feet in diam, wall 5 ft high and roof starting on that runs to a peak 8 ft in the center. Roof is thatched and wall is plastered on inside with clay spread with the hand. All the light you get is through the door. The floor is plastered with a specially prepared clay, I think ox blood enters into the composition, makes a hard and smooth floor. B.B. thinks she will have her next house built in that way. . . . I think it is all visionary and will end by building a 4 roomed brick house. She has been visiting a lady friend who lived in these Kaffir huts but hers are each separate and B. thinks she can improve on the lady by setting them so she can go from the living room into the others without going out of doors. She thinks of starting on the steamer Nov. 8th from Biera. Will go via Cairo. G. and Pete going that far with her and Fred. I presume Uncle J. and Mrs. B. will start about middle of Nov. or 1st of Dec and they will do London in shape and maybe Paris. Hard to tell, depends on how rich F. and B feel. Now, if I had my pile, how I would like to take the trip with them and then cross the briny deep to see my best girl and her baby girl. That would be too good for poor mortals like us, would it not? So we must jog along till we can turn something up or we strike a rich mine and then we will make things buzz and go to Mt. Lowe,

Wilson's Peak or Catalina Island. Won't we cut a great swell? The large rivers here are full of fish as well [as] crocodile. Yesterday Homer saw one stick its head out of the water, and he shot, but being so far off, it was a glancing shot, but hurt it so that it turned up its whole length 10 feet and through the belly it was 14 or 15 in, about as large as I am.

I quit at this point and made a table. Filled the lamp and am now writing on the new table with the new lamp giving me the light. I think I scorched my nose today as it feels quite sore to the touch. I can't see it as the glass is not up yet, so I must go by feeling. You may want to know how we came to have a hut, but I think I told you that when we selected the site for the house a Cape Kaffir and his wife have built 3 huts, one to live in, one to sleep in, and the one we have as a storeroom. Just married. No children. He fought against the Matabeles and then married a Matabele girl. You need not fear me talking to her as she can't say yes even in English. As we drove out in front of the crawl (sic) she came out and saluted us. She knew Homer but had not seen me. She knew F. B. and I had been here from some of the other crawls folks. 23 crawls on this farm, but you can't talk to any of them. The Cape man at this crawl can talk and read English. Went to school 5 years. Was a Sergeant Major in the Native Contingent of the Salisbury Column—Matabele war. So all Homer or I can say to the Mistress we must first say it to her husband and he to her or to our ox driver who is also from Cape Town and he tells her she is not bad looking, as all the young men and women have pleasant features. I can't say as I admire the dress of the ladies. It is too [indecipherable]—the upper part of the body is low as the middle is entirely naked, unless now and then one has earrings and a strand or two of beads around the neck and bracelets. Then comes a girdle around the loins and a short petticoat reaching half way to the knees. Then some have anklets of brass or copper, no shoes, with this exception, the limb from middle of thigh is naked. Some have a little top knot on crown of head about 1½ in. long. Balance of hair is cut as short as the men's. The women do all the water carrying, hoe up all the ground and plant the corn, Egyptian corn, millet and whatever they may raise. I passed quite a number of women out with their big rude hoes digging up the ground and planting the seed to be ready for the rains. They get all the wood so I don't know what the men do, unless it is to work for the white man of whom they have a fear. You can hire a big stout man for 10 shillings a month and his scoff. We expect to work 30 or 40 of them this winter and next summer in fitting up this 18000 acres of land. Our boy John will have to do the talk act and our two Cape boys. Homer thinks he can soon learn enough to make them understand him. Will start the foundation of the house in the morning and the stable.

Team stuck in creek last night. Just got back 7 P.M. I hear the other team coming now. So I must go and show them where to offload. He has been rather unfortunate. Two days he has laid up to hunt his oxen as they left him. Homer did not tie up our cattle last night and I had to pay a runner 1 s to run and get them, so I did not get started till 11 o'clock A.M. and landed here by then. The Cape nigger bake us two nice loaves of bread this P.M. in the big dutch oven of B's we brought down with us. Will get fresh milk from the Cape boy in this crawl. You see I am spelling the word the way it is pronounced. Kraal is the correct way. I will now bid you good night.

Yours &c.

J. S. Blick

———

James Blick to Blick family

Bulawayo Post Office
Centerbank Farm Oct 5th, 95

My Dear Ducks at Home,

This is one of those raw chilly days that we dread so much at home. Just rain enough to go to the marrow bones. Oh! of all the homes give me back my dear old California home. So you can bank on me coming back. You know mother the old saying a bad penny will return, so if I live you need not think you are rid of me yet. Now you may think from the above I am homesick. I can't say that. Of course when I am talking to you through the pen it makes me wish I was with you, although I could not ask for better treatment than is accorded me. I must stop now and drink my cup of coffee, the darkey has just brought in. Homer is still in bed. You can tell Linnie that he will be so badly spoiled that she will have to get up, make a cup of coffee and take it to bed to him before he gets up. I know she will kick and maybe carry the point against him, so that he will have to get up and make the coffee for her. The darkey maids and dames are very busy now getting in the corn crop, as spring is now on us. Had one big rain so as to raise the *spruits* (creeks) and rivers. The rain was north and east of us on the heads of the spruits. I look for a downpour on this 36000 acre farm before we are ready for it. Have quite an amount of work to do before we are ready to move into the house, so I fear the rains will be on us before we are ready for them. We were delayed on account of the iron being so long enroute. Breakfast is now about ready and I will have to knock off.

Breakfast over. Two white men called, one a Mr. Woods, who was acquainted with John, had met him at the Filembusa Mines, was on his way from Belingua (I spell these words the way they sound to me—not the Kaffir way). The mist has cleared up but the wind is blowing cold from the east but I think we will have some storm this P.M. Have just got back from a trip to a Kraal northwest of us to make arrangements for a runner to Bulawayo to take and bring our mail. To get a man you must see the *Induna* or head man who will select a black man or boy and of course is responsible for his behavior. Will hire him for one year, £12, and furnish him an overcoat to protect him and the mail during a storm. If he fails to run during the year, he forfeits the coat to his successor.

. . . Oct. 9—This one more of those hot days. Yesterday was one so that I took off my over shirt and went about my work in the flannel undershirt we bought off Al Heiff and today I took it off wearing my overshirt only. The big bucks at work for us are without shirt or pants and are sweating like everything so you see when there is no air stirring it is simply hot. It cools off after sundown and the night is so that you can lay under two blankets. John and King have not put in an appearance yet. Can't say what keeps them. I have just been out to start the blacks to work. Homer has gone to see his sore patient and take him more medicine. One of the denizens of the camp is playing on a one stringed instrument the sounding box of which is a gourd. One of my Cape boys bought a pot of Kaffir beer and wanted a shilling to pay the young *dusky damsel* for it. I did not have the change so he and she are having a go over it. All in greek to me. She is a plump piece of humanity, clothed with a short apron in front and one in the rear showing she is still unmarried. As soon as she is married the husband must furnish her a skirt reaching from over the thigh half way to the knee, made of skin curried on both sides so that it looks like cloth and wears for 5 or 6 years, so you see a buck can afford to keep from 2 to 6 wives. The father of the child Homer is doctoring has two wives, one bears children, the other none, so far. She is a woman weighing about 150#.

John and King came at 10 o'clock Oct 10 all well but empty. I will now say good-by as this is the day for the mail to leave. John and King start to the Filembusa.

Yours in love,

J. S. Blick

James S. Blick to Blick family

> Fairbank Centerbank Farm
> Bulawayo Rhodesia
> Oct 14th 1895

My Dear Folks at Home,

Today Monday we raised the frame of the house. I will sleep in the storeroom in the barn. It has a floor, one door, no windows, but I think it will be cool enough as there is quite a breeze from the east and the air is quite cool so I will not suffer from the heat. I think it will take two weeks to finish the house as we are going to brick the inside with sundried brick and dogered with (or plastered) with clay. . . . King took dinner with us today. Is on the road to Bulawayo to turn over some mining claims that he and John bought. They think they can make a thousand pounds sterling a piece in the next month. That is why John is not with us this month. They are at work on their own account, furnish their own donkeys and scoff and pay all their own bills. The English are crazy to own mines in this country, so if the prospectors can find a mine that will yield a few pennyweights they stake it out into claims and let the anxious investors have it at a good price. Many of the mines that are sold I don't believe will ever be worked. Our post boy will be here tomorrow, so I will look for a letter from home giving an account of yours and Mazzie's trip to the beach. I am writing in the shed which is open on the west side and the flying ants about pester the life out of me attracted by the lamp light so I will bid you good night, and as soon as the mail comes I will jaw you again.

Oct. 16th—No mail yet. I do not know what has become of the post boy unless F. is holding him for some important news for us. Every preparation is being made for war. All the police are being called in. A thousand or more horses have been brought into Bulawayo for the use of the calvary. No one seems to know who is to be whipped but surmise it is Kahama or his general who is in command of Mashonaland.[1] Others think it is the Dutch (Boors). England you know wants to own all of South Africa so they try to possess it through the British South African Co. Now this is as much guess on my part as any of the rest. Dr. Jameson is a close mouthed old chap, but makes a confident of no one so the movements and intentions do not leak out. F. and Pete say if it is the niggers they are going to fight they are not in it. So you know more than we do if you read the papers as to what Parliament is doing. The conservative element may hold them in check. They are anxious though to control all of this country so we will wait and see.

Oct 18th 1895—Well we got the mail today. A letter from my best girl, Joe and Kitty so you see I am happy again. We received an invitation to Pete and Grace's wedding which is to take place on the 23rd of this month at Bulawayo. We will go up leaving the farm Sunday P.M., getting there Tuesday P.M. They will leave on their wedding trip Sat for Cairo, Egypt, so you see they will visit the pyramids and many historic places &c &c. We commenced the roof of our house today. Think we will get it on tomorrow. Well Mother you wished to know what we were doing on the 25th of Aug. We arrived in Bulawayo on the morning of Aug 24 at 2:30 A.M. and on the 25th we were talking over old times. . . .

. . . Ma, I don't think I will send for you to come to this country as I know you would never like it, so I will come home to you as soon as I can get things in shape. It may take a year or less so live in hope and we will meet again. John and King, I think, are on the high road to fortune. Am glad the boys are in good luck. Judd I can't say, as he left for the north with the best of prospects. May be

1. Blick is wrong. Khama ruled in Bechuanaland.

back before Pete and Grace go Northeast. When he left he said if he struck something good he would come back before Pete and Fred went away. Will know when we go to Bulawayo. John is as fat and brown as you find any of them. Goes with his sleeves up to his elbows, shirt collar open, so that arms and breast are as brown as his face, nor does King look like a clerk or school boy any more, but has a good healthy color and is as rugged as can be. Has not been sick an hour.

Yours in love and fear,

J. S. Blick

James C. Blick to Blick family

November 15th 1895
South Africa

My Dear Folks at Home,

I expect ere the above date is written again to be with you. I am now in mind if not in body. I can't say that this would be the land of my choice although we have enjoyed good health since here. Have had several good rains and the grass is coming up nicely and we are getting along nicely. I thought I must write a line or two to let you know that I had not forgotten Nov. 15th or will I forget the 18th the day my little duxie came to light. Homer and I thought of the many births and wedding days as they pass, not forgetting Sep 29th 1858 when I claimed my own sweet wife Phebe E. Dunning. This seems foolish for an old man 62 years old to be talking of love affairs so many years gone by, but when you are alone and so far from those you loved so long ago it makes you feel like writing a love letter even if you are old and ugly. That is one comfort. We can love if we are ugly and most always find someone or something to return the love if nothing but a dumb brute.

Pete and Grace went off as happy as two clams in the same shell. I think all must be well on the way to Cairo by this time. I think P & G will go on to England with B.B. and F. Let them enjoy life while they can. We would have done the same had we possessed the wherewithal. I am going to give this to a friend to mail for me if he don't forget it. He is now ready to go and so I

must say good morning. Our mail facilities are not all that we could wish for. Hoping this will find all well I am as ever,
Your old lover,
James S. Blickensdorfer[1]

━━━━━━━

Judd Blick to Madge Blick Ford

Bulawayo Nov. 30, 95
Cumming Ranch

My dear sister Madge,

You wrote me one letter which I never received. It was lost when they sent my mail up to the Zambezi river. So I can't answer any of [your] questions. I am now with King. We are baching it on the Cumming farm a mile and a half from Bulawayo till the rains are over. I am farming 60 acres of land for Fred and dip my line as well so am not idle. I have done better in this country than I expected to do, so don't be surprised if you hear of me in Paris on a trip with a plug hat and low neck shoes a year from now. I have had a pretty hard time of it here. Have had the fever terrible but am all O.K. now. *This is no country to live in.* You can't get anything to eat. I have not tasted a potato since I have been in the country. Everything must be hauled with oxen 500 miles which takes 4 months to make a trip, so all of the fresh fish spoil by the time it gets here. If you plant anything, the locusts eat it right up so that is no go. The oxen all get so poor in the fall of the year that they can't pull their own weight and the horses die of the horse sickness, so we have to walk most of the time. I have walked over 1000 miles this season so you see it is no snap to make a stake in Africa. I expect you will think that I am getting homesick if I don't stop telling you the good points of my adopted home, for I will never leave here as long as the money comes in as it has been doing in the last seven months. King and I talk about $200 and $300 as if it was $1 at home. We bought a few groceries the other day for a month, the bill was only $60. That was not bad for bacon and corn meal. I will tell you something that you won't believe. I killed a big male lion on this last trip, 14 ft. from tip to tip, and how is that for a boy? He

1. The family name had been shortened to Blick.

charged me. I was so frightened I couldn't run so had to shoot and hit him in the eye not two feet away.

It is dark now and King wants me to go to bed. Will write a long letter next time.

Love,
Judd

———

Part IV
1896
Rebellion

Sketch of Fred Burnham made by Sir Robert Baden Powell in June, 1896.
From *Scouting on Two Continents*.

John Blick to Kate Blick

Bulawayo
Altyre Store, Insezi P.O.
Jan 5th 1896

Dear Flushy,

Well you are a brick Flushy. I am bound to admit. It's not enough for you not to write to your poor little boy who used to be so good to you, take you to church &c, but when it comes to not writing to your own Pard its a positive sin. . . .

Some of our boys ran away the other day before their month was up so I sent down to the police station to the native commissioner who sent up two native police and appointed me JP for the occasion. The police caught two yesterday and we held a trial out under some trees. After all the evidence was in I rose up and spoke thus, "Guilty, fetch um and tie um and give em ten."

The police then ran a rope through them, handcuffed them up through the crotch of a tree about two ft above the victim's head and then lashed his feet to the trunk of the tree and then stood off and laid on ten with a hearty good will. There are three more not caught yet but the white man's arm is long and he sees in the dark, and vengeance is mine sayeth Johnney. Nigs don't like to work and if you don't lick those that run away they will all run.

I am going to make a plum duff for dinner or rather what you would call a suet pudding. The two little kids Spot and Cash are down to the spruit washing. Do you do the cooking Pork or do you let mother do it all.

I dreamt I came home last night and that I was such a horrid looking sight I wouldn't come downstairs. I thought I had only a pair of pants and a shirt on and no shoes and that there were a lot of people downstairs to see me. I had a hard time of it. I hope it will be different. . . .

Tuesday Jan 7—Homer is going to mail this tomorrow so must finish it now or never. I am baking bread as usual. That's because the days I bake bread I have to stay at the house a good deal and not work so have time to write. Yesterday P.M. I caught three nice big cat fish. One was so large that I had to play him a long line before I could get him out. He was as long as your leg if not as large around.

257

We had a bushing big rain last night and the river was so high, Johnston couldn't get across to where the boys are working. A white man close to here shot a nig in the ribs with a shot gun and it has about done for him. He is now out in one of our huts ready to be taken into town.

It's awfully hot today. I am going to try and bake my bread without a fire. I know I can do it. . . .

Take good care of Mag and the others
With lots of love,
John

———

BBB to Blick family

25 Margaret Street
Cavendish Square W.
Jan 31, 96

Dear folks at home,

Oh dear, another short letter but you know what a lazy, careless scribe I am getting to be. So glad to hear from you at N.Y. and that you had such a pleasant trip over. Thank you for the advice about the seasick cure, but you know I am pigheaded on that point. You see we have changed our abode. We have a *very* pretty little drawing room and two bedrooms on the second floor, order what we like for meals, and it is nicely served in our drawing room. Fred and I dined with Mr. and Mrs. Rider Haggard last Tuesday. Four other guests. I had the seat of honor on Mr. H's right. Had a very enjoyable time. I like him very much. We took the Greenes out to dinner at the Holborn last night and then to The Sign of the Cross to hear Wilson Barrett. It was *grand*. I like tragedy better than comedy. We all dine with the Marriotts on Monday evening. Enclosed find copy of paper which Fred has sent to Uncle to put in our strong box. He sent the money last week and Uncle will loan as soon as possible. I believe I gave you three months interest did I not? Hope the boys can soon make up the sum to $5000 and we won't have to think of our dear old daddy working at the bench. It will keep you alive if it does not give many luxuries. I have commenced shopping for Bula and will be very busy for a week. Bushels of love.
Your loving,
B.B.B

—————

Blanche Blick Burnham to Phebe Blick

25 Margaret Street
Cavendish Sq.
Feb. 16, 1896

My dearest little mother,

I am going to write a little letter all for you and shall commence it in good time. Were you not glad to see dear old daddy?[1] You were so good to let us have such a good visit from him. We thoroughly enjoyed him and he was so good to me on that long sea voyage. I should have been very lonesome many times without him. It gave Fred the headache to stay in the stateroom too long and anyway he has not had the experience in nursing that father has. But I expect he has told you how he used to wash my face and hands, comb my hair and read and talk to me by the hour. I really expect we had more good talks than we would have had had I been able to be up. I was not so ill when in bed but I could not get up and I was *so* tired. It must have been malaria which we contracted in Beira because Grace was almost as bad as I, and now she was not a bit ill going to Cape Town. I suffered some with indigestion when I first came here, but have entirely recovered and am looking fine, Fred tells me, especially when I wear my new evening dress of pale pink and blue shot, alpaca trimmed with white silk chiffon and such dainty iridescent trimming. . . . We are going to have two dressmakers come to the house this week. Labor is so cheap here. We only pay one 3s a day and the other 1s 8d per day. Isn't it outrageous? Have already had one dress made for mother [Burnham] and will have two more, good ones made and then we will be *sure* that she is decently clothed for the next year or two. . . .

Fred seems determined that we shall have a good time here. He says that we are getting our pay for some of the hard times that we have gone through both singly and alone. And we have seen some pretty close times. He says that I have written long enough now, to give you oceans of love from him and to come to bed, and as it is 11:30 I think so myself, so good night. Can you feel me kissing you?

1. Within a few months of his arrival, James Blick tired of Africa and returned to the United States.

Monday evening—Well this has been a busy day. Two sewing women in the house. Miss Greene here for luncheon and Mr. and Mrs. Borrow and Mrs. and Miss Meiggs called this P.M. Fred and I dined with the Meiggs last Wednesday and we are all going there to lunch on Sunday. We dine with the Borrows on Thursday. Miss Borrow came out to Bulawayo and married Capt. Spreckley and Harry Borrow was killed with Major Wilson. Father will remember about Mrs. Spreckley's wedding. She has been very ill. The Meiggs are Americans but have lived in London for many years. This Mr. Meiggs and his brother are great railroad men. Built a number of roads in South America and the south of North America. Mother and Mr. Burnham knew Harry Meiggs that first time they were in California. Like them ever so much. More than any ladies I have met here. Did I tell you that we dined with Mr. and Mrs. Rider Haggard? Have dined with a number of other friends of Fred's. Are going down to see Mrs. Doré before we go back. Mr. Raunchman leaves Bulawayo on the 18th and is bringing all the papers with him, so we do not know whether Homer and John's contract have been stopped or not. I fear times have been rather dull there, but Mr. Rhodes is on his way there and things will brighten up a bit. If we can get a berth we are going back on the 29th on the "Scott." The steamers are all so full. I am getting *very anxious* to see my baby again. It was best to leave her but you would not . . . [page missing].

Heard Charlies Aunt, The Club Widow and went to the Olympia last week and I believe went to Robinson Crusoe or maybe that was the week before. Heard Carmen by the Carol Rose Company on Saturday P.M. Going to the Prisoner of Zenda tomorrow night. I really must stop now so goodnight dear little mother. Kiss daddy for me. With lots of love to all the children from all of us.

Your loving daughter, son and grandson

———

FRB to Kate Blick

[undated]

My dear Kate,

From your father and brothers tales of a sedate maidenhood, long dresses, dead languages, hard study &c. have reached my ears and I am scared to write to you. A sneaking dread that you might turn up as a new woman or some faddist creeps over me at times and I want you to throw down your Greek some night and write me a good letter so I can see if you are still "Kate." In fact unless you intend without fail to be a teacher tis such a pity to squeeze into your cranium the language of the dead. We have it already written in our own and can see that they were swayed by and controlled by the same hope and passions as we are today in spite of cycles and the new photography.

The other evening I heard Rider Haggard read a translation from the Egyptian scrolls of 5000 years ago, a government document that with slight changes might have been taken from the Blue books of the English capitol. Also a chapter from their ancient works that was almost a chapter from the Bible and showed where the Jews got their knowledge and the Old Testament. Well your Pa can fill you up on tales of Egypt. Tis a rare and wonderful old country and even Westminster Abbey seems as a house of yesterday in comparison. Soon we will return to this ancient, new, country where our race is planting its flag, midst blood and tears. Yesterday I held the hand of my friend Jefferson Clark (your father will know him) while the shadow of death settled. He met it as a man should, steadfast and brave. Rhodesia needed him and many mourn him. Our hearts are all sore over poor Dr. Jim.[1] But he will come out with honor, which is more than can be said of a lot of the cowards and curs who failed to come to his assistance in their hour of need.

Well, write me and tell me all the latest fashions and fads, slang and novels, anything that pops into your massive brain.
Your as ever,
Fred

———

Pearl (Pete) Ingram to James C. Blick

Cape Town
21/2/96

Dear Dad,
We received your kind letter yesterday. Was glad to hear you arrived on U.S. soil all O.K. Very glad to hear you liked the

---

1. Dr. Leander Starr Jameson was now under arrest following his failed raid, which was aimed at overthrowing the Boer government in the Transvaal.

White Star line. We received a letter from King. Everybody is well up in Rhodesia. He and Judd are fencing the ten acre lot out by Cumming farm. He says the baby is well and is the boss of the ranch. Everything is very unsettled in Johannesburg. My opinion is they will have another war within 12 months. Rhodes and Jameson are more thought of than ever and they will both come out with flying colors. Rhodes is on his way back to Rhodesia. He will make a flying trip through the northern country and get back to London in time for Jameson's trial. Well Dad, excuse me for writing with a pencil but Grace is writing with "the" pen. Well, kind regards to all.
I remain,
Yours &c &c
P. Ingram

━━━━━━━━

BBB to Rebecca Russell Burnham

March 28 1896
On board the train
Bound for Mafeking

Dear Mother,

As the old Grantully was nearing the dock at 7 A.M. yesterday who should we see waving his hand to us but Pete. I went straight up to Schroeders to see Grace and left them to attend to business. We were very busy all day and left for Mafeking at 9 that evening. Of course you have heard the telegraphic news about the Matabeles attacking the whites in certain outside camps and the great excitement. We know all the men that are reported killed, and are hoping against hope that it is some other Cumming than our Art Cumming. It will seem terrible without our very best friend. It was fearful news to meet us was it not? Fred says it was not very near where our boys were, even if they were yet there they would go into Bulawayo at once.

He thinks the uprising will be quelled quickly. We will learn more at Mafeking. You see I cannot write on the trains. We are wild to get to Bulawayo. Will try to send a line from Mafeking.
Your loving,
Blanche

The attack of the Matabele on Cummings's store, where about thirty-eight settlers had taken refuge. From *Scouting on Two Continents*

FRB to BBB

April, 1896

My Darling BB,

There is so much to write about I don't know where to begin. Great excitement in Bula. Gifford lost an arm and the boys were with him. Heavy fight on Insezi River. Homer lost £68 in burned house. John slightly wounded twice. Homer powder burnt slightly. Natives right up against this laager. Gifford saved them, and Harry Cumming gave them warning and in 30 minutes after, the house was attacked.[1] [Captain George] Brand just in last night. Heavy patrol defeated. 30 horses killed. 5 men including Grier and 15 wounded including Dr. Levy. All patrols so far defeated. No more will go out. Big reinforcements coming up. I am offered a commission in scouts under Grey[2] or an independent command if I chose

1. There was a fight at Harry Cumming's store in which the Blicks and others stood off a Matabele attack.
2. George Grey, who raised a company, Grey's scouts.

it, but I prefer to be unattached and go on staff of Sampson[3] who will have a big command. Dr. Sauer is not treacherous to Rhodes and he has done a great deal to put things in shape up here. So much so that I must forgive him somewhat for his financial rascality. He is going to bring down his two children he says on coach if we open pass O.K.[4] And he has a soft spot in his hard old heart for children and offered to take Nada down to you. Now for a man to offer that is a good deal and he will come and see you at Kimberly Central Hotel. He will wire you what train he leaves Mafeking on. Reynolds is killed. He was Conup's and Morrell's friend. I did not send Nada because of the danger and because Pete and I want you folks up here as soon as pass is opened. Better cable home, all boys safe. A. R. Hammond and 5 Americans with him killed.[5] Hammond killed five with his six shooter. Many killed in all parts of country. I at last got off to Mangwe Pass with Capt Sampson and 50 men to build fort at Fig Tree, another at middle of pass and Mangwe. With 3 forts and patrols we can hold the pass open and get up supplies and men. 10 maxims and other cannon are coming up and we will have 1500 men in field in two or three months. The coach has just overtaken us. The Kaffirs sent word that they were going to attack this place so a small patrol was sent with coach. We (Capt Sampson and Pete) leave at midnight to go through pass and we expect to meet Capt Armstrong and 50 men coming up. We will put them in the middle fort. I wish I could talk to you a while. I am awful anxious for you to come up. Bulawayo looks queer. All arms and cannon and forts. Fine rain today and grass up here is very good. Homer left £68 in the farm house. Now burnt. I don't know if the boys are in laager or not. Our fence is finished and well sunk 30 ft. It needs 10 ft more to finish. The Chartered Co. must pay losses of war, I believe, so John and Homer may get something out of it. Of course Homer never put one darn penny in bank for me. He drew £50. Neither did he give John a cent, so Judd says, and John is broke, but of course there is money due on contracts, about £800 in all and it must be paid by the estate. I ought to write a letter to Uncle. Everybody was glad to see us roll up in Bulawayo and they expect us to kill lots of Kaffirs.

3. Captain Wools Sampson.
4. Mangwe Pass.
5. Andrew (Doc) Hammond.

Oh my dear I must quit and with these last few pencil strokes convey to you my undying love and tell you that through all and over all you dwell in my heart of hearts and the purest impulses of my soul are entwined in you, no matter into how many bypaths I may wander or pitfalls catch my unguarded moments.
Fred

We will have you up in about a month or so.
F.

———

BBB to Phebe Blick

Savoy Hotel
10:40 April 12

Dear little mother,
    I have written to Roderick, Mother B., Uncle J and Howard B., and Grace has written you what little news there is but I must just write a few lines to tell you how much I think of you and poor Linnie and how very, very sorry I am for you. If anything should happen to Homer, Judd, or John I should never be able to forgive myself for asking them to come to Africa.
    But we wanted to help them and never dreamed of such a thing as a Matabele uprising. Pray give Linnie my love and tell her how sorry I feel. I can never be too thankful for my happy thought which took father home with us. It is hard enough now but it seems as though I could not have borne it had father been up there. There are enough of our loved ones there now, God knows. But I must not write this way for everything will be settled by the time this letter reaches you and we will all be happy together in Bulawayo. I am so glad Roderick is spared all this and dear little Baby is too young for it to leave any impression on her mind. If I only had her in my arms this minute. I will *never* leave her in Africa alone again. Good night dear little mother with love to all.
Your loving daughter,
Blanche

FRB to Rebecca Russell Burnham

Mangwe Pass
April 14, 96

Dear Mother,

On stepping off the steamer at Cape Town you can imagine the astonishment and sorrow with which I read the news and bulletin. The natives were on the war path in red Indian style this time and had murdered and mutilated the whole family next door to Homer Blick's, a farm 45 miles from Bulawayo. Also Percy Cumming and dozens of others. Cables were waiting for me to rush to Bulawayo and spare no expense. My heart is in the work as you know and Ingram went with me. Great excitement at all the towns and many young men wanted me to enlist them. We arrived at Mafeking and end of R.R. and there left B.B. and Grace much to their chagrin for they swore they could shoot better than some of the men in the country.[1] Here we heard that Bulawayo was in laager, many more people killed, food supplies short. So far the government had made no effort beyond unwinding a lot of red tape. I met here a few friends of B.S.A. and we resolved to go on at once. The coach was running and we became its escort, purchased arms at Mafeking and with 2500 lbs of mail sped north. As if war was not enough for a new country, we are this year swamped by a cattle plague from Russia (Rindepest). It has swept the game off in thousands and cattle as well. For 300 miles the stench of dead cattle is never out of your nostrils. All transport is blocked and 1000 wagons standing by the roadside to Bula. All oxen dead. At Palapya, a huge nigger town of 25,000, we purchased all the horses in the place, eight head. I was forced to pay $600 for my horse. Such is war prices. We rode night and day and hearing war news that Mangwe was short of ammunition we threw away the government mail and took on 12,000 rounds of ammunition on the coach. At Tati we found first laager, but no Matabele in neighborhood. At Mangwe, 60 miles further, another laager of about 100 wagons and a small fort. They had sent out a patrol and had a fight with natives, but needed ammunition and were very glad to get what we brought them. At Mangwe begins a pass 30 miles long leading up to the Bulawayo Plateau. It is about

---

1. The government forbade women going north into the war zone.

such a pass as Arroyo Seco Canon and is key to whole country. This pass was not in possession of the whites through a grave military blunder. With us came a Capt. Sampson a man who has fought Kaffirs for 20 years and a trained military man. He wired the government the necessity of seizing this pass and was commissioned to do so and I was ordered to assist him at once. So we have been on the jump night and day building three forts and rushing 50 men down from Bulawayo and 100 up from the south and as I write this letter to you I can see the smoke of the campfires of the enemy. Ingram and myself are now near upper portion of pass and men are working as hard as possible to complete the upper and middle forts, set dynamite mines and buried shells in good position and hold the pass at all hazards for if taken by the enemy 600 women and children must starve in Bulawayo. I shall leave tonight for Bulawayo. I am offered several important commands but think there are better men who should have them. I prefer to serve under Sampson, not being hungry for a military handle to my name, but I will have a free hand and be able to utilize my knowledge of the country in planning out the coming campaign. From Homer and John I learn the following. At about 1 o'clock A.M. on Mar 23rd they were awakened by a friend riding up to the house and saying, "For God sake Blick jump up, the Kaffirs have risen and murdered Maddox and others. I will go to Bulawayo and you must run up the river and warn the families there." They did so, having many narrow escapes and gathered at a store about 6 miles off. 38 men women and children. They tore off and burned the thatch roof, filled and loopholed the windows, and fortunately found 400 rounds of ammunition and waited. Maurice Gifford raised a small force of 20 men and came to aid them, arrived at their laager at night, but before day the Kaffirs attacked it. It was a misty night and black as pitch. They rushed right up to the laager stabbing one man through a port hole. The fighting was very hot for a few minutes. Homer was powder burned and John received two buckshot, but not deeply, so he is all right. O'Leary was killed and several wounded. At daylight they charged the Kaffirs and drove them from the rocks and finally all fell back on Bulawayo safely. Next King, John, Homer, and Judd joined Spreckley's Patrol and had some fighting down the river. Kaffirs in large numbers, many ex-policemen, armed with Winchesters and shooting like a white man.[2] Andrew R. Hammond of Los Angeles and several American engineers were met going out to their mines and all killed. Their black servant alone escaping. He says Hammond had a six shooter and killed 5 niggers with it. Bob White is one among the killed and two men from Los Angeles. Also Alex Anderson of Daggett and San Bernadino reported killed but not found. Several San Francisco men are missing and there is little chance for them. Many women and children tortured or mutilated. Gwelo, my old camp, is in laager with 250 men and can hold its own. Capt Brand went out with 100 men. Had desperate fighting losing 25 men killed and wounded and 30 horses. But I fear he was not cautious. My dear friend Gifford has had his shoulder shattered and lost an arm. His second in command is killed, a Capt Lumsden, a handsome brave young fellow just out for a hunting trip from home but always ready to help his countrymen in distress. Reynolds, whose horse I am now riding, is killed. He lived next house to us in Bulawayo. Chappie Grier, one of my men who served under me last year, also killed. 200 in all so far.

Now reinforcements are coming up and we will settle this score. These brutes who were treated better under the white than they ever knew have neither gratitude or pity. At the attack on the Insezi laager they killed a man who two days before came and received medicine for his wife and various presents claiming friendship for the whites. 700 niggers took service under the government and mutinied, escaping with all their rifles and ammunition and joining the hostiles. But this time, if Exeter Hall don't again spoil all, we will make a quiet country of it. If the miserable fools who sat at home and dictated the terms of native settlement at close of last war were now here to have their toe nails and finger nails drawn out by these well meaning and harmless savages, they would understand more that it is the white who needs the protection.

But this is a grand country and well worth fighting for. We will fight the savages, the missionaries, the Aborigines Protective Society, and may some day have to fight the Imperial Government

2. The B.S.A. employed Matabele in their police force, instructing them in the use of firearms, something the Matabele were unfamiliar with in 1893.

for the right to rule ourselves, though I think the latter looks more favorably on colonies than a decade back.

So in spite of wars, plague, drought, locusts and the loss of our leader Jameson, we will fight on and win. R.R.s are coming as fast as possible and Rhodesia has the backing of the greatest financiers of the age and the sympathy of many English at home. Her gold veins are numerous and rich and it's the coming country. An empire to be proud of and claim citizenship in. I am writing this note with my gun laying beside me and O'Bern has just arrived to say that the Kaffirs have looted the next place above this so they need a little patrol. I also received news that another of my men is killed defending a house on the Shangani. His name was Hurlstone. He went north of Zambezi last [letter torn] with me. We will make a strong patrol of 250 picked men and attack the Kaffirs inside next few days. I am to take an important part, I hope, and may God give keenness to my eye and cunning to my hand. My blood surges in my veins. I wish the patrol was tonight.

Well Mother this may be my last letter to any of you. But to Roderick give him as my last wish that he take up the work I have begun.
I am as always
F.

I may get a chance to add a line to this again but more news is coming in—not of the best. Rhodes, our greatest chief, is sick at Salisbury. May God spare him for he is the friend of all the Americans here and in fact of all settlers and pioneers. A Grand Young Man and greatly needed in these times when the hearts of many turn to water and in their cowardice they abuse those who would help them. But all of the Pasadena boys have fought like men so far.

———

John Blick to Phebe Blick

Bulawayo
April 18th 1896

My Dear Mother,
This may be the last letter you will get from me for a long time. The mails are very uncertain now. The road is pretty well

opened up but still there is a lot of dangers of the coach being stopped all together. But the nigs don't seem to be in that direction.

Since the 23rd of last month we have had a very exciting time and one that we are not likely to forget. We are still in the ring and are likely to remain there. I will write and tell you all about it later but now a fellow don't have any time.

We are in a fort at present and are likely to remain here until reinforcements come up from below. Fred and Pete arrived last week and are itching for a fight. I have been in five already and have bagged more than one nigger all by my lonesome. Gosh but its sport and lots more exciting than shooting big buck. I must stop now.
With lots of love from,
Your loving Son
John

———

BBB to Roderick Burnham and Rebecca Russell Burnham
Mafeking
April 19, 1896

Dear Little Roderick and Mother,

You will see by this that we are in Mafeking again and it is Sunday. Last Thursday we received the following wire from Pete dated Bulawayo. "Have wired for seats on coach leaving 19. No answer yet. Be ready." We received it Friday morning and left Kimberley Saturday morning for Mafeking. I had wired to know whether our seats had been secured and got an answer at Vryburg saying that our seats were secured for Wednesday. So we have to wait here until then. We traveled up with some very nice people who were going to the Zambezi for a pleasure trip from London. Of course this Matabele trouble upsets their plans. One of the party is a genuine American and several of the others have spent some time there. One of them is going up on the coach with us if we go. People are very much astonished that Fred and Pete have sent for us and think that we will have to undergo all sorts of hardships up there and perhaps be massacred, but they have sent and we are going unless they wire telling us not to come. I would not refuse to go now for anything, for if anything should happen to them we could never forgive ourselves for refusing to go.

They must have some good arrangements for us or they would not have sent. I shall wire this morning that we are here and will leave Wednesday unless we hear from them to the contrary. Mangwe Pass, the only dangerous place, is guarded by three forts so there is no danger on the road. Twenty wagons had arrived last week so there is not such fear of famine. The people have laid a dynamite train all around the town to be fired by electricity if the Matabele masses are seen approaching. The town is well fortified and considered safe from an outside attack but there are so many natives on the inside and they have been seen smuggling clothes out to give to the Matabele, it is supposed, so that they can enter the town without being known. And women have been found bringing assegais into the town hidden in bundles of wood. I fear the natives in the town more than the ones outside. The Matabele are killing the natives who will not join them, so a great many have gone to Bulawayo for protection. I do not know what will come of it all. Troops are being sent up as fast as possible but father can tell you what a difficult country it is to travel through and water is so scarce this year. Capt. White went up on the coach yesterday with the new administrator Earl Grey. Capt White came to see us yesterday. We feel very unsettled and wish we were started on our journey. In a little town like this everyone knows everyone else's business, and they all know who we are and say they cannot imagine what Burnham and Ingram are thinking of to send for us. It does not make us very pleasant to know they are all talking about you. The town is full of soldiers and officers. They are being sent up in detachments every day. I shall put almost £700 in the Standard Bank here before I leave and Grace over £300 so if you never hear from any of us again you will know that it is here. I do not think that anything will happen but it is foolish to give the negroes a chance to get any money. It is mean of me and selfish to write this way but somehow I cannot help it. But do not let this letter worry you for if anything should happen you will hear of it long, long before this reaches you.

I suppose it is only one of the little experiences through which we have to go here below. My family are so scattered now that it makes me homesick but I will soon be with Fred and Nada and I know my dear little man is safe among our own family. I am glad he is not in England. I must go over now and send off that wire to

Fred. I have a great mind not to send this letter at all but you will not like it if you do not receive any letter and I cannot write a cheerful one. Only please don't worry, for as I say you will know before this reaches you if anything goes wrong. I cannot write to Uncle this week so let him read this if he wants to. We have not had any letter from the boys only the wires saying they were all well. We will be so glad to see them all and our dear little baby. Oh, how I wish I had brought her with me but one never knows what is going to happen. I am glad that we all had such a good visit together in London.

With love and kisses under the chin,
For my dear little man from his loving mother,
Blanche Burnham and daughter B.

———

Grace Blick Ingram to Blick family

Mafeking, Africa
April 20, 1896

My Dear Family,

I have another chance to write to you as we could not go on the coach yesterday and will not be leaving until Wednesday the 22nd. We hear no good news from Bulawayo but as they do not send us any message to the contrary we will go. They surely know what they are about and if it was so dangerous they surely would not send for us. All the men here think they must be mad to send for us to go in this danger all the way and then get to Bulawayo and be in still more danger but we will do as they say as they surely know best and if something should happen to them we want it to happen to us as well. I can never be happy without Pete in this world. If he dies, I don't want to live. They know we did not make any fuss at being left behind and were in a comfortable place so they must have a place for us there not in the laager. Anyway, we are going. There are some awfully nice men going in the coach with us and they are *all* going to take care of us so we will fare well that way. The one who has the seat with us called this morning and told us he didn't mind going with us but there were some ladies he would not go with for any amount of money. Someone told him we had been all over this country and were so brave. Alas! Poor man! He may be fooled about us. Everyone is so nice to us and they all know Burnham and Ingram which makes it much pleasanter for us. But its no fun traveling alone. Your own men are best. I hope we will never have to be alone again. This is the first time.

You are all worried enough about this fearful war but this news will come much later after all is over. Mafeking is swarming with men, all going to the war. Every day a large troop leaves and marches, and men are coming from the south every day. Of course we know a good many of them. Capt. White left yesterday. He said he would see Fred and Pete and tell them we were coming. We will have to join the troops he says if the coach has to stop on the way. We are going for a bicycle ride this afternoon anyway and must soon start.

April 26th—Well you see we are still here. We were all ready to leave and late the evening before we were visited by a number of men and among them a B.S.A. agent who said he thought it his duty to come and see us and advise us not to go. We had been tormented nearly to death and B. gave in and said we would not go. I said I'd go alone then and they left us. In a few more minutes our seat partner came over and as he had heard so much talk he turned and said he was afraid it was unwise. That was too much for me and I gave up. I couldn't leave B. Since then we have had three wires telling us to come or why did we *not* come. And today we received one telling us seats were engaged through permission of the administrator. So now I think people will mind their own business and let us go to "sure death" if we like and Fred and Pete want us to. We must wait now until Wednesday and if nothing happens before then we will be off as sure as fate. We got letters today and of course you have heard of the boys escape and how the nigs were right on them when Gifford saved them. You will hear some fine tales when this is over. I'll write again before we leave and tell you how we got off this time or didn't get off. In the meantime we are killing as much time as we can. We know an awfully jolly lot and have as many picnics as we can. Some lawyers who are all bound for Bulawayo tomorrow and one of them has such a sweet Scotch girl out on her honeymoon. They are all admirers of Fred and Pete and have taken us right in. Money is no object to them and they have the finest outfit you ever saw for camping. We went out to a camp yesterday where there were 300 men and donkeys. One of

the men who was a cowboy in the States for a few years (sent out by his dad to see life), threw lassos, and we had a fine time. They had a severe engagement yesterday 3 miles from Bulawayo. Five white men killed. Another fight is expected today. The town is safe they all say. They have a dynamite mine all around it. We are very anxious to be there and if anything happens to the boys we can be with them. I hope you are all well at home and in two years we will have a grand reunion and all be there. With love to all.
Your loving daughter,
G.I.

———

BBB to Roderick and Rebecca Russell Burnham

Mafeking
April 26

Dear Roderick and Mother,

I believe in my last we were going to Bulawayo at once but you will see in Grace's letter to father how we were stopped. Everyone interfering in our affairs and late Tuesday evening after our luggage was all over to the coach office Mr. Kennedy, the B.S.A. agent, and Mr. Jaegars, one of the coach owners, came over to see us and almost forbade us to go. Pete's wire telling us to come was four days old and they said very likely Fred and Pete were out of town and the despatches from there kept getting more serious. I wanted to give up but Grace would not until Mr. Lopez, who was going to take charge of us on the coach and had been almost the only one in favor of our going, came over and said he really did not think we ought to go. We gave up and sent letters by Mr. Lopez to the boys and then cried ourselves to sleep. The next morning we sent them a wire telling them we were not coming, but if any of them were wounded or ill to send and we would come at once. We did not think they would send again but had a wire yesterday from Fred saying he had all arrangements made and for us to come on as soon as we could and to wire when we started. And then another wire came this morning too late for us to go on the coach saying "Latest seats secured. Sundays coach. Special permission from administrator. Wire." We will make another attempt on Wednesday. I am not nervous. I do not think anyone is hurt or he would have said so. They simply think the cam-

paign will be a long one. That they will be in Bulawayo more or less and that they want us up there. Another engagement yesterday. Five killed and another engagement expected today. Tomorrow is the time of the full moon and the natives will be sure to attempt something. I had a letter from Fred today but it was two weeks old. Homer has doubtless written how Harry Cumming warned them that the Matabeles were coming and they were attacked in thirty minutes. Gifford saved them and they were with him when he was wounded. The farm house was burned. I shall be glad when we are up there so we can hear what is going on every day. The coach trip will be something to forget. The roads are strewn with dead cattle from this rinderpest. Water and food scarce and mules poor. My mind is too upset to write any more. . . .
Lovingly,
Mother

BBB to Roderick Burnham

25 miles from Mafeking
May 3, 96

My darling Roderick,

At last we are on our way to Bulawayo by special permission of Earl Grey, the administrator. He wired down to the B.S.A. agent in Mafeking that Messrs Burnham and Ingram had been of invaluable service to the Company, and he wanted to oblige them in any way he could, so he wanted the agent to give us seats on the first coach, so here we are quite important persons. Seven passengers but none allowed to go beyond Palapya except a doctor and Grace and I. Have just had luncheon. Lots of love. I will kiss Nada for you my sweetheart.
Love to grandma,
Your loving Mother

Hello Chum. Don't you wish you were on the old coach bound for Bulawayo and all the boys. I wish you were. Time is up.
Your Aunt Grace

BBB to Roderick Burnham

Bulawayo
May 14 or 15 [1896]

Dear Roderick,

Well here I am at last after three attempts and an eleven day coach ride. Dear little Nada had been ill for two days and this is the fifth day and I am thankful to say that she is better. Bronchitis the doctor says. All the children in the laager had the whooping cough. Mrs. Cumming, who is quite a doctor herself, gave Nada a preventative which keeps them from whooping if they do have it. Baby has had a cough for a week or more but only the fever for the last five days, and she has been very ill and grown so very thin they say. She knew Fred by the way she acts, and although she scarcely opened her eyes until yesterday she seems to know me for she will come to me at any time and will not go to some of the others. She has kissed me several times and tickled me under the chin, one of her love pats. I think that she will be all right in a few days. I could not write before and am sorry to send such a short note but hope Baby will be well enough for me to write a long one for next mail.

Fred came down to Fig Tree (35 miles) to meet me. The coach stopped there all night as it is not considered safe to come in at night, and the next morning an escort rode before us. Tell grandpa that there are seven forts between Mangwe and Bulawayo. We reached here Wednesday noon, and Thursday noon Fred rode out 12 miles to overtake the patrol of 500 that have gone toward Gwelo to meet Rhodes. They had had a scrap before Fred reached them and killed almost 100. The natives seem to be losing heart and they will soon be hungry. I hope the men will kill thousands of them. Judd and John are with Fred. Homer is here in town but on duty so much that I seldom see him. We have two rooms, but I shall sleep in the laager while Fred is away. A great many people sleep outside, but I do not like to when Fred is away. We were fortunate enough to get a good sized room in the laager so we are by ourselves, the Cummings ladies and Nada and I. The Cummings live in rooms near the laager but come here at night. Have kept Nada here all day as we were afraid to carry her over to the rooms.

Pete met us 12 miles the other side of Palapya and took Grace back to Kimberley with him where he has to go on business, so I was the only lady on the coach for six days, but the gentlemen were all very good to me. Could not have asked for more pleasant people to travel with. It was a special coach for Earl Grey's friends, brothers and cousins of Lords and Ladies. Eleven days without ever going to bed until the tenth night you might think rather tiring, but I was "as right as rain" which seemed to be the word on the coach. They gave me the entire back seat so often for a nap that I never felt the loss of sleep. We were only able to get six meals from hotels, had to cook all the others ourselves. I had a little spirit lamp and got along finely. The coach was loaded with rifles and very heavy and we stuck so many many times in the sand or mud. It rained one night, but we could not capsize.

There, a lot of company came and I am afraid this is too late for the post. Please let Grandma Blick read it because I cannot write this week. The doctor has just been again and says she is getting along nicely. Of course we cannot expect her to be well all at once. She is so sweet and pretty. I will tell her all about you as soon as she is well enough.
With heaps of love and kisses,
Your loving Mother,
Kisses from little sister to you.

━━━━━━━

BBB to Rebecca Russell Burnham

Bulawayo
May 18, 1896

Dear mother,

Only a line to let you know why I cannot write more this week. I sent Roderick a letter last Saturday which I told him to let you see. In that I thought Nada would be well by this time but last night was the worst night she has had. She really seems better today but we have thought she was improving so many times before. This is the eighth day. A mild attack of whooping cough developed last Monday a week ago into fever and bronchitis the doctor said, but it seems now more like inflammation of the lungs. The doctor comes two and three times a day but I do not think he knows much, but he is open to suggestions finally, so we have hopes of pulling her through but the little darling is very ill. Mrs. Cumming is so glad that I am here and you may be sure I am, but

how I wish she could have been well until two or three days after I came so I could have seen all the cute little ways they tell me about. I must write a note to Grace. I see Homer every day but Fred, Judd and John are with the patrol sent to meet Rhodes. With lots of love.
Your loving daughter,
Blanche

———

Cable Message [sent by BBB]
Western Union Telegraph Company
Received at Pasadena California
6.35 P.M. May 19 1896

To Blicks
Pasadena Cal.
Nada died today.
Burnham

———

BBB to Blick family

Bulawayo
May 25, 1896

My dear ones at home,

In my letter last week we all thought dear baby was better that afternoon, but she grew much worse in the evening and went *home* about three in the morning of May 19. I am sure she knew me about midnight from the way she kissed me. Oh my little darling. I cannot write about it now. I look for Fred tomorrow. It will be such a blow to him for he was so proud of her. I cannot write to anyone by this mail. Homer sent you a cable on the 20. I am so lonely,
With love from your loving,
Blanche

———

Grace Blick Ingram to Blick family

Bloemfontein
Orange Free State
May 28, 1896

My Dear Dad, Mom and Kitten,

. . . Pete and King have been gone two days.[1] They went to Prince Albert by rail and from there they were going all over the colony on horseback. Of course I couldn't go with them and as this is one of Africa's health resorts (not that I needed recuperating) and I had a good place to stay I thought it best to remain here. Pete wanted me to go to the Cape but I am not stuck on running about this country myself so I'll remain here. . . .

I am going to hear Mark Twain tonight. Our own Markie Twain. Dad, you remember in Cairo? There has been a splendid speaker here the last week, one of the best I have ever heard. I went twice to see or I mean to hear him. I'm so frivolous when Pete is away! He always stays at home in the evening and we prefer it to going out, but when he is away I don't stay in if I can help it. I'll have a letter today and I am anxious for the train to get in. This is much better than having him away up in Bulawayo where it takes so long to get a letter. He can't tell how long I'll be here as this business is uncertain. All the donkeys have been bought up in this part of the country and if there are more there I am sure I don't know what they will do. Pete is thinking of South America as a great scheme. Donkeys and mules will have to [be] brought into this country some way. If Pete had had this idea before he went to Bulawayo this time or at the first of the rinderpest outbreak he would have made £10,000 by this time.

June 4th—A long time since I began this letter but I found I was too late for the mail and so much has bothered me since. I haven't felt like writing. I only heard yesterday that our dear Baby had died so long ago. You have been told all about it. My heart aches for my poor B. If I were only with her, but here I am all alone with no one who cares anything about your troubles. I can only sit and think by myself day after day. I get lots of letters from Pete and in his yesterday's letter he said I could look for a change any day

1. The B.S.A. sent Ingram south to buy horses and mules for the war.

now but all our plans are changed so quickly that I am not going to count on seeing him very soon. I may get a letter today quite to the contrary. Hoping you are all well and happy. I am as always
Your loving,
Grace

I sent a book of views today. Tell me if you get them.

––––––––

FRB to Roderick Burnham

Bulawayo
May 31, 1896
My darling Roderick,

I little thought when we parted on the pier at Southampton how much of life's stream of events would pass in so few months. Another war is upon us and a hard one, all the town is forts and cannon, marching men, blowing bugles, and tramp of horses, all the women and children gathered in the big market building in the square, and little Nada among them. But the hardships were too much for her and a cold settled on her lungs and she died in a few days. She always knew and kissed your photograph and was as bright and strong as possible. Many of the men you knew have been killed by the Matabele. Old Longman is still with us. He is not hostile. I have been very busy fighting and riding and gathering men into forts ever since I arrived and of course Pete is with me. Judd, John, Homer and King have all had lots of fighting and killed many of the savages.

I am in hopes your mother and I can come to Pasadena next year. You are now the only one to bear the name and dwell in our hearts always.

It is not often in war time that I can write you as you know and just now I wish you were here to comfort your mother. But for your own good, you must be away from us and do the duties each day that come upon you. I hope you still remember all I said to you in London. With unbounded love for you my dear boy
I am your
Papa

––––––––

FRB to H. Ridder Haggard[1]

Bulawayo
May 31st 1896

My dear Haggard,

It is very kind of you to wire as you did and this war has brought out the fact that England and Rhodesia are not far apart. Personally, I fear some of us will be utterly ruined and get the swelled head from the many kind attentions and messages from England. But it is a cheering thought when hungry and worn to feel that the people of the homeland are watching every effort and ready to aid us in every way.

This war was a complete surprise to all and shows what a grain of fanaticism will do in a savage. It came within a hair's breadth of being a second Sepoy[2] mutiny. Each servant in Bulawayo was to kill his master and each district to kill all whites in it on a certain hour and day. But certain hotheaded ones sprung the trap too soon, else I think it possible to have succeeded so quiet was the country considered to be. It does seem this year of 96 was destined to be a dark one for Africa. Ambitions and reputations, the brightest turning to ashes.

A bitter cup of woe pressed to the lips of each one in turn whose heart was bound up holding her from the grasp of savages. Our Nada died in laager of inflammation of the lungs caused by the drafty market buildings into which the women and children were huddled during the siege. Mrs. Burnham arrived on first possible coach and had the consolation of being with her at the last. I, on the day of her death, was making a desperate ride through the Ingobo regiment and knew nothing until my arrival in Bulawayo.

You know the tempest that is raging in my soul. The circumstances of her birth tied her to me in a strange way, and like the Nada of your brain she bound all to her and leaves us all in deepest sorrow.

I am hit awful hard, but for Africa and the Empire I will fight on. Even the ten plagues of Egypt had an end.

Rhodes is in good health and says he will see the country through.

1. In the papers of H. Rider Haggard, Henry L. Huntington Library, San Mateo, California.

2. A reference to the Indian mutiny in 1857, when Sepoy troops rose against the English.

The political sky is still very dark and those abominable telegrams are a club in the enemy's hand. Still they show that there was a dearth of real leaders and some of the men talked of revolution and rifles who never intended to use them.[3] A man who goes into a revolution must expect to fight. The end is not yet though postponed. But why all this bosh about friendship between Boer and Briton? There is none until the matter of supremacy is settled. So I say throw off our masks and fight it out like men at once. It is not a war of extermination but a trial of strength between two systems of government. Let's clear away this fog. May the strongest and best win. I see Mr. Wills[4] nearly every day.

Yours very sincerely,

F. R. Burnham

━━━━━━━━━━

BBB to Roderick Burnham

Bulawayo
June 5, 1896

My dear little sweetheart,

Do not think that I have not thought of you because I have not written for the last two weeks. When I think of you it makes me think so much of the little sister that you will never see again in this world and I think of all the plans we had made of soon having a home in London or somewhere in England where you children could go to school and I could stay with you while your Papa made quick trips out to Africa and back. It seems as though my heart would break. I am so lonely without either of my children and I cannot have you here because there is no school for you. I have to give you up for that for a time but I had fully made up my mind before I reached Bulawayo to never leave Baby again. I could have taught her until she had to go to a finishing school and then we would all have been together and how she would have loved her brother Roderick.

Fred says before I came that it was not safe enough to send Baby down to me. There had not been much illness here then and

3. Reference to the Jameson raid.
4. W. A. Wills, copublisher of *The African Review*.

Baby was so healthy and well and was so loved and taken care of that it seemed much the wiser plan to keep her here. The laager was kept very clean but it was very draughty, but they kept her so well dressed and she wore a little flannel night cap, but it had to be I suppose. The Cummings were so good to her and mourn for her like she was their own child. Everyone in town seemed to know and love her and say she was always so very happy. Mrs. Cumming's black boys cried terribly. Old Pete who dug the well and Delagoa Bay Tom came to tell me how sorry they were and old Longboy is working for me and came to the laager twice a day to see how she was and afterward to Cumming's to see how I was. I did not come up here to these rooms opposite Napier's meat market until after Fred came back. There are a great many gardens in town and everyone brought flowers and she loved them so well Mrs. Cumming tells me. She had grown so very, very pretty and had such lovely curved lips.

She had been ill two days when I arrived so I never saw her walk or play and she seemed unconscious most of the time, but I am sure she knew me, especially the last night when she kissed me and I kissed her for you and Papa. God gave me that to remember and I am very thankful for it but oh it was so hard to give her up so soon and I was *all* alone. When she was born I had you with me but when she died neither you or Papa. I seemed stunned, dazed at first, until Fred came home ten days afterwards. It seemed I had been such a long time getting to her, that I had not found her but must surely find her soon. But now I realize every hour that we will never see her until we meet in heaven and it is very, very hard to think it is for the best and say God's will be done.

So many little children have died here during the last two months. The coach road is considered safe now and those who can are leaving Bulawayo with their children, but it is a very long hard trip.

Mrs. C. was going to have her photo taken. They do them very well here now, but then thought she would wait until I came so all we have is the baby one we had in Cape Town, but she had changed so much, grown so much thinner and had such dainty decided features. She frowned just as Fred does when he is thinking deeply and nodded her head when you talked to her just as they say I do. Our little war baby, born just at the close of one war and buried in the middle of another, with the Matabele so close that she could not be taken to the cemetery but was buried just over the ridge from the police camp. Another baby buried there the day before and a great many people since then. You would not know Bulawayo now. I must send those photos I promised grandma and will get you some of Bulawayo as it looks now or did yesterday. They are breaking up the laager now. There are sixteen hundred fighting men in the country now and three big patrols went out to beat out the country for a number of miles. The natives will not attack a big column but run. They are going to try decoying them with small parties with a big one in reserve but they are very cute and will be hard to catch. Our men burn all the kraals and grain and they will not fight. They will soon be starved into small bands whom the police can dispatch. Judd and John just got home yesterday and Judd did not need to go out again, but when he found Art Cumming was going, why he must go too. I am so sorry for I thought I would have a good visit with them all. John was unattached from Gifford's horse to act as guide in this last patrol so Col. Napier, who is left in command here, said he would keep him here as he wants to visit the forts bye and bye and wants Fred and John. Fred was going with McFarlane but last night Col. Napier came around to the house and told him he must stay with him as he needed him, and I shall love Col. Napier forever for that act, for Fred says he thinks he just did it for my sake. When they go to inspect the forts they will only be gone a few days. So John is living here with us. Homer takes his meals here but has to sleep at the barracks as he is left in charge.

I brought John the gum you bought for him and he was so pleased. I have been telling him and Homer about your school, swimming, rowing and gymnasium. They are so glad that you are at home so they can see you when they go home next year. If we go to England this year, I do not believe I can stand it to be so near home again without running over for a little while even if Fred cannot come. London would not be so pleasant as it was last year with Fred gone all day and me alone with sad thoughts.

I shall wish for you so much my darling boy. How strange it is. I know you and grandma must write every week as you said you would and yet we have only got the first letter you wrote after our leaving England. Some of the mail have gone off to Johannesburg

and they have not troubled to send it back yet. The Matabele were so bad they had to stop the coach on that road. We will get them all someday so please don't stop writing. A letter came to Judd this week and one to Fred from Howard. They were written the 15 and 18 of April and you were not in Pasadena yet and no one knew where you were. What in the world are you and grandma doing? Your father is thinking of cabling to find out where you are. You ought to be in school. I was right about the schools. John tells me that you can enter the public school *any* time so I do hope you are in Pasadena and going to school every day for the sooner that is well done the sooner you can come to us and you do not know how much I need you now, so be a good boy and learn good long lessons. Mrs. Greenfield and Bertie have gone away and so have Mrs. Rorke and Edgar and Mrs. Nelson and Annie but the Austins had to come in from their farm and are living here in town. The children have grown so tall. They all ask about you and send you love and so does Art Cumming, Bob, Judd, John, Homer and your father—heaps of it. Aunt Grace and Pete would but they are down in the Free State and your mother—you know how much love she sends you don't you my darling and I wish I could have forty kisses in my favorite place. Save that little chin for me until I come home. Your loving mother,
B.B.B.

June 6 Evening—While Fred was out on horseback last evening with Sir Charles Metcalf they ran square on to an impi of about eight or ten hundred within six miles of Bulawayo. The Salisbury column were expected near town that night so they rode right up to it thinking it was Beales men. It was seven in the evening. They rode parallel with part of the schermes thinking they were Beales friendlies when all at once one Kaffir jumped up and called to the others and in an instant the place was swarming like a bee hive so they knew it could not be friendlies so came back at once and reported. Sir Frederick Carrington believed them. He is chief in command and telephoned at once to Rhodes to send out Cape boys from the government house as no one knew where exactly the Salisbury column was. However when Sir Charles Metcalf got down to Gov. house Rhodes laughed at him and Burnham's niggers and no one was sent until early this morning, and John was sent out on the road he came in on to see if Beale was there, and sure enough he was, but he did not think an impi would dare come in so close with so many troops around and rather pooh poohed this idea, but sent scouts out to investigate. Just about this time the Cape boys also returned and reported an impi right where Fred and Metcalf said and the whole town was bustle. John was sent out on a race horse to tell Beale to join the column which was going from town under Capt. Spreckley at a certain place which was successfully done and 230 mounted men, three maxims and a seven pounder rushed on them. They got so close that they never used one of the big guns. The Kaffirs made one stand, ran, and were in a panic and ran and fell down, but fought. John saw one cling with his arms around a horses neck but the man blew his head off. John had such a good horse he could chase them up well and killed six at close range but could not tell about the longer range shots. He did some fine work and has got a lot of praise for it. Homer's troop did not get to go. Fred only knows of three he killed this time for sure and captured a horse. Two men killed nine each and one was fortunate enough, they say, to get twenty. In all three hundred were killed. The men marched in in triumph loaded with guns, assegais and shields. John had a beautiful assegai but his Col. Gifford begged for it and he gave it to him. You know Col. Gifford lost his right arm in the first of the campaign. They chased them as far as the horses could go. It is too bad that the horses are so poor. Burnham's niggers, as they call it, is considered one of the best engagements of the campaign, only six hours absent from town. Fred was skirmishing around and went back to the field with Colenbrander's blacks and killed twenty-five more who were wounded or playing dead. John stabbed one through the side with an assegai. It all sounds awful but when the men think of the women and children who were brutally murdered they could do anything and then think of all the deaths that have been caused there by people leaving to go into the laager. Our dear little Nada. I could kill the black beasts myself.

Do you know Roderick, that I dream about her almost every night, and she always comes back to me from heaven and says that she will stay with me a little longer, and then she kisses and loves me and sometimes stays a long while and plays about the house. Last night when I was looking through the tin box I found a big envelope with all of your letters in it and the picture of you taken at the Alvord mill and a photo of your father. They are the photos that set on the ledge over the bed all the while Fred was north of the Zambezi and every morning regularly baby would get these two pictures and kiss and kiss them and then she would eat a biscuit and perhaps kiss you again. When I found she loved them so well I let her call them hers. There are little bits of biscuits on them yet left by her loving lips. When we used to ask her where Roderick and her Papa were she would point to the bedroom and run to get them. They are among my most precious mementoes.

They say she always knew you lying on the rug. We have someone waiting in heaven for us now, haven't we, and she met good friends at once for four of her great friends were murdered, one Mr. Bentley, do you remember him? He lived out on the new farm with our Mr. Cumming. Percy Cumming, Albert Barragwamath and Mr. Carpenter. She was the last one to whom they all said goodbye and kissed. She was a great favorite and is missed so much by all. She was so bright and happy but oh was so ill when I saw her, perhaps that is why God lets her come back *well* to me in my dreams. Here comes your father and I must hear whether there is any war news. No, there is nothing new but he says for me to send you lots of love and to be good to grandma.
With love, oceans of love,
From your mother
Blanche Burnham

Dear Mother,
I intended to write half that letter to you but it is so hard to tell where to begin and where to stop in a letter that goes to the same house especially when the one has to read it all. You won't care will you dear if I address most of my letters to Roderick because you have to read them to him and they are meant equally for both of you. Poor mother. You always wanted a little granddaughter so much and then to have such a fine one and never to be able to see her seems very, very hard does it not. We were going to be so proud to take home our African baby. I cannot write any more about it. You would have loved her so much. Good night dear mother. I know you will take good care of our only one now.
Your loving daughter,
Blanche

John Blick to Phebe Blick

June 7th, 1896

My Dear Mother,

    Well Mamma, if you haven't changed any since I left, you are still worrying about us boys. Imagining us with arms and legs off and almost everything else. Homer and I are all right and I am pretty sure Judd is also. He is with Col. MacFarlane who has over 500 men with him. B. and Fred are just turning in. I can see them through the door. I live with them you know when I am in town. It's awfully difficult to say where one lives during these war times. You are here and there everywhere.

    Talk about fighting. Sport? Gosh it beats football or lawn tennis. It's grand to hear a nigger say "My ba bo" and put a bullet into him or stick him with an assegai. You and the people of Pasadena may think it rather cruel, but if you or any of them had of seen the murdered women and children that we have seen you would hate anything black. Tell Roy to lick some little nig for me and I will kill one for him.

    You know that it takes an artist to describe a battle, and that I am not one, so don't expect me to write anything. I can talk to you for hours but writing is all together a different thing. I am sending some papers to Mr. Conger and Fred is sending some to J. Russell so you can get some from them.

    Night before last was the first night that I slept with my clothes off since the 23rd of March. What do you think of that? Father, all that is left of the house at the Insezi is the chimney. A few pieces of your spring bed, but nothing more. . . .

Your loving son,

John C. Blick

In the dark

    Next day—The light went out on me last night so had to chaw off before filling up the sheet. Tell Mr. Conger that I am sending another paper by next coach.

    B. is looking awfully well and pretty. It doesn't seem possible about little Fattey. The day I left to go out with Col. Napier just 8 days before she died, she got or rather was lifted up on the saddle in front of me and rode all around a block with me.

I'll say good bye again,

John

FRB to Roderick Burnham

June 19, 1896
Bulawayo

My dear Roderick,

The war news is still coming in and patrol after patrol is being sent out. I leave again in the morning to go into the Matopa Mountains. Aunt Grace and Pete are still down country but may be up here soon. You would hardly know the town so full of soldiers and forts. But we do not have to sleep in laager now. . . .

I hope you will get into an advanced grade at school for you are getting very old and far behind and must study hard to catch up with all those little roosters above you.

I think this war will last all this year as the Mashonas are now rising.

Yours as ever,
Papa

BBB to Blick family

Bulawayo, June 21, 96

To the dear ones at home,

Johnny is much interested in talking about his girls so I do not know whether I will be able to write much of a letter. He is a great dear old chatterbox now he has switched off on to the difference between English and American pronunciation and I have let several minutes slip by. It is such a comfort to me to have him around all day long and I shall always thank Col. Napier for his thoughtfulness in attaching John for his special service. I know he thought of me and my great sorrow when he kept both Fred and John in Bulawayo. They have never been sent away at the same time except one night and then Homer got off and came and stayed with me. Fred was sent away on a secret mission yesterday and expects to be gone five or six days. I am so uneasy about him now when he is away for it seems as though Africa has more trouble in store for me. And we are surrounded by war for the Mashona have broken out and killed nine at LoMagunda 80 miles from Salisbury, three, twelve miles from

Salisbury, and today a despatch came that ten men went out to relieve thirteen at Mazoe and had an encounter in which six were killed and also 16 mules. Do not know how many were wounded. Relief came just in time to save them all from being cut to pieces. Now if the Boers would declare war against the Uitlander and Khama would close up the road to Mafeking—but I do not think that all this will happen. I think the boys will soon go home. There will be nothing doing here for a good many months, perhaps not until the railway is here. That will be in less than eighteen months for they are pushing it fast from the other end and are using it for fifty miles this side of Mafeking. I had thought of being so busy and happy here with dear little baby to look after and now the days are so long and I miss her so much although I keep talk, talk, talking to keep from thinking for then I realize how much I have lost and what she had meant to me in my dreams for the future. I thought and had thoroughly made up my mind that I would never leave her again that I would stay here next year and then after that she would be large enough to go everywhere with us, and I was always so glad that we had her, although you know I am not demonstrative in my love toward anyone. Roderick, I knew I had to practically give up for his education, but baby was a girl and I meant to cling to her through thick and thin after this one trip to see Roderick who rather felt in Cape Town that I had neglected him for baby. Poor little man! I know he will feel very sorry. I have written long letters to him about her. Do you ever see his letter from me? I cannot write to you about her tonight for I have cried today until my eyes ache but I will talk when I see you. I was going to be so proud to bring her home next year. Perhaps we planned too much over our little war baby. Ah but it was hard to give her up so soon after having been away so long. She comes to me often in my dreams and tells me she has come back to stay with me a little while and then she will love and kiss me and I hate to wake up.

Monday morning—While Homer and John are here writing I might as well talk a little more to you. . . . Col. Napier has just called and taken John over to his office. I hope he is not going to send him out any place. We had such a nice old visit last night after we finished writing we cooked us a nice little supper at 9:30 and after that John brushed my hair until tired and we talked until midnight and did not get up until 9:30 this morning.

Yes, John has to go at 2:30 this afternoon and expects to be gone four or five days. He goes to the Springs twelve miles from here. Homer says that this is an off week with him and that he will come and stay with me all the time. Now when Judd comes if I can just keep him for a few days I will have had a good visit with each one and that is something that I feel as though I never had had in Africa because it was always bustle and preparation to go off somewhere on a trip.

You would not mind seeing me a year before the time I set for making a visit, would you, you dear old darlings? I am trying not to count on it too much but it may happen sometime next winter. I would not mind so much having Fred in London, but I will not leave him while he stays here.

. . . John has gone to get his horse and I must see about some luncheon. Our cooking is very easy now. Nothing to do but warm over tinned goods.
With lots of love from your poor old loving daughter Blanche

Monday Morning and we are moving into a more comfortable house. John and Homer are helping me. John goes off on a two weeks patrol either this afternoon or tomorrow morning. It was a mistake about Judd's column coming in, but they will be here soon. You know our boys belong to Gifford's Horse but are often sent out as scouts. Gifford is going home in three weeks if his wound is well enough. How the papers lie. The poor man has only just come out of the hospital instead of leading a charge. It was three days before he got in to have his arm amputated. He has wonderful vitality. John is going with Plumer's Column. Judd is with McFarlane's. Homer is leaving for home Thursday July 2. John wants to wait for King, and I do not know what Judd will do. No letter from Grace this week so I do not know what she is doing. We are sending you a roll of papers this mail. Fred's secret mission was to kill the M'Limo which he did as you will see by the paper but the war has gone on so long that I doubt if it will have any *immediate* effect.[1] The officials are very well pleased with him. He has had congratulations

1. On June 23 Burnham, accompanied by Assistant Native Commissioner Bonar Armstrong, killed a priest of the M'Limo cult at Njelele, in the Matopos. The incident became clouded with controversy. There is no question Burnham killed the man, and it may have had more effect on ending the war than Burnham's detractors care to admit. Burnham himself thought there would be no immediate effect, and Blanche is probably repeating his evaluation.

from the High Commissioner and different cables from London friends. It makes me homesick to think of Homer going so soon. With heaps of love to all of you.
Your loving daughter,
Blanche

John Blick to Phebe Blick

Bulawayo Matabeleland
June 26th, 1896

My Dear Mamma,

It's only a short time mother until the 14th of August and then it will be just two years since I left my happy happy home. It's probably been two long years to you but to me, great heavens it seemed but yesterday. Time flies in this country. When I go back and think what I have done and what I have seen since leaving Pasadena it seems an age. I do hope that I won't find things so very much changed. People all grow up so that I will have to call them Miss and Mr. Do you want me to come back and get married and settle down in Pasadena to always live near you? Well if you have got me a nice girl picked out I may do it. Strange things have happened. . . .

Fred has gone to a big swell dinner tonight and B and I are here alone. B. is reading "David Grieve" by Mrs. H. Ward. I have just finished the "Refugees" by Conan Doyle, the first book I have had time to read for a good many months.

Judd will be in town I think by tomorrow. He has been out for the past fortnight but has had very little fighting. I will be going out in a very few days but only for a few weeks. They wanted me to go to Salisbury awfully bad, but I knew they would be gone for several months and that probably I would get as much fighting by staying close to Bulawayo where I can be with B. and Fred a good portion of the time. I can tell you B is an angel and if I can only find a wife as good I won't ever grumble or have cause to.

We are going to move to some rooms a short distance from here on Monday. We are rather in an out of the way place here, in a backyard as it were. And you know that we have Colonels, Generals, and Lords to come see us nearly every day. Not all together but one or the other. Fred is exceedingly a high muck-a-muck with a ringed tail out here and is greatly respected. That green-eyed villain that put that article in the Star can thank his stars that he lives as far away as he does and he had better give me a wide birth when I come back.

Mother I can think of a lot more to tell you than I can to write so "Garselech Vecham"

Your loving son,

John C. Blick

———

FRB to Roderick Burnham

Bulawayo
June 27, 1896

My dear Roderick,

In spite of the dark war cloud that still hangs over all this land, I find time to think often of you and of what you are doing. You must write to me every week, never mind where. I am address Bulawayo, and it will finally reach me no matter in what part of the world I may happen to be. You will see by the papers that I have been doing all in my power to crush this rebellion and have succeeded in killing the great M'Limo in his big cave in the Matopa Mountains. It will be a tale I can tell you sometime when I come home to Pasadena.

Write me what books you are studying and the names of each book you read, and of course I am always interested in any gymnastics you may perform or any scores you may make with the rifle. Make a spot or target on a piece of paper, shoot 5 shots at it, and send the paper to me with the range at which you shot. I suppose you have the 22 rifle O.K.

Uncle Judd will be in with the patrol day after tomorrow.

Uncle Howard also writes me occasionally.

I am going up with your Mama now to look at a new house so will say

Goodbye

My dear boy,

Papa

FRB and BBB to Rebecca Russell Burnham

Bulawayo
July 5th 96

Dear Mother,

We are coming home for a trip. Will leave Bulawayo July 11th and should arrive in Pasadena about two weeks or so after this letter. But I will be in London about a week and will wire Uncle date of my leaving New York.

Tell Roderick to meet us at depot as I will need a guide to show me round probably as I hear the town is grown so. Pete and Grace will come with us I expect. I think I will come southern route. Can't say. Will wire from N.Y.

Well how is this for a surprise to you?
Fred

Isn't this a lovely surprise—if only we could have brought our African lily, but Africa claims her own. Sometimes I just *hate* the country but I must not let myself do that for Fred's sake. Please tell my mother that I will write from Mafeking to let her know whether Grace and Paddy are coming. Tell Roderick I will bring his assegai and shield and grandma Blick, Judd's lion skin.
Lovingly,
B.

POSTSCRIPT

The Burnhams returned to Bulawayo the following year and attempted to resume their old life. It was not the same. For Blanche Africa was a place of sorrow. Even Fred Burnham seemed less satisfied. Rumor of a new land of Ophir—Alaska—was on the wind; Klondike fever replaced African fever.

In January 1898 the Burnhams left Rhodesia for the last time. For two years Fred prospected in Alaska on behalf of a London syndicate. He brought Blanche and Roderick north and built a home in Skagway. But polar regions were not his natural element. He and the Blicks mined claims but the results were not good

Africa called again. The conflict Burnham had long anticipated between Britain and the Boer states broke out in October 1899. Burnham believed the war would achieve Cecil Rhodes's vision of a United States of Africa, Briton and Boer under one flag. Anxious to gain a place in what he considered the latest advance of civilization, he wrote high-placed London friends asking for an appointment in the British Army. In the end, however, he was the beneficiary of luck. Field Marshal Frederick Lord Roberts was en route to his new assignment as British commander-in-chief in South Africa when he heard Burnham's former Rhodesian commander, Major General Sir Frederick Carrington, speak of the American's scouting ability. The British Army needed to improve its scouting, for the press was blaming its early defeats on poor intelligence. Roberts immediately proposed that they bring Burnham to South Africa.

During his Christmas vacation in Skagway in 1899, newsboy Roderick Burnham was waiting to pick up American newspapers arriving on the steamship *City of Seattle*. A purser handed him a telegram from London addressed to his father. He ran home. The message read: "Lord Roberts appoints you to his personal staff, all expenses paid. If you accept, start shortest way to Cape Town and report yourself to him. London Naval and Military Club." Burnham immediately wired his acceptance.

From mid-February to June 1900, Burnham served as chief of scouts for the British Army. Captured by the Boers, he escaped. He led raiding parties and carried out lone expeditions to dynamite Boer rail lines. On the last of these excursions he was severely injured but succeeded in destroying the railroad before making his way back to British lines. The wounds ended his role in the war.

British society lionized Burnham for a time. Queen Victoria invited him to visit Osborne, and after her death King Edward VII awarded him the Distinguished Service Order and promoted him to the rank of major in the British Army. Burnham made public predictions about how wars would be fought in the future and began to write a book on scouting, but he was not a scholar. He returned to prospecting for the Wah Syndicate, seeking concessions in West Africa.

The Burnhams moved to Kenya, where Fred prospected from 1902–1904. They returned to the United States, and Burnham entered the service of the Guggenheim Syndicate and made friends with the leading mining expert of the day, John Hays Hammond. From 1908 to 1914, Burnham directed an American colony in Mexico, mixed in that nation's revolution, and dealt with an insurrection by Yaqui Indians. When the colony disintegrated under the mounting cost of doing business amidst revolution, he returned to the United States, broke.

After World War I Burnham found his gold of Ophir—black gold—in the oil field at Dominguez Hills, California, where he had ridden his pony and herded cattle fifty years before. The Burnhams were finally rich. They lived in palatial style atop Hollywood Hills. In 1929 they returned to Africa to revisit the sites of earlier adventures.

During the 1930s, the Burnhams were among Southern California's leading citizens. Blanche Burnham died in 1939. Before America's entry into World War II, Fred worked with pro-British groups in the United States; after the attack on Pearl Harbor he offered his advice and services to the newly formed Rangers of the U.S. Army, but his fighting days were past, and his offer was rejected. He died September 1, 1947.

Roderick Burnham, the little boy, who named the donkeys, cracked his whip atop giant ant hills, and promised to hand his father cartridges, lived for another twenty-nine years. He too had become a prospector and a respected mining engineer. On May 10, 1952, in the mountains east of Pasadena, Roderick officiated at a ceremony honoring his father, in which the Department of the Interior named an 8,853-foot peak Mount Burnham. Roderick Burnham died July 1, 1976, eighty-three years after the trek to Rhodesia, and joined his parents in crossing the last and greatest frontier.

INDEX